Parents, Schools and the State

This book maps globally shifting relations between families, schools and the state across a range of nations (Australia, Germany, India, Norway, Singapore, Sweden, USA) in the late twentieth and early twenty-first centuries.

Featuring contributions from leading international experts, the book's eight chapters reflect upon the apparently vital responsibility of parents for choosing the rights sort of educational pathways for their children, offering comparative insights into several different kinds of state, with different contexts for the practices of 'educational' parenting. The contributors consider the proposition that a significant focus of the material, emotional and occupational investment of contemporary parents is the formal education of their children, re-shaping not only the relationship between parents and schools but also the nature of parenthood itself. Parents are analysed both as local actors in schools and as subjects of national and international policy regimes, particularly recent and contemporary imperatives of marketisation. With a focus on social change, the chapters examine the operation of global educational programmes and ideas in national and local settings. The collected national and local studies attend to different confluences of the local, regional and transnational, considering a variety of social and cultural patterns as well as national and local educational structures and policy regimes.

Parents, Schools and the State: Global Perspectives will be a useful resource for academics, researchers and advanced students of comparative education, educational policy and leadership, educational research, history of education, sociology, research methods and politics. This book was originally published as a special issue of *Comparative Education*.

Helen Proctor is Professor of Education at the University of Sydney, Australia. Her research examines the historical formation and reformation of the relationships between schools, families and 'communities' from the late nineteenth to the early twenty-first centuries.

Anna Roch is Research Associate at the Martin Luther University of Halle-Wittenberg, Germany. Her research interests include schooling, school choice, parenthood and the methodological potential of discourse analysis and ethnography.

Georg Breidenstein is Professor of Education at Martin Luther University of Halle-Wittenberg, Germany. His main interests and areas of research are ethnography of schooling and education, childhood research and school choice and parenthood.

Martin Forsey is Professor of Anthropology and Sociology at Edith Cowan University, Australia. His research focuses on educational systems, their impacts on individuals within society and their role in social change.

Parents, Schools and the State
Global Perspectives

Edited by
Helen Proctor, Anna Roch, Georg Breidenstein and Martin Forsey

LONDON AND NEW YORK

First published 2024
by Routledge
4 Park Square, Milton Park, Abingdon, Oxon, OX14 4RN

and by Routledge
605 Third Avenue, New York NY 10158

Routledge is an imprint of the Taylor & Francis Group, an informa business

Chapters 1, 2, 4, 6–8 © 2024 Taylor & Francis
Chapter 3 © 2020 Synnøve Bendixsen and Hilde Danielsen. Originally published as Open Access.
Chapter 5 © 2020 Susanne Dodillet and Ditte Storck Christensen. Originally published as Open Access.

With the exception of Chapters 3 and 5, no part of this book may be reprinted or reproduced or utilised in any form or by any electronic, mechanical, or other means, now known or hereafter invented, including photocopying and recording, or in any information storage or retrieval system, without permission in writing from the publishers. For details on the rights for Chapters 3 and 5, please see the chapters' Open Access footnotes.

Trademark notice: Product or corporate names may be trademarks or registered trademarks, and are used only for identification and explanation without intent to infringe.

British Library Cataloguing in Publication Data
A catalogue record for this book is available from the British Library

ISBN13: 978-1-032-59951-9 (hbk)
ISBN13: 978-1-032-59952-6 (pbk)
ISBN13: 978-1-003-45695-7 (ebk)

DOI: 10.4324/9781003456957

Typeset in Myriad Pro
by Newgen Publishing UK

Publisher's Note
The publisher accepts responsibility for any inconsistencies that may have arisen during the conversion of this book from journal articles to book chapters, namely the inclusion of journal terminology.

Disclaimer
Every effort has been made to contact copyright holders for their permission to reprint material in this book. The publishers would be grateful to hear from any copyright holder who is not here acknowledged and will undertake to rectify any errors or omissions in future editions of this book.

Contents

Citation Information		vi
Notes on Contributors		viii

1   Parents, schools and the twenty-first century state: comparative perspectives   1
Helen Proctor, Anna Roch, Georg Breidenstein and Martin Forsey

2   Normative development in rural India: 'school readiness' and early childhood care and education   15
Arathi Sriprakash, R. Maithreyi, Akash Kumar, Pallawi Sinha and Ketaki Prabha

3   Great expectations: migrant parents and parent–school cooperation in Norway   33
Synnøve Bendixsen and Hilde Danielsen

4   What parents know: risk and responsibility in United States education policy and parents' responses   49
Amy Shuffelton

5   Parents as a problem: on the marginalisation of democratic parental involvement in Swedish school policy   63
Susanne Dodillet and Ditte Storck Christensen

6   Building trust: how low-income parents navigate neoliberalism in Singapore's education system   78
Charleen Chiong and Clive Dimmock

7   Parents as 'customers'? The perspective of the 'providers' of school education. A case study from Germany   93
Georg Breidenstein, Jens Oliver Krüger and Anna Roch

8   Practising autonomy in a local eduscape: schools, families and educational choice   107
Martin Forsey

Index   125

Citation Information

The chapters in this book were originally published in the journal *Comparative Education*, volume 56, issue 3 (2020). When citing this material, please use the original page numbering for each article, as follows:

Chapter 1
Parents, schools and the twenty-first century state: comparative perspectives
Helen Proctor, Anna Roch, Georg Breidenstein and Martin Forsey
Comparative Education, volume 56, issue 3 (2020), pp. 317–330

Chapter 2
Normative development in rural India: 'school readiness' and early childhood care and education
Arathi Sriprakash, R. Maithreyi, Akash Kumar, Pallawi Sinha and Ketaki Prabha
Comparative Education, volume 56, issue 3 (2020), pp. 331–348

Chapter 3
Great expectations: migrant parents and parent-school cooperation in Norway
Synnøve Bendixsen and Hilde Danielsen
Comparative Education, volume 56, issue 3 (2020), pp. 349–364

Chapter 4
What parents know: risk and responsibility in United States education policy and parents' responses
Amy Shuffelton
Comparative Education, volume 56, issue 3 (2020), pp. 365–378

Chapter 5
Parents as a problem: on the marginalisation of democratic parental involvement in Swedish school policy
Susanne Dodillet and Ditte Storck Christensen
Comparative Education, volume 56, issue 3 (2020), pp. 379–393

Chapter 6
Building trust: how low-income parents navigate neoliberalism in Singapore's education system
Charleen Chiong and Clive Dimmock
Comparative Education, volume 56, issue 3 (2020), pp. 394–408

Chapter 7
Parents as 'customers'? The perspective of the 'providers' of school education. A case study from Germany
Georg Breidenstein, Jens Oliver Krüger and Anna Roch
Comparative Education, volume 56, issue 3 (2020), pp. 409–422

Chapter 8
Practicing autonomy in a local eduscape: schools, families and educational choice
Martin Forsey
Comparative Education, volume 56, issue 3 (2020), pp. 423–440

For any permission-related enquiries please visit:
www.tandfonline.com/page/help/permissions

Notes on Contributors

Synnøve Bendixsen is Professor in the Department of Social Anthropology at the University of Bergen, Norway. Her specialist area of research is migration and refugees, and within this, she focuses on issues relating to marginalisation, differentiation and migrant containment.

Georg Breidenstein is Professor of Education at Martin Luther University of Halle-Wittenberg, Germany. His main interests and areas of research are ethnography of schooling and education, childhood research and school choice and parenthood.

Charleen Chiong is Senior Researcher at Australian Education Research Organization (AERO), Australia. Her research interests include societal relations, families, the state and social and educational inequalities.

Ditte Storck Christensen is PhD student in education at the Department of Education and Special Education, University of Gothenburg, Sweden. Her research concerns parents who, due to the strict regulation of home education in Sweden, have chosen to home educate in Åland, an archipelago province belonging to Finland.

Hilde Danielsen is Associate Professor at NLA, Bergen, Norway, and Research Professor at NORCE Norwegian Research Institute, Bergen, Norway. She has a Dr.art in Cultural Studies and is working with both historically and contemporary perspectives on family-life, gender and equality, the welfare-state, diversity and inclusion and exclusion.

Clive Dimmock is Professor of Leadership and Professional Learning in the School of Education, University of Glasgow. His research concentrates on cross-cultural comparative leadership and schooling in Asian contexts, especially Singapore, Hong Kong and Vietnam.

Susanne Dodillet is Senior Lecturer at the Department of Education and Special Education, University of Gothenburg, Sweden. Her research is focused on the intellectual history of the present.

Martin Forsey is Professor of Anthropology and Sociology at Edith Cowan University, Australia. His research focuses on educational systems, their impacts on individuals within society and their role in social change.

Jens Oliver Krüger is Professor for Educational Research at the University of Koblenz-Landau, Germany. His research focus is on choice and competition in the German school system, discourse analysis parenthood and advice book literature.

Akash Kumar is an independent researcher and consultant based in Delhi. His focus areas are education and gender, and he is currently Communication Consultant, La Via Campesina, South Asia.

R. Maithreyi works in the area of childhood studies and was formerly a practising child psychologist. She is Strategic Lead-Adolescent Thematic at Karnataka Health Promotion Trust, India.

Ketaki Prabha is PhD student at the Camden College of Arts and Sciences, Rutgers University, USA. She hopes to explore the contemporary 'skills' landscape in India, at the intersection of youth, learning-for-work and neoliberalism.

Helen Proctor is Professor of Education at the University of Sydney, Australia. Her research examines the historical formation and reformation of the relationships between schools, families and 'communities' from the late nineteenth to the early twenty-first centuries.

Anna Roch is Research Associate at the Martin Luther University of Halle-Wittenberg, Germany. Her research interests include schooling, school choice, parenthood and the methodological potential of discourse analysis and ethnography.

Amy Shuffelton is Professor in the Philosophy Department at Loyola University Chicago, USA. Her primary areas of research are democracy and democratic education, feminism and parental engagement in schools.

Pallawi Sinha is a researcher interested in education and international development with a particular focus on inequalities in the Global South.

Arathi Sriprakash is Professor of Sociology and Education at the University of Oxford. Her research focuses on racial and epistemic justice in education.

Parents, schools and the twenty-first-century state: comparative perspectives

Helen Proctor, Anna Roch, Georg Breidenstein and Martin Forsey

ABSTRACT
This article introduces a collection of papers comprising the special issue, *Competing interests: Parents, Schools and Nation States*. Drawing on the seven papers in the collection, and situating them in recent developments in the sociological field, the article discusses globally shifting relations between families, schools and the state across a range of nations in the late twentieth and early twenty-first centuries (Australia, Germany, India, Norway, Singapore, Sweden, USA). The article proposes that the school is a crucial site for relations between family and state, and argues that a significant focus of the material and occupational investment of contemporary parents is the formal education of their children, re-shaping not only the relationship between parents and schools but also the nature of parenthood itself. In the contemporary context of global neoliberal education reform, parents are analysed both as local actors in schools and as subjects of national and international policy regimes.

The focus of this introductory article, and of this Special Issue, *Competing interests: parents, schools and nation states*, is the often fraught and always complex relationship between family, schooling and the contemporary state. The idea that parents should not only send their children to school each day (fed and clothed), but also take active responsibility for supporting and nurturing their children's formal educational success, is, in the twenty-first century, a matter of principle in schooling systems across the world, and encompasses such activity as choosing a school (e.g. see Forsey, Davies, and Walford 2008; Campbell, Proctor, and Sherington 2009; Breidenstein et al. 2017; Carrasco and Gunter 2019), and helping with homework (e.g. see Kim 2020; Hutchison 2012). Strong discourses of parental obligation operate, even if expressed in different ways, under different state regimes of schooling provision and support, in places where parents have themselves probably experienced high levels of formal education and in places where that is less likely. The supplementary labour and pro-schooling orientation of parents, especially mothers, are constituted as a national resource for modernisation and/or international competitiveness in many educational jurisdictions (e.g. see Maithreyi and Sriprakash 2018), and parent–school interactions are frequently shaped by education policies that encourage or require schools and teachers to establish formal systems of parent 'involvement', requiring support from both parents and teachers (e.g. see Blackmore and Hutchison 2010; Stacey 2016).

Nationally mandated standards for teacher professional accreditation in Australia include the capacity and willingness to 'engage' with parents (e.g. see Saltmarsh, Barr, and Chapman 2015). In the US a significant element of the 2002 No Child Left Behind Act of the George W. Bush presidency was the requirement for states, districts and schools to establish and maintain formal structures for parent 'involvement', particularly aimed at poor and minority families, as part of an accountability agenda (e.g. see Auerbach and Collier 2012). Among other outcomes, public policy interventions like these have accelerated the growth of an already extensive practice-oriented literature within the field of school effectiveness, offering guidance for 'goal-oriented and comprehensive parent involvement programs to involve all families for student success' (Hutchins 2012, 1; see also Epstein 2011). This collection is situated in a different and more critical strand of the literature, in which the value of parent–school connectedness is not necessarily doubted, but in which sociological, historical and above all political questions about parents' relations with schooling are prioritised.

Parents for most of the twentieth century were of marginal interest to the fields of critical sociology and history of schooling, becoming more visible from about the 1980s in new Marxist and post-Marxist sociological studies of the implication of the school-family relationship in the making of inequalities of social class and gender (e.g. see Connell et al. 1982; David 1980). Foundational to the contemporary field of critical parenting studies were the Bourdieusian analyses by Annette Lareau (2003), whose term 'concerted cultivation' encapsulated an explication of the purposefulness and intensity of the educational labour of middle-class mothers (also see Reay 1998). Relatedly, a new focus on understanding the centrality of formal education to the intergenerational persistence of metropolitan middle-class privilege (e.g. Ball 2003; Campbell, Proctor, and Sherington 2009) supplemented older studies of how working-class kids 'fail' (e.g. Willis 1977). The question of how the contemporary practices and expectations of parent–school relations can be understood as 'neoliberal', or as responses to neoliberal policy reforms, is an important one for this collection. Many scholars this century have identified a phenomenon of parenting 'intensification' as a strategic response to new regimes of risk and responsibilisation (e.g. Vincent 2017; Crozier and Symeou 2017; Faircloth 2020; see also Hays 1996). The literature (in English) of parenting under neoliberalism has been dominated by studies coming out of the US and the UK, which are also national settings in which neoliberal reforms have been embraced by national governments.

Each of the articles in this collection captures aspects or elements of parental labour in the service of children's schooling, reflecting upon an apparently vital responsibility of parents for choosing the rights sort of educational pathways for their children and accompanying them on those pathways. The authors examine the present-day investments by parents in their children's schooling, and how parents' educational activities, and in some cases activism, are shaped and influenced by the education histories and policy landscapes of the various nations and regions that provide their empirical settings (in Australia, Germany, India, Norway, Singapore, Sweden, and the USA). In each of these setting, global education trends and practices interact in different ways with longer standing local and national schooling systems and arrangements.

Each of the states represented in the collection is governed by a form of electoral democracy. Using the (contestable) typology of Esping-Andersen's *Three Worlds of Welfare Capitalism* (1990), these include two Nordic 'social democratic' states, Norway and Sweden, which have significantly diverged since the 1990s, in terms of privatisation of social infrastructure (e.g. see Lundahl et al. 2013; Bæck 2019); Germany, 'corporatist', 'conservative' and, in common with a number of OECD nations, affected by 'PISA shock' after the first iteration of that international measure in 2001 (e.g. see Paseka and Killus 2019); as well as two non-European 'liberal welfare' states, the US and Australia, both enthusiastic proponents, albeit under differently governed school systems of the 'Global Education Reform Movement' (Sahlberg 2011). The education systems of the two Asian nations included in the collection, one South Asian, one South East Asian, have also been shaped by neoliberal education reforms. Singapore is a PISA 'winner' and has been described as a state in which neoliberal economic policy and the responsibilisation of citizenry coexist with visible state ownership and social control (Liow 2011). The Indian study is located in a (pseudonymous) village in the north eastern state of Bihar in which both family aspirations and parental decision making about education are constrained by the restricted set of possibilities on offer.

This introductory article brings the seven papers into a cross-national conversation, placing the family at the centre of a comparative analysis of schooling and the state through consideration of the labour of 'parenting for schooling'. It is animated by a set of questions including, 'Who precisely is being referred to in school and policy talk about parents and family?', 'What is intended or achieved by policies of parent engagement or involvement in different national settings or kinds of states?' and What do these studies reveal about the tensions between the classic territorial claims of the nation state over the people within its political borders, and the globalising impetuses of such international processes as human migration, educational assessment, and policy borrowing and transfer? Central to the comparative analysis is the question of how school-family relations operate to make and/or disrupt relative privilege and inequality in different settings and under a variety of policy regimes.

We have grouped the papers according to three overarching themes, empirically derived from reading the papers together and deployed here as useful heuristics. These are: (1) 'Opportunity and advancement', (2) 'Participation and citizenship' and (3) 'Choice and trust'.

Theme 1: opportunity and advancement

Schools have historically encouraged the prolongation of childhood dependence by alienating children and young people from making early contributions to household economies. They have also by design or default normalised specific kinds of family arrangements, notably the dyadic intergenerational relation of adult parent with dependent child. This is despite in many places, a formal school policy language that acknowledges 'carers' who may or may not be parents. Schools and schooling systems thus reinforce a modern 'generational order' (e.g. Alanen 2009) in which agency is allocated or attributed to parents in a structural relationship with their offspring who are the object and purpose of this agency. In educational discourses parents can be subject to moral judgments which depend upon how expertly and carefully they are seen to be engaging with the schooling project. Social and cultural deficit views of racially diverse parents, or parents living in poverty, have a long history (e.g. see Hayes et al. 2017; Haebich 2000; Proctor and Weaver, forthcoming). 'Pushy' parents can also be taken to be a problem (Beauvais 2017) and also racialised, for example as 'tiger' parents (e.g. see Ho 2020). As Dehli (2004) pointed out more than a decade ago, however, for Canada and other similar Anglophone nations, twenty-first-century neoliberal education reforms have created new ways of understanding parents as 'stakeholders' or 'consumers'. As she also points out, these arrangements come with both constraints and opportunities. What is clear, however, is that parents have become central both to familial and national agendas of competition and advancement in new ways.

The idea that schools are places for social and economic opportunity is firmly established in all kinds of formal and informal education discourse. Many foundational statements of mass elementary and secondary schooling – from the periods in which these systems were established across the globe in the nineteenth and twentieth centuries – describe metaphorical ladders of meritocratic opportunity, and this imagery has persisted to the present day. The promise of meritocratic educational systems – and indeed meritocratic armed forces, corporations and civil service departments – was that clever and hard-working individuals could rise through the system no matter their parentage, and that nations and other organisations would benefit from the more efficient distributions of human capital. By the late twentieth century, these kinds of ideas were criticised on several grounds. These were (1) that ostensibly meritocratic school systems were never authentically based on effort and ability but were always distorted by hidden structures of social inequality; (2) that even in the best scenario meritocratic school systems could offer only mobility for select individual rather than equality for all and (3) that traditional meritocratic public education systems were fettered by inflexible bureaucratic forms of management and were thus offering poor quality education. The relationship between parents and children can be interpreted as an impediment in meritocratic discourses, because the point is that the child advances by its own intelligence and effort without undue help or hindrance from family. In neoliberal education discourses, by contrast, the parent is theorised as a crucial agent of accountability, in a system of education provision that cannot necessarily be trusted.

At the crux of the critical literature of parent–school relations is the conflict inherent in the relationship between the individual and the common good. Sociologist Philip Brown's classic 1990 paper, 'Education and the Ideology of Parentocracy' was one of the earliest to identify parents as a key 'problem' of neoliberal education reform (even though his paper predated the proliferation of 'neoliberalism' as a term). Brown (1990, 66) proposed in a now well-known formulation that certain countries, notably Britain, were at that time entering a new historical phase 'where a child's education is increasingly dependent upon the *wealth* and *wishes* of parents, rather than the *efforts* and *ability* of pupils'. The logical development of this argument was a number of studies which argued that the exercise of educational privilege by middle-class parents contributed to schooling inequality (e.g. see Cucchiara 2013; Posey-Maddox 2014). Brown and others also argued that the power that parents were given under 'parentocracy' was limited, and did not include 'what is taught in schools', and that in fact the 'state' had strengthened its power over the school curriculum even as it appeared to involve parents in their children's schooling by distributing certain kinds of choice.

Focussing on the circumstances, education relationships and labour of parents, each of the papers in this collection has a different story to tell about educational parenthood. The focus for most of the material in the collection is on parents with limited power who do what they can with the conditions in which they find themselves to secure their children's futures through schooling. The two articles grouped under Theme 1, reporting on research conducted in Norway and India, respectively (Bendixsen and Danielsen 2020; Sriprakash et al. 2020) examine the strategies and contexts of non-privileged parents in navigating school systems they have not experienced themselves, and in which they do not necessaryily feel at home or at ease. Both of these papers examine the identification of parental competence or inadequacy with children's educational success or struggle, in the pursuit of opportunity and advancement.

Norway is distinct from other settings in this collection by virtue of the relative homogeneity of its population, especially in comparison with such places as India and the US, and the relative modesty of its uptake of neoliberal education reforms, such as school privatisation and high stakes national assessment. The introduction of state policies ostensibly aimed at increasing parents' rights and responsibilities to influence schools can be seen as partly neoliberal but also as a reform of democratisation, and family rights (Bæck 2019). These reforms, and the school practices that accompany them have, however, according to Bendixsen and Danielsen (2020), contributed to the normalisation of middle-class styles of intensive parenting, and discursively rendered other kinds of parenting as deficient in the view of some or perhaps many elementary school teachers. Bendixsen and Danielsen's article, reporting on part of a larger ethnographic study conducted in the city of Bergen, describes the unease experienced by some non-Nordic migrant parents from Africa and the Middle East, who were strongly invested in their children's scholastic success, but resistant to what they interpreted as the school's efforts to reach into their personal lives and dictate their parenting practices beyond the classroom. Where some teachers identified the biggest risk to immigrant children's advancement as lack of a particular individualised form of parent–school engagement, a number of parents were most worried about things such as the safety of the neighbourhoods in which they lived, and the obstacles to acquiring Norwegian language proficiency presented by living in immigrant neighbourhood and working in unskilled jobs.

The setting for the article by Sriprakash et al. (2020) is a small village in Bihar, an Indian state characterised by significant educational and economic disadvantage with literacy rates below fifty per cent for some groups. Drawing on rich ethnographic data collected over several months, the authors found that discourses of 'good' parenting for schooling were culturally restricted to middle- or upper- caste/class book-based intellectual enrichment such that they were rendered unreachable or irrelevant for some village families. By the same token, the knowledge and cultures of families living in rural poverty were understood as having little or no educational value, and home and village were often construed as simply places to leave behind. Focussing on early childhood care and education, the authors describe a case in which a deeply competitive educational system has rendered early childhood education a site of market competition, low quality institutional provision, and deepening inequality. Under neoliberal resource-allocation reasoning and fiscal austerity the value of early education is overly calculated in relation to potential future economic effects and rights, and justice-based rationales are subdued. In a local context where public early childhood education was so poorly supported by the state as to be functionally inoperable, a for-profit private market had flourished, characterised by narrowly conceived and pedagogically impoverished practices of 'school readiness' such as learning by rote. With no acceptable alternatives, marginalised parents were prepared to pay for such tuition, understanding the educational capital on offer to be necessary for their children's future.

Theme 2: participation and citizenship

The school has been a crucial site over many decades – or longer, depending of the history of schooling in each place – for encounter and negotiation between the private worlds of the family and the public, larger scale collectivities of states and governments. Schools have been key institutions in the ascription and legitimisation of citizenship, advancing social and political agendas of national harmonisation around shared language, religion and values – as well as the exclusion or differentiation of others whether within or outside national borders (e.g. see Myers 2020). While conventionally authoritarian in internal form, schools in democratic states often include citizenship education to promote forms of civic participation.

That parent engagement with schooling can be individualistic is fundamental to the critique of neoliberal education reform, as described above. Articles by Amy Shuffelton (2020) and Dodillet and Christensen (2020), however, raise the possibility of parental engagement with schools as a form of grassroots democracy. The question posed by each of the papers in this section is whether and how parents might become involved in their children's schooling in a way that is supportive of the collective good, whether within or beyond the classroom. The papers comprise a Deweyan influenced analysis of democratic citizenship and parent participation in local public school politics in the US (Shuffelton 2020); and a proposal that the historical weight of Swedish collectivist, statist education policy continues to frustrate any kind of meaningful parent participation, despite significant neoliberal reform that promises to empower parents in some ways (Dodillet and Christensen 2020). These cases offer insights into the ways in which different forms of statecraft impact upon how schools are constructed and configured, and how, in turn, parents are positioned in relation to the forms of state values and practices that schools represent.

Research in the field of parent–school relations is dominated by ethnographic studies for good reasons – not the least of which is the access to the informal and routine social interactions between parents and schools that ethnographically based research can provide. The paper by Dodillet and Christensen (2020), however, employs an historical policy discourse methodology, examining representations of parents, schools, and the Swedish state from the 1940s to the present in order to understand what the authors argue are deeply sedimented anti-parent 'attitudes' and 'mind-sets' that continue to shape parent–school relations despite Sweden's radical education policy shifts over the past thirty years. Parents, they maintain, have been very narrowly empowered by the post-1990s reforms; their field of action mainly restricted to making a public complaint or choosing from amongst an array of private and public schools for their children. According to Dodillet and Christensen, parents are effectively blocked from productive participation in a collective educational project because they are viewed as overly invested in the personal and lacking in professional expertise. The paper can be read as partly a manifesto, urging systems and teachers to invite parents into schools as allies and collaborators, including as political allies.

Amy Shuffelton's (2020) paper draws on an interviewing project with US school parents who were activist participants in their children's schooling in ways perhaps dreamt about by Dodillet and Christensen (2020) for Sweden, but were also compelled by intolerable circumstances. Shuffelton's research was conducted in Chicago, a city where schooling inequality is acute, and resources are typically scarce where they are most needed. Educational problems and anxieties, she argues, cannot be disentangled from endemic racism and poverty, high levels of gun ownership, and a widespread lack of heath, economic and housing security. Chicago Public Schools was a pioneer of neoliberal education reform in the 1990s, introducing measures such as test-based accountability some years ahead of No Child Left Behind (2002), and closing schools whose students performed poorly on them. At the same time, the adoption of centralised corporate governance models, and the replacement of many public schools by charter schools has resulted in existential challenges to the US tradition of locally distributed democracy in the form of elected school boards. While No Child Left Behind opened certain forms of parental agency, it helped to close down others. Whether despite or because of such challenges Chicago is well known for the political engagement of parent groups (and teacher unions) and Shuffelton profiles two activist parents in the paper, both mothers, in order to demonstrate the value of their affective connectedness with their local schools, and the legitimacy and value of what she theorises as their democratically grown 'social knowledge'.

Theme 3: choice and trust

A means by which parents have become central to national programmes of neoliberal education reform has been the introduction of new kinds of choice and responsibilisation. According to much of the research in the field, market-oriented school reform has been associated with a popular loss of trust both in the efficacy of bureaucratic public administration and in the expertise of schoolteachers (e.g. see Connell 2013; Gobby, Keddie, and Blackmore 2018; Windle 2015; Lupton 2011). The three papers in this section add fresh perspectives to this discussion by (1) demonstrating how well-developed practices of choice and competition operate *within* an 'architecture of trust' in the state in the case of the 'hybrid neoliberal-developmental' city–state of Singapore (Chiong and Dimmock 2020); (2) examining public school devolution and parental choice in relation to geography in the vast and sparsely populated region of Western Australia (Forsey 2020) and (3) analysing the reflections of school administrators in a German city – where market-oriented schooling reform has a relatively short history – as they negotiate the complexities of treating parents as both partners and 'customers' (Breidenstein, Krüger, and Roch 2020).

If Luhmann's (1979) assertions about trust being central to the functioning of any society can be taken at face value, it is not surprising that most of the articles in this collection dwell upon the notion of trust, or its opposite, at one point or another. Public institutions rely on public trust for legitimacy, and while a relatively recent rise in home-schooling in some parts of the world points to a loss of trust in formal, usually government-run education systems (Apple 2020), it is well to remember that home-schooling remains a minority practice. It would be a mistake to take mere attendance as a mark of significant trust in a school; however, it is the case that the vast bulk of parents around the globe hand their children over to the care of teachers and assistants on a daily basis, and they would not, and indeed could not, do so without some degree of surety that their child will be safe in the school. (Even though, as Sriprakash et al. 2020 and her colleagues point out in this collection, for some parents there is not much they can rely on educationally in the school.) The fact that most governments require that parents do this handing over, and that they tend to limit, or in some cases ban, home-schooling, suggests a lack of trust by government of parents' abilities to adequately address the educational needs of their offspring. Nevertheless, as already indicated, there have always been expectations that parents act in partnership with the school their children attend, in some way. Breidenstein, Krüger, and Roch (2020) capture the situation eloquently in describing how in Germany, the institutionalisation of compulsory schooling in the nineteenth century instigated the formation of a complementary relationship between family and school through which parents take responsibility for the upbringing, if not always the wellbeing, of children.

This collection of papers quickly disabuses the reader of ideas of there being any sort of steady-state 'complementarity' associated with a teacher-parent relationship – a reality Breidenstein, Krüger, and Roch (2020) readily acknowledge. By virtue of the professional training of its key personnel, schools often set themselves at some distance from parents. Dodillet and Christensen link this distancing in Swedish schools to distrust of parental involvement on the part of teachers in Swedish school policy. Breidenstein, Krüger and Roch write of school leaders who, in the face of shifts towards relationships transacted through a market-focused imaginary, expressly identify the importance of maintaining their professional identity as educators with specialist knowledge. The relationship between school personnel and parents is as characterised by its unevenness and contestations as it is by cooperation and partnership – both dimensions are extant often simultaneously. As reported through this collection, teachers and school administrators often express distrust of the professional judgment of parents in a variety of settings, while parents are reported in all but one of the studies in this collection as distrustful in some way about schools and what they are offering to them. The exception is Chiong and Dimmock (2020) thoughtful exploration of the trust invested by low-income families in the forms of institutional schooling supported by the 'strong state' of Singapore.

In thinking through the notion of political trust and its educational practices, Chiong and Dimmock (2020) demonstrate how their interlocutors, drawn from a small cohort of low-income Malay families, display significant trust in the Singaporean state as generous providers of educational opportunities for their offspring. According to the parents interviewed for the study, the factor determining a comfortable future for their child is the child's response to the opportunities offered. Success or failure depends upon how well she/he/they make use of the resources bestowed more or less equally upon all students by a beneficent state. The meritocratic myth of formal education has been absorbed by the particular parents involved in the study, which Chiong and Dimmock explain as a consequence of the significant levels of trust in the school that they argue is conflated with the high levels of political trust garnered by the strong 'neoliberal-developmental' state that is Singapore.

The observation that political trust is promoted rather than negated by neoliberal responsibilisation of children and parents could be a direct response to Breidenstein,

Krüger and Roch's (2020) argument that the increasing emphasis on school choice in Germany reflects and responds to a loss of parental trust in some of the structures and forms of the nation's schools. This particular binary, highlighting different inflections, if not forms, of democratic structure practised in the two nations, suggests an important research agenda exploring links between parental beliefs and actions and the ongoing reproduction of national values and practices promoted through school systems.

School choice is a relatively new phenomenon in Germany, and Breidenstein, Krüger, and Roch (2020) make it clear that moves towards devolutionary reform, school autonomy, competition and parental participation are much more tentative and contested than they appear to be in much of the Anglosphere – particularly England, the USA, Australia and New Zealand. Indeed, they argue that many parents do not trust these moves, picking up earlier writing focussed on the ongoing problems associated with legitimising school choice by parents associating hesitantly with the practice of choice (Breidenstein et al. 2017).

In their paper in this collection, Breidenstein, Krüger, and Roch (2020) offer a unique perspective in the school choice literature in focussing on the providers of choice, or more specifically the views of the administrators of three different types of school competing with various degrees of enthusiasm for the newly constituted consumers of educational services. The three 'providers' are positioned by the researchers in terms reflecting their relationship to the quasi-educational market in the ways in which the school people in turn position parents as either 'customer', 'client' or 'amateurs' (non-professionals). Each of these educational professionals relates differently to the parents seeking places in the educational establishment for which they are the main gatekeeper. Nevertheless, the researchers identify a consensus among their interlocutors that makes it impossible for these educational leasers to conceptualise parents as customers – with the limiting of educators' professional authority that that implies. Ultimately, the three educational leaders embrace the distance created from parents by virtue of their privileged view of educational practices as leaders in their respective learning communities; parents are usually not qualified to make sound judgements of the complex field that is school education.

Martin Forsey (2020) takes a more traditional parent-eye view of school choice in his construction of the educational systems of the vast Australian state of Western Australia – Government, Catholic and Independent – as part of a broader eduscape. The notion of eduscape is drawn from Appadurai's highly influential portrait of globalisation as a complex multi-dimensional flow of material goods, people and ideas (e.g. Appadurai 1996). According to Forsey, the local destination this 'matter' flows towards determines in no small part the particular form and function it takes on as a consequence of the peculiar conditions of the places into which they embed. The notion of eduscape is used as a metaphor enabling appreciation of the shaping influences of the broader policy flows: the ideas they reflect and promote and the practices they enable at their 'destination'. In a jurisdiction that slowly embraced late modern ideas of the state school system of decentralisation and autonomisation, Forsey reflects upon how socio-economic status and geo-location impacts the sorts of decisions families are able to make in relation to how and where they want to be in relationship to schools. The more significant contribution of his work here relates to his mobilising and merging of the ideas of Bourdieu and Beck in a formulation of reflexive habitus that draws attention to larger social processes of 'cultured structured agency' often understood and represented as matters of individual choice alone.

Conclusion

Contemporary nation states invest enormous amounts of money, time and human resources (the labour of children and adults) in formal education systems, of which schools are the largest and most consequential part. In complex, modern (or postmodern) city-dominated economies, it is hard to imagine that changing anytime soon. Administrative and policy responsibility is allocated differently in different states to centralised or smaller units of government jurisdiction and civic organisation, but despite considerable change in service provision over the past half century or so across a number of sectors that directly address or enrol the 'public', the twenty-first-century state remains preeminent in the provision, organisation and regulation of mass education. The two cases with which the editors of this special issue are most familiar are Germany and Australia. Germany, as discussed in this collection, has engaged with such neoliberal strategies as 'school choice' comparatively recently and hesitantly. Part of the contribution of the paper by Breidenstein, Krüger, and Roch (2020) are accounts of the reasoning of school administrators as they weigh up some of the features of a choice-based system almost from first principles. Australia by contrast, is often analytically grouped with Britain, the US and New Zealand as an entrenched case of the application of the neoliberal 'Global Education Reform Movement' (e.g. see Proctor, Brownlee, and Freebody 2015). In both of these instances and in each of the five other cases collected in this journal issue, the state remains a strong actor, even where there is a flourishing of private and even commercial institutions and organisations. There is some historical continuity in how the school operates as a bridge between family and state, even as the lives and labour of parents have been affected by neoliberal transformations to the state-school-family relationship in the late twentieth and/or early twenty-first centuries.

Despite the international pervasiveness of 'neoliberalism' as an analytic frame, the literature of 'parenting for schooling' has tended to remain grounded in the national and the local. Certainly, each of the seven studies in this special issue of *Comparative Education* benefits from its detailed analysis of particular and distinctive circumstances and interactions of parents with schools and states – in Asia, Europe, North America and Oceania. The aim and contribution of this special issue, and this introductory essay, however are to bring these similar and different perspectives into closer conversation, not as glibly representative of their respective systems, but for the purpose of teasing out some of the intricacies of the relations described and examined. We are aware that the terms 'neoliberal' and 'neoliberalism' can be used imprecisely, or in a way that ignores historical continuities of educational practice. The studies collected here demonstrate the untidiness and impurity of neoliberal education reform, as global discourses of choice, competition and responsibilisation meet local practices and local histories.

Looking across the studies, there are some elements that are common to all. For each of the cases, the public provision of schooling remains a fundamental principle. Even in the Indian case, the commercial providers, no matter how mainstream they had become, operated in gaps left by public institutions that were theoretically open to all, even if effectively non-functional. All of the parents represented in the research were not only compliant with the obligation to send their children to school, but also seemed to agree that they should actively work to support and to encourage their children's prolonged schooling and scholastic success. In these ways family, school and state goals were in strong alignment and the educational work of these twenty-first-century parents had indeed intensified, in comparison with some earlier generations. Their daily lives and their affective lives – their hopes and fears for the future of their children – have been shaped by contemporary education imperatives that demand a lot more than passive obedience to school attendance laws. Some of the parent participants expressed the conviction that doing well at school was an essential requirement for their children's future security, and by implication, that school failure could have serious consequences.

Some of the studies documented tensions between parents and teachers. (The Singapore study offered an important exception to this.) In the Norwegian case, for example, some teachers and parents were at cross purposes about how best to address the needs of non-Nordic migrant and refugee children. For these teachers, the signal strategy was to try to persuade parents that they should spend more time doing schoolwork with their children after hours, in the classic middle-class model. Several of the parents explained to the researchers, however, that what they most worried about in terms of their children's future success were economic security, better housing and capacity in the Norwegian language. These were the priorities that were occupying their time and energy. At the same time, it would be an oversimplification to conclude that parents and teachers remain in binary opposition entirely in the same old ways, along the fault-lines of professional expertise, and race and social class. As a problem of neoliberalism, such discordancy is shaped by new pressures on both parents and teachers to which, as the Swedish and US papers suggest, a new collective politics might be part of the answer.

Parents have to some extent come into their own in recent years as objects of sociological study in schooling, partly because of a recognition that families have always been important in schooling, and partly because of the new agency parents are theoretically accorded under market-oriented education reform. The studies in this journal issue demonstrate several ways in which parents, including non-middle-class parents, have taken seriously the idea that they have responsibility for their children's schooling, and that this responsibility extends to much more than a simple observance of forms. While the means and strategies of parents varied substantially depending on local and national economic, social and political structures, however, these studies also show how individualised, local parent power tends to be limited by both structural forces and interpersonal dynamics. (This is quite distinct from the structural cultural power exercised by privileged parents by way of their membership of a social class, or from the successful exercise by parents of voting and lobbying power in some places, for example the religious right in the US.)

Overall the purpose of this collection, and this introductory paper, is to offer greater precision, detail and variety to the figure of the parent, both 'real' and as an imagined figure of education discourse, and to scope out some of the array of conditions and systems under which parents and schools meet each other. Taken collectively, these studies show the school to be a crucial site for intimate and complex relations between family and state and demonstrate how the job of 'parenting' is made, or at least shaped, by the contemporary meanings and practices of schooling.

Disclosure statement

No potential conflict of interest was reported by the author(s).

References

Alanen, Leena. 2009. "Generational Order." In *Palgrave Handbook of Childhood Studies*, edited by Jens Qvortrup, William A. Corsaro, and Michael-Sebastian Honig, 159–174. London: Palgrave Macmillan.

Appadurai, Arjun. 1996. *Modernity at Large: Cultural Dimensions of Globalization*. Minneapolis: University of Minnesota Press.

Apple, Michael W. 2020. "Homeschooling, Democracy, and Regulation: An Essay Review of *Homeschooling: The History and Philosophy of a Controversial Practice by S. F. Peters & J. G. Dwyer*." *Education Review* 27. doi:10.14507/er.v27.2931.

Auerbach, Susan, and Shartriya Collier. 2012. "Bringing High Stakes from the Classroom to the Parent Center: Lessons from an Intervention Program for Immigrant Families." *Teachers College Record* 114 (3): 1–40. Accessed May 19, 2020. https://www.tcrecord.org ID Number: 16292.

Ball, Stephen J. 2003. *Class Strategies and the Education Marketplace: The Middle Classes and Social Advantage*. London: Routledge.

Bæck, Unn-Doris K. 2019. "Parental Involvement in Norway: Ideas and Realities." In *Parental Involvement Across European Education Systems: Critical Perspectives*, edited by Angelika Paseka and Delma Byrne, 77–89. London: Routledge.

Beauvais, Clementine. 2017. "An Exploration of the 'Pushy Parent' Label in Educational Discourse." *Discourse: Studies in the Cultural Politics of Education* 38 (2): 159–171. doi:10.1080/01596306. 2015.1064098.

Bendixsen, Synnøve, and Hilde Danielsen. 2020. "'Great Expectations: Migrant Parents and Parent-School Cooperation in Norway." *Comparative Education*. doi:10.1080/03050068.2020.1724486.

Blackmore, Jill, and Kirsten Hutchison. 2010. "Ambivalent Relations: The 'Tricky Footwork' of Parental Involvement in School Communities." *International Journal of Inclusive Education* 14 (5): 499–515. doi:10.1080/13603110802657685.

Breidenstein, Georg, Martin Forsey, Fenna La Gro, Jens Oliver Krüger, and Anna Roch. 2017. "Choosing International: A Case Study of Globally Mobile Parents." In *Elite Education and Internationalisation: From the Early Years to Higher Education*, edited by Claire Maxwell, Ulrike Deppe, Heinz-Hermann Krüger, and Werner Helsper, 161–179. Houndmills: Palgrave Macmillan.

Breidenstein, Georg, Jens Oliver Krüger, and Anna Roch. 2020. "Parents as "Customers"? The Perspective of the 'Providers' of School Education: A Case Study from Germany." *Comparative Education*. doi:10.1080/03050068.2020.1724485.

Brown, Phillip. 1990. "The 'Third Wave': Education and the Ideology of Parentocracy." *British Journal of Sociology of Education* 11 (1): 65–85.

Campbell, Craig, Helen Proctor, and Geoffrey Sherington. 2009. *School Choice: How Parents Negotiate the New School Market in Australia*. Sydney: Allen and Unwin.

Carrasco, Alejandro, and Helen M. Gunter. 2019. "The 'Private' in the Privatisation of Schools: The Case of Chile." *Educational Review* 71 (1): 67–80. doi:10.1080/00131911.2019.1522035.

Chiong, Charleen, and Clive Dimmock. 2020. "'Building Trust: How Low-Income Parents Navigate Neoliberalism in Singapore's Education System'." *Comparative Education*, doi:10.1080/03050068.2020.1724487.

Connell, Raewyn. 2013. "The Neoliberal Cascade and Education: An Essay on the Market Agenda and its Consequences." *Critical Studies in Education* 54 (2): 99–112.

Connell, R. W., Dean Ashenden, Sandra Kessler, and Gary Dowsett. 1982. *Making the Difference: Schools, Families and Social Division*. Sydney: Allen and Unwin.

Crozier, Gill, and Loizos Symeou. 2017. "Editorial." *Gender and Education* 29 (5): 537–540. doi:10.1080/09540253.2017.1325994.

Cucchiara, Maia Bloomfield. 2013. *Marketing Schools, Marketing Cities: Who Wins and Who Loses When Schools Become Urban Amenities*. Chicago, IL: University of Chicago Press.

David, Miriam E. 1980. *The State, the Family and Education*. London: Routledge and Kegan Paul.

Dehli, Kari. 2004. "Parental Involvement and Neoliberal Government: Critical Analyses of Contemporary Education Reform." *Comparative and International Education / Éducation Comparée et Internationale* 33 (1): Article 4. http://ir.lib.uwo.ca/cie-eci/vol33/iss1/4.

Dodillet, Susanne, and Ditte Storck Christensen. 2020. "Parents, a Swedish Problem: On the Marginalisation of Democratic Parental Involvement in Swedish School Policy." *Comparative Education*. doi:10.1080/03050068.2020.1724489.

Epstein, Joyce Levy. 2011. *School, Family, and Community Partnerships: Preparing Educators and Improving Schools*. 2nd ed. Boulder, CO: Westview Press.

Esping-Andersen, Gøsta. 1990. *The Three Worlds of Welfare Capitalism*. Cambridge: Polity Press.

Faircloth, Charlotte. 2020. "Parenting and Social Solidarity in Cross-Cultural Perspective." *Families, Relationships and Societies* 9 (1): 143–159. doi:10.1332/204674319X15668430693616.

Forsey, Martin. 2020. "Practicing Autonomy in a Local Eduscape: Schools, Families and Educational Choice." *Comparative Education*. doi:10.1080/03050068.2020.1776467.

Forsey, Martin, Scott Davies, and Geoffrey Walford, eds. 2008. *The Globalisation of School Choice?* Oxford: Symposium Books.

Gobby, Brad, Amanda Keddie, and Jill Blackmore. 2018. "Professionalism and Competing Responsibilities: Moderating Competitive Performativity in School Autonomy Reform." *Journal of Educational Administration and History* 50 (3): 159–173.

Haebich, Anna. 2000. *Broken Circles: Fragmenting Indigenous Families, 1800–2000*. Fremantle: Fremantle Arts Centre Press.

Hayes, Debra, Robert Hattam, Barbara Comber, Lyn Kerkham, Ruth Lupton, and Pat Thomson. 2017. *Literacy, Leading and Learning: Beyond Pedagogies of Poverty*. Abingdon: Routledge.

Hays, Sharon. 1996. *The Cultural Contradictions of Motherhood*. New Haven, CT: Yale University Press.

Ho, Christina. 2020. *Aspiration and Anxiety: Asian Migrants and Australian Schooling*. Melbourne: Melbourne University Press.

Hutchins, Darcy J. 2012. "Families and Schools." In *Encyclopedia of Diversity in Education*, edited by James A. Banks. Thousand Oaks, CA: Sage. doi:10.4135/9781452218533.n279.

Hutchison, Kirsten. 2012. "A Labour of Love: Mothers, Emotional Capital and Homework." *Gender and Education* 24 (2): 195–212.

Kim, Sung Won. 2020. "Meta-Analysis of Parental Involvement and Achievement in East Asian Countries." *Education and Urban Society* 52 (2): 312–337. doi:10.1177/0013124519842654.

Lareau, Annette. 2003. *Unequal Childhoods: Class, Race, and Family Life*. Berkeley: University of California Press.

Liow, Eugene Dili. 2011. "The Neoliberal-Developmental State: Singapore as Case Study." *Critical Sociology* 38 (2): 241–264.

Luhmann, Niklas. 1979. *Trust and Power*. Chichester: Wiley.

Lundahl, Lisbeth, Inger Erixon Arreman, Ann-Sofie Holm, and Ulf Lundström. 2013. "Educational Marketization the Swedish Way." *Education Inquiry* 4 (3): 497–517. doi:10.3402/edui.v4i3.22620.

Lupton, Ruth. 2011. "'No Change There Then!' (?): The Onward March of School Markets and Competition." *Journal of Educational Administration and History* 43 (4): 309–323.

Maithreyi, R., and Arathi Sriprakash. 2018. "The Governance of Families in India: Education, Rights and Responsibility." *Comparative Education* 54 (3): 352–369. doi:10.1080/03050068.2018.1430299.

Myers, Kevin. 2020. "Citizenship, Curricula, and Mass Schooling." In *Handbook of Historical Studies in Education: Debates, Tensions and Directions*, edited by Tanya Fitzgerald. Singapore: Springer.

Paseka, Angelika, and Dagmar Killus. 2019. "Parental Involvement in Germany." In *Parental Involvement Across European Education Systems: Critical Perspectives*, edited by Angelika Paseka and Delma Byrne, 21–34. Milton: Routledge.

Posey-Maddox, Linn. 2014. *When Middle-Class Parents Choose Urban Schools: Class, Race, and the Challenge of Equity in Public Education*. Chicago, IL: University of Chicago Press.

Proctor, Helen, Patrick Brownlee, and Peter Freebody, eds. 2015. *Controversies in Education: Orthodoxy and Heresy in Policy and Practice*. Cham: Springer.

Proctor, Helen, and Heather Weaver. Forthcoming. "Family, Community and Sociability, 1920-Present." In *A Cultural History of Education in the Modern Age (1920-Present)*, edited by Judith Hartford and Tom O'Donoghue. Bloomsbury.

Reay, Diane. 1998. *Class Work: Mothers' Involvement in Their Children's Primary Schooling*. London: UCL Press.

Sahlberg, Pasi. 2011. *Finnish Lessons: What Can the World Learn From Educational Change in Finland*. New York: Teachers College Press.

Saltmarsh, Sue, Jenny Barr, and Amy Chapman. 2015. "Preparing for Parents: How Australian Teacher Education Is Addressing the Question of Parent-School Engagement." *Asia Pacific Journal of Education* 35 (1): 69–84. doi:10.1080/02188791.2014.906385.

Shuffelton, Amy. 2020. "What Parents Know: Risk and Responsibility in United States Education Policy and Parents' Responses." *Comparative Education*. doi:10.1080/03050068.2020.1724490.

Sriprakash, Arathi, R. Maithreyi, Akash Kumar, Pallawi Sinha, and Ketaki Prabha. 2020. "Normative Development in Rural India: 'School Readiness' and Early Childhood Care and Education." *Comparative Education*. doi:10.1080/03050068.2020.1725350.

Stacey, Meghan. 2016. "'Middle-Class Parents' Educational Work in an Academically Selective Public High School'." *Critical Studies in Education* 57 (2): 209–223. doi:10.1080/17508487.2015.1043312.

Vincent, Carol. 2017. "'The Children Have Only Got One Education and You Have to Make Sure It's a Good One': Parenting and Parent-School Relations in a Neoliberal Age." *Gender and Education* 29 (5): 541–557.

Willis, Paul. 1977. *Learning to Labour: How Working Class Kids Get Working Class Jobs*. Farnborough: Saxon House.

Windle, Joel A. 2015. *Making Sense of School Choice: Politics, Policies and Practice Under Conditions of Cultural Diversity*. New York: Palgrave Macmillan.

Normative development in rural India: 'school readiness' and early childhood care and education

Arathi Sriprakash ⓘ, R. Maithreyi, Akash Kumar, Pallawi Sinha and Ketaki Prabha

ABSTRACT
Global education agendas frequently draw on the construct of 'school readiness', indexing the developmental trajectories of children to the expectations of school systems. Through in-depth ethnographic research in a village in Bihar, India, this paper examines how normative discourses of 'school readiness' govern family strategies for early childhood care and education (ECCE). To navigate the demandsof a competitive and socially stratified school system, marginalised families saw it as crucial for their young children to access multiple forms of educational capital: written literacy, discipline, and dominant caste-class codes. In the absence of functioning provision of ECCE by the state, the low-fee and low-quality private market of early childhood education was seen as a key site through which 'school readiness' could be secured. The paper illustrates how normative developmentalism in education, and the 'hegemonic aspirations' it enshrines, has entrenched the marketisation of ECCE and reinscribed forms of caste-class domination.

Introduction

This paper examines how norms relating to both child development and global development have come together in the field of early childhood care and education (ECCE). Within international development policy, concerns about early childhood development are often narrowly framed in relation to systems of formal education. For example, the construct of school readiness, drawn from educational psychology, indexes the developmental trajectory of the child to the political and social norms of schooling. As we discuss, such discourses of school readiness not only establish developmental norms for children, but also for families, who are expected to participate in specific ways in the projects of national/global development. We explore the implications of these expectations in rural India among families who have faced their own structural exclusion from formal education and who are living in contexts of significant deprivation.

The paper reports on ethnographic research that took place in Gajwa village in the district of Katihar, in the state of Bihar.[1] In Gajwa, three *anganwadi* centres were to provide fee-free pre-school education for 3–6 year olds, as well as health services and supplementary feeding programmes for children under six years, as part of the government's

Integrated Child Development Scheme (ICDS). These centres were observed to be largely non-functioning, with few resources, little pedagogic engagement, and irregular staffing and student attendance. Many families emphasised that the anganwadi was a place for children to receive midday-meals and health-checks rather than being a space for school-relevant learning (see also Kapoor 2006; Alcott et al. 2018). Seeking opportunities for their children to be 'school ready', then, those who had the financial means tended to turn to low-fee options for ECCE provision, usually in the form of English-medium private kindergartens or private tutoring.[2]

The research shows how the competitive, highly stratified, and increasingly marketized system of elementary and secondary school has profoundly influenced ideals and expectations of early childhood education in India. This is having several implications for marginalised families and the practice of ECCE. Firstly, pre-school-aged children were experiencing forms of instruction that did not meet the norms of developmentally appropriate practice, but which were nevertheless accepted as necessary preparation for the rigid, competitive structures of schooling.[3] Children as young as three and four years were required to sit for long periods engaged in rote-instruction[4] with little to no opportunity for play-based learning. Corporal punishment, at times severe, was frequently used by instructors as a disciplinary device. Secondly, parents and teachers alike widely interpreted institutional forms of ECCE as not only desirable but also as the only legitimate site of learning. The knowledge and pedagogies within families – most of whom had been excluded from formal education – were deemed irrelevant or deficient to the work of 'readying' children for school. Thirdly, and relatedly, strategies for school success often involved assimilating the cultures of educational consumption of the dominant middle-classes. In particular, sending young children to English-medium private pre-schools, including those with boarding facilities, was seen as desirable so that children would not be influenced by the 'village environment'. Through both coded and explicit casteism, parents expressed concern about their children picking up 'bad habits' from a perceived lack of cleanliness, discipline and literacy in the village. With caste domination explicitly shaping everyday life in Gajwa, participation in a differentiated system of ECCE was another way in which caste-class stratifications were being reproduced.[5]

As an account of the political economy of ECCE in Gajwa, we frame these findings through Leela Fernandes' and Patrick Heller's discussion of 'hegemonic aspirations' (Fernandes and Heller 2006). Dominant middle-class cultures of consumption in neoliberal India are explicitly shaping the aspirations of – and therefore new markets for – the emergent middle classes and also, as we show, the rural poor (see also Fernandes 2004). In education, the marked exit of the middle-classes from the government school system (Nambissan 2014),[6] alongside middle-class consumption of educational products and services (e.g. English medium instruction, private tuition), has circumscribed the imagination of 'good' education to the life-worlds and resources of the dominant caste-classes, and to the institutional priorities of schooling (e.g. written literacy and social discipline). These are ideals which the marginalised are expected to aspire to and assimilate; demands that see poor families incorporating themselves into a competitive, highly marketized system of low-quality and often developmentally inappropriate early childhood education (see also Donner 2006).

Here, we suggest, there is an underexamined confluence of development norms: those from educational psychology (vis a vis 'school readiness'), which sets out attitudes and practices that families should assimilate in order to participate appropriately in formal schooling, and; those from the political project of economic development, which establishes ideals for assimilating oneself into modern capitalist society. These norms govern life, not in a totalising sense, but through 'countless, often competing, local tactics of education, persuasion, inducement, management, incitation, motivation and encouragement' (Rose and Miller 1992, 175). As the fields of development and psychology continue to interact with each other and insert themselves into the lives of the poor, there is an ongoing need to more clearly identify and critically examine the forms and effects of such normative developmentalism in ECCE and in education more broadly.

The structure of the paper is as follows. We first examine the circulation of school readiness discourse in global development policy, identifying its normative assumptions and its rendering of the 'ready family' as a matter of concern for development intervention. Next, we elaborate on the research context and approach of the study, and then demonstrate how discourses of school readiness are reflected through parental aspirations and participation in ECCE and through the practices of ECCE institutions themselves. This is an analysis of how 'global forms' of expertise on early childhood development are translated through, in Collier and Ong's words, 'new material, collective and discursive relationships' within specific local contexts (Collier and Ong 2005, 4; see also Newberry 2017). By foregrounding relations of casteism and capitalism in ECCE, the paper sheds light on how school readiness is a discourse that not only governs families, children, and ECCE institutions but is also rendered intelligible through a framework for 'development' that is enmeshed in, and arguably sustains, systems of social domination.

ECCE and school readiness in global development policy

Early childhood development has become a major priority of global development.[7] Target 4.2 of the Sustainable Development Goals makes clear the instrumentalism behind such concerns: by 2030 countries should 'ensure that all girls and boys should have access to quality early childhood development, care and pre-primary education *so that children are ready for primary education*' (emphasis added). Investing in early years education is often underscored an effective strategy for promoting economic growth (cf. World Bank 2018; UNICEF 2019), and early childhood development is sometimes predictively linked to a sweeping array of social concerns: 'school success and completion; higher earnings; active participation in communities and society; and reduced odds of delinquency, crime, and chronic and non-communicable disease' (Young Lives 2016, 2; see also Penn 2011).[8] Often less apparent in such development discourses are rights- or justice-based frameworks for child development.

The rendering of ECCE as a global development priority and an effective economic investment, and sometimes as a moral panic, has had implications for how childhood and families across the world are imagined as subjects of intervention. The concept of 'parenting' has gained prominence within international development policy and research agencies, with 2019 seeing the first Global Parenting Month launched by UNICEF. Dahlberg and colleagues note that a language of standardisation, efficiency and control permeates the now very public – and explicitly scientised – discourse on early childhood care and education, which has shifted away from the vocabularies of home or community learning and care practices (Dahlberg, Moss, and Pence 2005). Drawing attention to the geographically confined, and thus conceptually narrow, empirical basis of early childhood development research, Helen Penn (2004) argues that

> almost all the evidence about the effectiveness of ECD in determining cognitive, social and economic outcomes for children is drawn either directly from the North, particularly from the USA, or relies on the assumptions of work carried out in the North as a basis for programming and recommendations in the South. (Penn 2004, iv; see also Serpell and Nsamenang 2014)

To be clear, early childhood development matters. But there is a need for critical inspection of the norms that become hitched to children and families in the global south through the take-up of child development as a matter of international development. The notion of 'school readiness' from educational psychology has, in particular, gained significant traction within global development discourse and has narrowly framed early childhood development in terms of the priorities of the institution of schooling (see, for example, reports by UNICEF on *School Readiness and Transitions* (2012) and *A World Ready to Learn* (2019)).[9] In broad terms, school readiness refers to 'the state of child competencies at the time of school entry that are important for later success' (Snow 2006, 9). However, there is little consensus within educational psychology about the constitutive components and theoretical underpinning of the concept.[10] The model of school readiness put forward by UNICEF identifies 'ready children', 'ready schools', and 'ready families' to suggest that each dimension would be 'considered ready when they have gained the competencies and skills required to interface with the other dimensions and support smooth transitions' (UNICEF 2012, 3).

What are the competencies and skills required of 'ready children'? UNICEF rather loosely suggests that school readiness is linked to broad domains of development and learning: 'physical well-being and motor development; social and emotional development; approaches to learning; language development; cognition and general knowledge; spiritual and moral development; appreciation for diversity and national pride' (UNICEF 2012, 4). Here, social norms such as 'spiritual and moral development' and 'national pride' have been included, without critical discussion, as a 'domain' of child development. This illustrates how the school-ready child is required to embody state and dominant-group interests, and in the context of the violent resurgence of ethno-nationalism in India and elsewhere, it also stands as a warning of how such norms can be depoliticised through their inclusion in 'scientific' frameworks.

What is also striking in such policy discourses is that preparation for formal schooling is uncritically positioned as the principal basis for early child development, producing narrow directions in which children's unfolding developmental maturities must be harnessed. Evaluative schemas to assesses children's and families' 'readiness' for institutional norms are thus produced and circulated as part of the target-driven, metric-based approach to education and international development. For example, the UNICEF report offers guidelines for policy-makers and practitioners to monitor and evaluate school readiness within families, including the degree to which parents understand the importance of education. Decontextualised statements about the predictive relationship between 'supportive parenting and stimulating home environments' and 'school performance during primary school and beyond' (UNICEF 2012, 4), enable development actors to position poor families as a key site of reform.

The educational dispositions and practices of families have thus become subjects of development inquiry. For example, UNICEF defines 'ready families' as having educational goals, beliefs, attitudes and commitment, and a supportive learning environment in the home, specifically parental engagement with 'singing, reading books, telling stories, and playing games' (UNICEF 2012, 4). Within Indian ECCE policy too, the need to strengthen the 'capabilities' of families is emphasised, particularly through programmes and provisions for 'balanced parenting' (MWCD 2013, Section 2.1.2). India's 2014 National Early Childhood Care and Education Curriculum Framework (NECCECF) echoes almost verbatim UNICEF's statements on the ready family, emphasising the need for families to provide 'supportive parenting and a stimulating home environment' and be 'sensitised' to enrol their children in school (MWCD 2014, 23–24). Here, the good of formal education is assumed, even as the principle of education as a public good erodes under aggressive market liberalism.[11]

Family 'readiness', then, assumes middle-class material resources (like books), educational capital (the ability to read), and hegemonic aspirations to schooling (goals, beliefs, and commitment). To secure educational success for their children, families who have been structurally excluded from formal schooling are required to assimilate their attitudes and practices, in the face of significant material deprivation, to an education system still marked by social domination and stratification. The 'school readiness' discourse in ECCE policy, we suggest, enshrines normative relations between schools, children and families, whilst failing to attend to the structural conditions of poverty and exclusion on which these relations are contingent. How poor rural families navigated the norms of school readiness through their strategies for early childhood care and education was, as we set out below, a key focus of our research.

The research context and approach

The ethnographic research on which this paper is based took place in Gajwa village, in Korha block of the district of Katihar, in rural Bihar.[12] Bihar is one of the most economically disadvantaged states in India.[13] The average adult literacy rate in Korha block is 50.16%, and significantly lower for marginalised 'Scheduled Caste' and 'Scheduled Tribe' groups (37.68% and 39.24% respectively, with female literacy rates lower than male literacy rates across all groups). (GoI 2011). Gajwa village, with an approximate population of 2800, is divided into three wards or electoral constituencies, each with their own anganwadi, and two with a government primary school.[14] Each ward was informally clustered into different *tolas* (hamlets) by sub-castes/communities, creating some geographic segregation between different social groups.

The three anganwadis in Gajwa catered to a mixed population of Scheduled Caste (SC), Scheduled Tribe (ST), Other Backward Castes (OBC) and Muslim communities.[15] Some 42% of the population in the village were Mahadalits (SCs) from the Mushahar, Pasi, Turi and Dom communities.[16] Against an ongoing history of caste oppression and educational exclusion, these Mahadalit communities were mostly landless daily-wage labourers and they lived in visible poverty. Dominant caste groups such as Bhumihars, Rajputs, Poddars and Bhagats were numerically small in Gajwa but held considerable political and economic power as land owners. A large Muslim community also lived in the village, many of whom had some economic power also through land ownership or small businesses. About 10% of the population of Gajwa were Santhals, who were mostly agricultural labourers. Officially designated as a 'Scheduled Tribe', many referred to themselves as Santhal or as Adivasi – the latter a collective political identification for the indigenous peoples of India. Through the influence of Hindu-nationalist and Christian missionary 'charities' in the area, and a broader politics of Sanskritization, many Santhals in Gajwa had converted to Hinduism or Christianity.

The research focused on the three anganwadi centres within the village which operated under the government's Integrated Child Development Services (ICDS) as well as a low-fee private English-medium school called AJ International School which was located on the main road at the outskirts of the village.[17] These institutions were selected as the main ECCE providers serving children in Gajwa. While relatively few families from the village could afford the private school, many pre-school children attended private tutoring classes run within the homes of local villagers. Akash, one of the authors of this paper, was based in Gajwa for six months to lead the fieldwork, focusing on practices within ECCE centres and families' interactions with these institutions. The research team – the other authors of this paper – also made visits to Gajwa to observe ECCE centres, meet families, and conduct interviews. Extensive observational fieldnotes were constructed of village life and of the settings and practices of each ECCE institution. We also conducted interviews with parents, teachers/anganwadi workers in each ECCE centre, and school managers and local administrators. Interviews were conducted in Hindi or Theti and were translated into English.[18]

Poverty and casteism profoundly shaped life in Gajwa, including the functioning of educational institutions. Key resources such as schools, anganwadis, places of worship, public shelters and shops were located further away from the hamlets of the most marginalised groups like the Mahadalits and Santhals, particularly the Doms.[19] This impacted the ability of such communities to regularly access the anganwadi centre, and parents reported that young children were often not able to walk the 2–4 kilometres required to attend classes. As a means of encouraging attendance, anganwadi staff were meant to conduct home visits and collect children for class. However, as we observed, and as Mahadalit and Santhali participants frequently described, the Sahayikas (anganwadi 'helpers') would only visit homes of children from their own communities and not enter the hamlets of the most marginalised groups. Such discrimination was also observed in the daily practices of the anganwadis. For example, Kiran, the upper-caste Sahayika at one of the centres, would not cook food for the children's lunches unless one of the children fetched the water – a task she considered below her caste status.[20]

Analytically, the research focused on how relations of power in Gajwa (such as casteism, poverty, marketisation, and development norms such as 'school readiness') were shaping ECCE participation. Taking this approach, we departed from the psychological and anthropological research in India that has focused on 'cultural' models of family practices (Roopnarine, Lu, and Ahmeduzzaman 1989; Saraswathi and Pai 1997; Tuli 2012; Chaudhary 2013; Anandalakshmy 2014; Saraswathi, Menon, and Madan 2018). Such work often indexes family cultures, either implicitly or explicitly, to normative concepts of parenting and childhood. Arguably, using culture as an explanatory device lays open the rendering of difference as 'deviation' from the dominant group norm and as an inherent – thereby racialised – trait.[21] Such an approach turns away from, and thus permits the obfuscation of, the relations of social domination that have produced conditions of difference. In particular, research has paid too little attention to how casteism – as a structural, intergenerational system of domination – has shaped how families negotiate and experience early childhood care and education (Sriprakash 2018).

Strategies of the 'ready family': navigating ECCE norms in Gajwa

Families in Gajwa widely expressed the need for formal early childhood education so that their children would be prepared for and be competitive within the structures of schooling. As we discuss in the sections below, school 'readiness' for children in Gajwa was largely interpreted as developing written literacy skills as well as caste-class educational capital: learning to sit still, being disciplined, and assimilating dominant caste-class cultures. In the absence of functioning anganwadis, many families turned to low-fee private tutoring and some to private pre-schooling to help their children be ready for school. We look more closely at these strategies for securing early childhood education – as enactments of the 'ready family'.

School readiness as learning to sit and learning to write

Families in Gajwa were, like anywhere, actively socialising and teaching their children, relaying complex skills relating to life and livelihood. Children as young as six were observed to be routinely involved in makhana (fox nut) harvesting, fishing, weaving, farming, cooking, trading, sibling-care, tending to animals, as well as playing. However, the knowledge and pedagogies that underpinned these activities, that is, the learning that took place outside formal institutions, was not seen as relevant to becoming ready for school, nor to success in the modern economy. The cultures and lessons of the home were regularly described as distinct to that of schools, with parents emphasising the need for formal, institutional education in early childhood. Within the school readiness framework, marginalised families were not seen to have relevant skills and knowledge to educate their young children.

For example, Sheela Devi Bhagat, was a 28-year-old woman from an OBC community whose family ran a small shop in the village. She had three young daughters aged four, five and eight, and reflecting on their education, she explained,

> In this world, education is the most needed, is it not? Without education, can a person get anywhere? That is why getting education is very important, so that the child learns the culture and becomes educated. The family can only teach children family values, how to bring them up or mould them. But the teacher's job of teaching can only be done by the teacher, not the parents.

Sheela often emphasised the importance of early literacy instruction, and despite being literate herself with a Bachelor's degree, her distinction between what parents and teachers could impart to young children echoed the idea that early childhood care and education was a specialised field that relied on expert knowledge. For many families in Gajwa, these distinctions entrenched and sometimes internalised relations of social domination. For example, Kanti Devi, a 40 year old Mushahar (Mahadalit) woman with a five year old daughter who attended one of the anganwadis, described, 'in our community, most of us are illiterate, so how could we teach our children? We know nothing'. The dehumanising effects of caste oppression, regularly reinforced by states and development agencies through administrative language such as 'backward', 'illiterate' and 'uneducated', meant that families in Gajwa were having to struggle against such deficit frameworks as they navigated the demands of school readiness.

With early years learning so strongly framed as written literacy, what options did parents like Sheela or Kanti Devi have for securing this kind of early childhood education for their children? Observations of the three anganwadis in Gajwa revealed that the centres were not following a planned curriculum and children were rarely offered teacher-led pedagogic stimulus. There were no books or toys available for children in the bare facilities (see Figure 1). On rare occasions, children were asked to copy out letters in Hindi on slates, otherwise they would talk or play among themselves, or be asked to sit still. One of the few interactions observed between anganwadi teachers and children involved a ritualised performance about the importance of cutting nails, washing hands, and coming to class in clean clothes. The anganwadi centres were not regularly staffed and, when open, the focus appeared to be on administrative duties, the delivery of mid-day meals, and the distribution of nutritional supplies to infants and pregnant/lactating mothers as part of the ICDS scheme.[22]

While only a handful of the 45 children registered in each centre were in attendance on any given day, and despite these centres being largely non-functioning, most families in Gajwa with preschool aged children had some connection to the anganwadis. Mothers from the Mushahar and OBC communities explained during a focus group discussion that even if their children didn't regularly attend, they were registered so they could access the mid-day meal provision, and to facilitate school enrolment once their children turned six.[23] Parents frequently expressed that there was 'no education' in anganwadis and it was just for 'time-pass purpose'. The only educational opportunity within anganwadis, according to parents, was socialisation into an institutional environment, particularly for young children to 'learn to sit'. Learning to 'sit still' was seen as an important component of becoming ready for school, something parents often referred to. However, for academic learning, particularly 'learning to write', parents had to look elsewhere.

Figure 1. An anganwadi centre in Gajwa village; typical infrastructure of a one-room facility.

Learning to write, then, was almost universally seen to occur through private tuition. Private tuition was a ubiquitous feature of life in Gajwa, with children coming and going to tuition lessons each afternoon. There were also numerous billboards along the main road of Gajwa advertising more expensive English-medium private coaching centres in nearby towns, standing as an aspirational reminder, and marking private tuition as a main (not just supplementary) provider of education. Most families whose children were registered at the anganwadis would attend private tuition within the houses of more educated members of each community, many of whom were teachers themselves, working a second job after school hours. Classes were held in Santhali, Theti or Hindi, in make-shift rooms or sheds in courtyards for both pre-school and school aged children. For one to one-and-a-half hours each day, children would complete copy-writing, homework and mathematics exercises. Some parents would purchase workbooks for children to fill in; a resource not available in the anganwadi centres.

Parents described private tuition as an alternative to private schooling for those who could not afford the higher costs of the latter, and as unquestionably necessary in the face of non-functioning anganwadis. However, despite being 'low fee', private tuition bore a significant cost to many households, with fees reported to be between 100–300 rupees per month for primary school children and 50 rupees per month for pre-school children.[24] As we discuss below, such investments in formal pre-school education emerge not just from a prioritisation of written literacy in the early years as part of readying children for school. They also reflect family strategies to secure forms of caste-class educational capital, which was seen as particularly crucial for both school and economic success.

School readiness as class-caste distinction

In the context of an expanding market of ECCE services and centres, the 'ready family' was arguably being drawn into participating in a highly differentiated, stratified system of early childhood education. In Gajwa, ECCE had become a means for creating class-caste distinctions and enacting the 'hegemonic aspirations' of educational consumption. This was often expressed by parents in terms of their desire for their children to learn English and/or Hindi (as the languages of the dominant classes), and to seek pre-school education that would separate children from 'lower' caste-class communities.

Sushmita, a Santhal woman in her early thirties who was an agricultural labourer explained the importance of studying in English as it opened up the possibilities of different kinds of jobs. Her twelve-year-old boy was in a residential convent school in a nearby town and she was very pleased that he had learned English. Comparing his education to her own, she expressed, 'I'm uneducated and was married early. Now my body is broken from all the hard work I have done. What work can I do now?'. Her five-year-old daughter was currently registered at one of the anganwadi centres in the village, but Sushmita wanted her to attend the convent school too. The high costs were preventing her from doing so, but, like many in Gajwa, Sushmita aspired for her children to learn English – and emphasised the importance of doing so at a young age. Indeed, Bittu, a father from the Muslim hamlet whose six-year-old girl attended a private residential school in a town 13 kilometres from Gajwa, was pleased that her teachers talk only in Hindi or English. He went on to explain that his daughter no longer had to be reliant on Theti, which he described as the language of *gawar*, or provincial, people.

The turn to private provision for early childhood care and education was a conscious strategy for securing caste-class advantage. As another father from the Muslim hamlet in Gajwa explained, government schooling, including anganwadis, are mostly for the poor who were 'just going about the course of their life'. But private schools are for the rich and the middle classes, he added, where children can imagine getting a good job and life style: 'Their dreams go far. They'll be made to study outside, their scope will increase'. Families who sent their children to private pre-schools would also purchase private tutoring as a strategy to keep their children occupied and away from other children with 'bad habits'. As Kamala, mother of five year old Manav, who attended Gajwa's low-fee private school, AJ International, explained, 'the more time he spends in school and tuition, the more time he will be away from children in the village who don't go to school'. Coming from a land-owning Kushwaha (OBC) family with a relatively higher annual income of 35–40,000 rupees, implicit in Kamala's remarks was a desire for social class closure.

There was also an explicit desire held by many families, particularly among those in relatively better socio-economic positions, to keep children away from the 'village environment' in order for them to do well educationally. Parents explicitly mentioned that children learn a new culture ('sanskar') by attending private school. So strong was the desire among some families for children to leave the village environment, that some would look to residential boarding schools. Parents like Bittu felt conflicted about sending his young daughter to a residential private school, but he explained it was necessary to avoid the lack of discipline and education among other children in Gajwa. Mukhabir Mansoor, a father from the Muslim hamlet explained that he did not want to send his children to the anganwadis where they would mix with 'lower' caste children and be exposed to 'bad language' and a 'dirty' environment. Mukhabir's sons were now six and thirteen, and had attended private ECCE centres in a nearby village instead of the anganwadis in Gajwa. 'In an anganwadi children should learn sitting tolerance', he went on, 'but they go there and get spoilt'.[25]

Here, we see how families are navigating ECCE as a crucial, high-stakes part of their children's education. Family 'readiness' at times involved being 'ready' to send young children away – out of the village environment – in order to secure caste-class advantages in schooling. As we turn now to discuss, through both explicit and subtle forms of discipline, young children in Gajwa were being socialised into both the academic and caste-class norms of schooling, often in ways that belied the norms of developmentally appropriate practice. Learning discipline, we suggest, was as a means of making oneself 'school ready'.

School readiness as learning discipline

Despite policies, legislation, and public campaigns for child-friendly education that is free from corporal punishment, rigid and often violent disciplinary approaches are frequently reported in Indian schools (Iyer 2013; Morrow and Singh 2014). The notion of 'discipline' – connoting both social and personal regulation – carries historical and social significance within postcolonial India as part of the active legacies of colonial domination. Ranajit Guha (1997) argues that discipline was an 'obsession' of nationalist mobilisation – 'an attempt to compensate by discipline for what the bourgeoisie had failed to gain by persuasion' (135), and Krishna Kumar's (1991) accounts of the teacher as the 'meek dictator' point to the centrality of schools as sites of 'maintaining order'. In Gajwa, discipline was often seen as a legitimate pedagogic device for academic and social learning, and parents would regularly describe fear and corporal punishment as a normal and necessary part of education. To be school ready, parents expressed that preschool aged children needed to learn the disciplinary codes of schooling, and this was a key rationale for seeking institutional forms of early childhood care and education. As Kamala, the mother of five year old Manav, explained,

> we cannot teach children at home, if parents teach with love and affection, then the child will not listen. That is why we have to send them to school. There is fear in children at school, because of which they study.

Formal learning environments were not only seen to be more effective in imparting academic knowledge but also in helping children internalise a kind of social respectability. A number of families explained that private schools in particular taught good social behaviour and discipline, and many aspired to enrol their children in private pre-schools for this reason.

Manav attended the low-fee private AJ International primary school that had opened in 2018 in the premises of an old warehouse on the main road of Gajwa. The school had multiple pre-school classes as well as rudimentary boarding facilities (see Figure 2) which Manav's mother wanted him to stay in after a year or so. The school had approximately 150 children between 2–6 years of age enrolled in its pre-school sections, some coming from Gajwa but many from surrounding villages. Tuition and transport fees were approximately 1000 rupees per month, and books and uniforms cost 3000 rupees each year. The

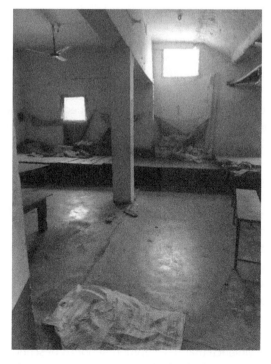

Figure 2. The boys' boarding room at AJ International School. There was a similar room for girls.

school had separate classes for pre-nursery, nursery, lower kindergarten, senior kindergarten and upper kindergarten, however, the curriculum was observed to be similar across these classes, and their physical arrangement and pedagogic interactions unmistakably mirrored that of upper-level primary and secondary schooling. Here, the desire to ready children for school, meant that ECCE was school-like, even though this often did not reflect developmentally appropriate practice.

For example, pre-school classrooms at AJ International consisted of long rows of metal benches attached to a desk which were too large for the smaller children. Subject periods (English, mathematics, science and Hindi) were of 45 minutes each and structured by the content of work books produced by the MBD Group, a publishing, real estate and hospitality company. Each child had books from MBD's 'Holy Faith' series in which they individually completed exercises such as identifying and writing letters and numbers, counting objects and naming shapes. Teachers read from the textbook and would mark children's written work. Pre-school children were observed reciting multiplication tables by memory without scaffolded instruction on the concepts involved. Inquiry-based or play-based learning was not observed as a pedagogic strategy within classrooms, and there were few resources to facilitate such approaches. Verbal and corporal punishment was regularly seen being used by teachers towards children who were not producing correct answers or who were distracted during lessons. Older children were made to squat on their haunches outside classrooms as a form of humiliation.

The 'chairman' of the school was Sirajuddin, an entrepreneur who had previously owned a molasses transportation business in Maharashtra and, like many who run such private schools, had no formal training in education.[26] He explained that poor families understood that it was important for children to come to schools such as his, not only to learn reading and writing but also to learn how to behave in society. He explained, 'uthana-baithana sikhte hain' – children should learn how to 'sit and stand', referring to embodiment of 'respectable' dominant caste-class behaviours. Sirajuddin went on to say that children at his school learned manners like wishing teachers good morning, and the first months of pre-schooling were spent socialising young children in these habits before moving on to 'writing A-B-C'. He echoed a commonly held view that village children needed to be disciplined because they came from 'uneducated' environments. Parents at AJ International, most of whom had not been to school beyond tenth standard, also expressed that it was important for their children to 'catch up' with the 'educated' classes. Speaking about the boarding facilities at the school, Sirajuddin explained that parents wanted their children to be 'away from the atmosphere of the village'. School readiness, as a form of disciplining oneself, called on social – and sometimes even physical – distance from families and communities.

Sohan Soren, a thirty-five year old Santhal man living in Gajwa, was sending his five year old son to AJ International School. He felt that Santhali language and culture wouldn't bring opportunities for his children or enable them to 'study further'. Nobody outside the hamlet spoke Santhali, he explained, so he wanted his son to learn Hindi and English. This may be read as a strategic decision by Sohan Soren to give his children access to the knowledge of the powerful, but it is also reflective of an internalisation of casteism; the symbolic violence that developmental norms of school readiness – and projects of mass education more broadly – are steeped in yet rarely address. As he went on to explain, *'Santhal dharm ka aadat chhoot jata hai toh bachche ache se shikshit hote hai'* ('Once they have gotten rid of the habit of Santhal *dharm* [way of life], children can get educated well'). For Sohan Soren, family readiness involved providing opportunities for children to access the social codes of the dominant caste-classes. He reiterated, *'Hindu dharm se padhayega tab bachcha ko shiksha milega'* ('If you teach using Hindu *dharm*, then the child will get educated').

Mirroring the rigid structures of formal schooling, the practices of early childhood education at AJ international had come to be accepted as a way in which young children should be disciplined in normative educational habits and practices. Such forms of socialisation were seen to enable children to access, internalise or embody dominant class-caste codes as a means of becoming 'ready' for social and educational success.

Interrogating normative development

This paper has sought to illustrate how marginalised families navigate development expectations of school readiness within specific political economies of early childhood care and education. The prioritisation of 'readying' young children for school, in both policy and community discourse, has circumscribed the kinds of practices and attitudes that are 'desirable' for young children and families. In particular, early childhood in Gajwa was predominately framed as a high-stakes period for the development of social discipline and educational capital. The downward extension of schooling into early childhood education was often at the expense of developmentally appropriate practices. In the absence of a functioning state system for ECCE and in a political economy that served caste-class 'hegemonic aspirations' of educational consumption, the preferred means for 'readying' children for school was through an unregulated private market of ECCE provision. Not only was the imagination of 'good' ECCE constrained to institutional forms, denying the care and education practices of the home, but it was also a means of creating and reinscribing caste-class distinctions. Enacting the developmental subject of the 'ready family', in this context, required families to incorporate themselves into a hierarchical, stratified, and marketized system of education.

It is through such an analysis that we argue for a sustained interrogation of the normative developmentalism that is brought to the lives of children and their families across the global south. Technocratic 'fixes' to make marginalised families and children 'ready' for schooling are ill equipped to identify, much less intervene in, the political economies that produce relations of social domination. It has become a norm for early child development to be attached to the structures of schooling, even when those structures produce both real and symbolic violence in marginalised communities (e.g. the internalisation of casteism, explicit disciplining in class-caste codes). It has become a norm for families to participate in institutional forms of early childhood education, even when this entrenches educational marketisation and a political economy that serves the dominant classes. It is assumed that the 'ready' child and the 'ready' family should be 'ready' to be included into the normative development project established by national and international elites. But it is precisely this project of 'development' that needs radical inspection if education – including early childhood care and education – is to dismantle rather than reproduce structures of inequality.

Notes

1. The village name is a pseudonym, as are all names of individuals and institutions reported in this paper.
2. The Annual Status of Education Report (ASER 2019) indicates 23% of children in rural Bihar are enrolled in private preschools or schools by age 5. Quantitative data on the nature and extent of private tuition across the state is unavailable.
3. The lack of developmentally appropriate practice in ECCE has been identified as a major concern in India (See Kaul and Sankar 2009; Swaminathan 2006). In 2014 the Ministry of Women and Child Development released the National Early Childhood Care and Education Curricular Framework (NECCECF) which put forward DAP guidelines for ECCE practitioners. However, the NECCECF is non-binding on private ECCE institutions, and as our research in Gajwa shows, it is not always implemented – or known about – in anganwadis.
4. Rote instruction refers to learning by repetitive instruction and memorisation. See Krishna Kumar's (1991) analysis of the historical significance of rote instruction in India, in the context of a broader 'textbook culture'. Sriprakash (2012) among others have documented the continued dominance of this pedagogic approach in formal schooling.
5. The conjoining of caste-class here refers to the 'nexus' between caste and class in processes of social stratification in India (See Sharma 2014).
6. National level data on school enrolment from 2015–16 indicate that 37.9% of children are enrolled in private schools in India, a growth of over 10% since 2007–08. (NUEPA 2016).
7. Funded under the British Academy's Early Childhood Development Programme in partnership with the UK Department for International Development (DFID), this project itself is a part of the UK Government's development interest in ECCE.
8. However, despite strong policy rhetoric of the importance of ECCE investment, research indicates that aid financing to ECCE has declined significantly in recent years (Zubairi and Rose 2019).
9. A recent collection by Kaul and Bhattacharjea (2019) on *Early Childhood Education and School Readiness in India* documents the normative purchase of 'school readiness' on Indian education research and policy intervention. The recently released draft National Education Policy identifies the lack of 'school preparedness' as a 'major cause' of low learning (or, the 'learning crisis') in schools (GoI 2019, 56).
10. For example, school readiness can refer to considerations of developmental maturation (such as fine and gross motor skills) and cognitive ability, as well as attitudes and emotional competence (Bowman, Donovan, and Burns 2001). Within educational psychology, the construct has largely moved away from narrow maturational perspectives which locate 'readiness' as a characteristic of a child. More often, 'readiness' is understood as a bi-directional socio-culturally mediated relationship between the child and their environment (Murphey and Burns 2002; Carlton and Winsler 1999). See Snow (2006) for a useful overview of the contested construct of school readiness.
11. In India, the 2009 Right to Education Act in effect accepts the privatisation of the education system. It legislates that all private schools (low-fee and elite) must admit at least 25% of students from disadvantaged backgrounds, with these places subsidised by the state (Maithreyi and Sriprakash 2018). Some states like Karnataka have recently amended admission processes such that enrolment to private schools under the 'RTE quota' can only occur if there is no government or aided school in the neighbourhood. The Right to Education legislates universal schooling for children aged 6–14 years which does not cover early childhood care and education. At the time of writing this paper, the Government of India's draft National Education Policy (2019) was released. Among many other significant reforms to the structure of education, it proposes to bring ECCE into the governance framework of school education. https://innovate.mygov.in/new-education-policy-2019/. The ICDS programme in India is currently overseen by the Ministry of Woman and Child Development, not the Ministry of Human Resource Development (the latter is responsible for education).

12. Ethical approval for the research was gained through the University of Cambridge Research Ethics process as well as the Institutional Ethics Committee of the Indian Institute of Management, Bangalore. Informed consent was gained by all participants in the study.
13. Bihar has the second lowest child development index (CDI) in the country at 0.296 (Dreze and Khera 2015) and an Infant Mortality Rate (IMR) of 48 (higher than the national average of 41), according to 2015–16 data (IIPS 2017). Thirty-four per cent of the population are reported to be living below the poverty line (World Bank 2016). The state average for pre-school attendance is 59.8%, compared to the national average of 69.4% (MWCD and UNICEF 2013-14).
14. At the time of the 2011 census, there were 555 children of pre-school age – between 0 and 6 years – in the village.
15. The terms SC, ST and OBC are official categories of the state for identifying populations that have been historically discriminated against and continue to be socially and economically marginalised. Muslims in India are also officially designated as minority populations who face widespread discrimination, particularly with the current resurgence of violent Hindu nationalism. The terms used for, and the boundaries between, different social groups are widely contested. For the rest of the paper, we use the terms that communities in Gajwa used when referring to themselves. These terms are explained along with their state classifications where necessary.
16. Though 'Dalit' is used as a term of self-identification and political recognition by SC groups across India, the term 'Mahadalit' is a state category specific to Bihar that participants in our research used to describe themselves. The term Mahadalit refers to the most marginalised among Dalit or SC groups.
17. AJ International is a pseudonym, but we have chosen a name that reflects the global and elite/middle-class branding used by the school to appeal to the aspirations of families in Gajwa and surrounding villages. While the school self-consciously marketed itself as an English medium school, most classes were conducted in Hindi as the language that teachers were most proficient in.
18. Theti is a dialect of the Maithili language spoken in several parts of Bihar.
19. A limitation of the research was that we were not able to access the Dom community to represent more fully their concepts and experiences of ECCE. The Dom community is one of the most marginalised of the Mahadalits in Gajwa, and they continue to be excluded from educational institutions. Since we used the ECCE centres as a means of contacting and building rapport with participants, we were not able to easily facilitate such connections with members of the Dom community. The empirical erasure of 'hardest to reach' populations is a significant issue for our future research to address.
20. Institutional accountability was also heavily mediated through relations of caste domination. For example, there was little opportunity for redress of the discriminatory actions by Kiran, the upper-caste helper. Her immediate supervisor, Yasmin, a 35 year old Muslim woman and the main teacher at the anganwadi, explained that Kiran took little heed of her requests to undertake her duties (such as cooking and home visits), intimating that Kiran's age and caste-status within the community provided her with a level of impunity. Yasmin, who would refer to Kiran as 'chachi' (aunty), expressed she was unable to do much to enforce her authority, since they lived within the same community and had known each other since childhood.
21. Projit Bihari Mukharji (2017) offers an historical account of a stagist view of cultural difference within Indian anthropology which 'encouraged comparisons between multiple cultures and their arrangement into hierarchies. Evolutionist thinking did not simply create hierarchies between the colonised and the coloniser; as the colonised urban elite gradually came to produce their own ethnographies, they created hierarchies that set themselves off from various subaltern groups' (465).
22. Anganwadi centres were meant to be open from 9am-1pm in summer and 10am-2pm in winter months, Monday to Saturday. However, the Anganwadi teacher and helper were rarely observed to be present for this duration at the three centres in Gajwa.
23. Parents reported that the government primary schools would use anganwadi records to identify children who could enrol into first standard.

24. The range of monthly household incomes reported by participants was 1600–3750 rupees.
25. 'Sitting tolerance' was how Mukhabir described the ability to sit still for long periods – a key marker of school readiness.
26. Chairman is the term used at AJ International, reflecting its corporate-style approach, to designate the school manager. Sirajuddin was also one of the eleven teachers at the school.

Acknowledgements

This paper is based on research undertaken for the project *Examining the contexts, practices and costs of early childhood care and education in India* funded by the British Academy. We also acknowledge the contributions made by the project's co-Principal Investigator, Jyotsna Jha, and team member, Arun Viknesh, to the overall development of this work.

Disclosure statement

No potential conflict of interest was reported by the author(s).

Funding

This work was supported by British Academy (GCRF Early Childhood Development).

ORCID

Arathi Sriprakash http://orcid.org/0000-0003-3655-0605

References

Alcott, B., M. Banerji, S. Bhattacharjea, M. Nanda, and P. Ramanujan. 2018. "One Step Forward, Two Steps Back: Transitions Between Home, pre-Primary and Primary Education in Rural India." *Compare: A Journal of Comparative and International Education*, 1–18. doi:10.1080/03057925.2018.1527214.
Anandalakshmy, S. 2014. *Thinking with the Heart: A Compilation of Writings 1970-2014*. Chennai: Sterling and Quadrapress.
ASER. 2019. Annual Status of Education Report (2018) Rural: Provisional. *ASER centre: New Delhi*.
Bowman, B., M. Donovan, and M. Burns. 2001. *Eager to Learn: Educating our Preschoolers*. Washington, DC: National Academy Press.

Carlton, M. P., and A. Winsler. 1999. "School Readiness: The Need for a Paradigm Shift." *School Psychology Review* 28 (3): 338–352.

Chaudhary, N. 2013. *Parent Beliefs, Socialisation Practices and Children's Development in Indian Families. Major Research Project Report 2010-2013*. New Delhi: University Grants Commission.

Collier, S., and A. Ong. 2005. "Global Assemblages as Anthropological Problems." In *Global Assemblages: Technology, Politics and Ethics as Anthropological Problems*, edited by A. Ong, and S. Collier, 3–21. London: Blackwell.

Dahlberg, G., P. Moss, and A. Pence. 2005. *Beyond Quality in Early Childhood Education and Care: Postmodern Perspectives*. London: Falmer Press.

Donner, H. 2006. "Committed Mothers and Well-Adjusted Children: Privatisation, Early-Years Education and Motherhood in Calcutta." *Modern Asian Studies* 40 (2): 371–395.

Dreze, J., and R. Khera. 2015. *Child Development: How are Indian States Faring?* http://www.ideasforindia.in/topics/human-development/child-development-how-are-indian-states-faring.html.

Fernandes, L. 2004. "The Politics of Forgetting: Class Politics, State Power and the Restructuring of Urban Space in India." *Urban Studies* 41 (12): 2415–2430.

Fernandes, L., and P. Heller. 2006. "Hegemonic Aspirations." *Critical Asian Studies* 38 (4): 495–522.

Government of India. 2011. *District Census Handbook XII-A and B: Village and Town Directory*. Series 11. Bihar: Directorate of Census Operations, Government of India.

Government of India. 2019. *Draft National Education Policy*. New Delhi: Ministry of Human Resource Development.

Guha, R. 1997. *Dominance Without Hegemony: History and Power in Colonial India*. Cambridge: Harvard University Press.

International Institute for Population Sciences (IIPS) and ICF. 2017. *National Family Health Survey (NFHS-4), India, 2015-16: Bihar*. Mumbai: IIPS. http://rchiips.org/nfhs/NFHS-4Reports/Bihar.pdf.

Iyer, S. 2013. "An Ethnographic Study of Disciplinary and Pedagogic Practices in a Primary Class." *Contemporary Education Dialogue* 10 (2): 163–195.

Kapoor, S. 2006. "Early Childhood Care and Education: An Indian Perspective." In *Early Childhood Care and Education: International Perspectives*, edited by Edward Melhuish, and Konstantinos Petrogiannis, 133–150. Oxon: Routledge.

Kaul, V., and S. Bhattacharjea, eds. 2019. *Early Childhood Education and School Readiness in India: Quality and Diversity*. Singapore: Springer.

Kaul, V., and D. Sankar. 2009. *Early Childhood Care and Education: Education for all – Mid Decade Assessment*. New Delhi: National University of Educational Planning and Administration.

Kumar, K. 1991. *Political Agenda of Education. A Study of Colonialist and Nationalist Ideas*. New Delhi: Sage Publications.

Maithreyi, R., and A. Sriprakash. 2018. "The Governance of Families in India: Education, Rights and Responsibility." *Comparative Education* 54 (3): 352–369.

Ministry of Women and Child Development. 2013. *National Early Childhood Care and Education (ECCE) Policy*. New Delhi: Ministry of Women and Child Development, Government of India. https://wcd.nic.in/sites/default/files/National%20Early%20Childhood%20Care%20and%20Education-Resolution.pdf.

Ministry of Women and Child Development. 2014. *National Early Childhood Care and Education Curriculum Framework (NECCECF)*. New Delhi: MWCD, Government of India. https://wcd.nic.in/sites/default/files/national_ecce_curr_framework_final_03022014%20%282%29.pdf.

Ministry of Women and Child Development and UNICEF. 2013-14. *Rapid Survey on Children (RSOC) 2013-14: National Report*. New Delhi: Ministry of Women and Child Development, Government of India. https://wcd.nic.in/sites/default/files/RSOC%20National%20Report%202013-14%20Final.pdf.

Morrow, V., and R. Singh. 2014. *Corporal Punishment in Schools in Andhra Pradesh, India: Children's and Parents' Views*. Young Lives Working Paper 123. https://ora.ox.ac.uk/objects/uuid:688ce8cc-aed1-4f6f-b56d-c0c89d3ffc0a.

Mukharji, P. B. 2017. "The Bengali Pharaoh: Upper-Caste Aryanism, Pan-Egyptianism, and the Contested History of Biometric Nationalism in Twentieth-Century Bengal." *Comparative Studies in Society and History* 59 (2): 446–476.

Murphey, D. A., and C. E. Burns. 2002. Development of a Comprehensive Community Assessment of School Readiness. Early Childhood Research & Practice: An Internet Journal on the Development, Care, and Education of Young Children, 4 (2).

Nambissan, G. B. 2014. Poverty, Markets and Elementary Education in India. *TRG Poverty and Education Working Paper Series, Max Weber Stiftung*.

Newberry, J. 2017. ""Anything Can Be Used to Stimulate Child Development": Early Childhood Education and Development in Indonesia as a Durable Assemblage." *The Journal of Asian Studies* 76 (1): 25–45.

NUEPA (National University for Educational Planning and Administration). 2016. *Elementary Education in India: Trends 2005-06 to 2015-16*. New Delhi: NUEPA.

Penn, H. 2004. *CHIP Report 8: Childcare and Early Childhood Development Programmes and Policies: Their Relationship to Eradicating Child Poverty*. London, UK: Childhood Poverty Research and Policy Centre (CHIP).

Penn, H. 2011. "Travelling Policies and Global Buzzwords: How International Non-governmental Organizations and Charities Spread the Word About Early Childhood in the Global South." *Childhood* 18 (1): 94–113.

Roopnarine, J. L., Maureen W. Lu, and Mohammed Ahmeduzzaman. 1989. "Parental Reports of Early Patterns of Caregiving, Play and Discipline in India and Malaysia." *Early Child Development and Care* 50: 109–120.

Rose, N., and P. Miller. 1992. "Political Power Beyond the State: Problematics of Government." *British Journal of Sociology* 43: 173–205.

Saraswathi, T. S., S. Menon, and A. Madan. 2018. *Childhoods in India: Traditions, Trends and Transformations*. London: Routledge.

Saraswathi, T. S., and S. Pai. 1997. "Socialisation in the Indian Context." In *Asian Perspectives on Psychology*, edited by H. S. R. Rao, and D. Sinha, 74–92. New Delhi: Sage.

Serpell, R., and A. B. Nsamenang. 2014. *Locally Relevant and Quality ECCE Programmes: Implications of Research on Indigenous African Child Development and Socialization*. Early Childhood Care and Education Working Paper Series 3. Paris: UNESCO.

Sharma, K. 2014. "Explaining Caste–Class Nexus: Continuity and Change." In *Subalternity, Exclusion and Social Change in India*, edited by A. Pankaj and A. Pandey, 338–354. New Delhi: Foundation Books.

Snow, K. 2006. "Measuring School Readiness: Conceptual and Practical Considerations." *Early Education and Development* 17 (1): 7–41.

Sriprakash, A. 2012. *Pedagogies for Development. The Politics and Practice of Child Centred Education in India*. Dordrecht: Springer.

Sriprakash, A. 2018, 26 May. "The Political Future of Childhood Studies." *Economic Political Weekly* 53 (21): 31–33.

Swaminathan, M. S. 2006. "Innovative Childcare Programme in India." *International Journal of Early Years Education* 4 (2): 41–56.

Tuli, M. 2012. "Beliefs on Parenting and Childhood in India." *Journal of Comparative Family Studies* 43 (1): 81–91.

UNICEF. 2012. *School Readiness and Transitions. A Companion to the Child Friendly Schools Manual*. New York: UNICEF.

UNICEF. 2019. *A World Ready to Learn: Prioritizing Quality Early Childhood Education*. New York: UNICEF.

World Bank. 2016. *Bihar - Poverty, Growth and Inequality (English)*. India state briefs. Washington, DC: World Bank Group. http://documents.worldbank.org/curated/en/781181467989480762/Bihar-Poverty-growth-and-inequality.

World Bank. 2018. *World Development Report 2018: Learning to Realize Education's Promise*. Washington, DC: World Bank.

Young Lives. 2016. *Early Childhood Development in the SDGs*. Young Lives Policy Brief no.28. Oxford: Young Lives.

Zubairi, A., and P. Rose. 2019. Leaving the Youngest Behind: Declining aid to Early Childhood Education. Theirworld. https://theirworld.org/resources/detail/leaving-the-youngest-behind.

Great expectations: migrant parents and parent–school cooperation in Norway

Synnøve Bendixsen and Hilde Danielsen

ABSTRACT
One long-standing characteristic of schools in Norway is inclusive education as a primary goal. The last years, the Norwegian government has emphasised increased parent-school cooperation as a way to limit risks, i.e. of drop-outs. This article focuses on how parent-school relationship is played out in an economic and socially diversified urban borough in Bergen, Norway. It draws on fieldwork and interviews among parents, teachers and principals in three different schools. As this article shows, the increased focus on parents' active engagement in the school encourages and creates expectations of an intensive parenting model. Yet, not all parents are ready, willing or have the capacity to pursue the intensive parenting model. We suggest that the current promotion of middle-class intensive parenting by schools, in practice, shifts the responsibilisation of equal education away from the state towards individual families and undermine the ideals of inclusive education and equal opportunities in Norway.

Introduction

In Norway, engaging in children's schooling has become an increasingly important part of the activities that define being a good parent, a pattern that is consistent with international trends (Crozier 1998; Crozier and Davies 2007; Hornby and Lafaele 2011; Turney and Kao 2009). Acceptable engagement includes following up on children's homework, keeping in touch with teachers, and taking part in activities at the school. The school reform often referred to as the 'Knowledge School', applied from the mid-2000s onwards, into Norwegian primary and lower secondary schools has shifted focus onto parents' contributions to their children's schooling and on the effects that parental involvement has on learning outcomes (Helgøy and Homme 2015). The formal rights of parents to influence schools increased further from around 2006 onwards as part of the democratisation and neoliberalisation of society (Bæck 2015). One consequence is that teachers encourage parents and pupils to embrace particular, middle-class views of what a 'good' parent and a 'good' pupil are, which often translates into an intensification of parenting

(Crozier 1998; Akselvoll 2016) and a school policy regime that has increased expectations of parental school involvement (Bæck 2015; Helgøy and Homme 2015).

In this article, we discuss how the school's expectations towards parent engagement are conveyed in encounters between parents and teachers, and how these expectations are experienced by parents with migrant backgrounds from Iraq, Ethiopia, West Africa and Somalia. In Norway, researchers have been concerned with how satisfied parents are with their level of cooperation with their children's schooling along with what their attitudes towards this cooperation may be (Bæck 2010b), and have evaluated the success of particular programmes designed to enhance parents' involvement in schools (Helgøy and Homme 2015). Researchers have also suggested the role of schools in generating perceptions of 'good parenting'. Very few studies have focused on the normative ideals of parenting that permeate home-school relations or on the increased expectations of parental involvement in students' education. This article aims to complement and contribute to previous literature by focusing on the relationship between migrant parents and schools.

We begin with a discussion of the shaping of current-day parent-school relationships in Norway before we discuss the research on parent-school cooperation and theories on intensive parenting. After presenting our method, we move on to discuss how schools frame their parental expectations. Next, we discuss how parents with migrant backgrounds understand the school's expectations. Finally, in the conclusion, we argue that while the school pursues parental engagement partly in order to limit the risks of future dropouts, 'pupils' under-achievement on tests, and low integration, this approach, risks increasing the effects of existing social and economic inequality in educational outcomes by putting too much responsibility on parents who despite the egalitarian vision of Norwegian population (Bendixsen, Bringslid, and Vike 2018), have different resources (economic, social and cultural capital) and prerequisites to provide their child with the best possible educational outcomes.

Parent-school collaboration in the Norwegian welfare state

In line with social democratic values, most schools in Norway are fully publicly funded and there are few privately run schools compared to many EU countries. Schools are considered to be a tool for promoting social equality and inclusion, and education is seen as one of the most important measures for reducing socio-economic inequality in society (Norwegian Ministry of Children, Equality and Social Inclusion 2012-2013, 10-11). Further, schools and kindergartens are presented as institutions in which the 'integration' of migrants and refugees should be pursued (Norwegian Ministry of Children, Equality and Social Inclusion 2012-2013, 10-11). Simultaneously, in spite of their foundational, egalitarian ambitions, schools in Norway reflect largely middle-class values (Rugkåsa 2012), and schools (generally) are recognised as one of the main sites for the reproduction of social class (Brison 2011) and thus social inequality.

During the past two decades, parents' formal rights have strengthened, for example, through parents' representation in cooperative and decision-making bodies in schools and through parent-teacher meetings and student-parent-teacher conferences.[1] This move towards increased parent-school cooperation can be explained in various ways. The Regulations to the Education Act § 20-1 states that the collaboration between schools and parents must have the student in focus and should bring about a good follow-up (of parents and the school) of the individual student's academic and social development. Several governmental reports highlight parental cooperation as an important area that promotes students' learning.[2] On the Norwegian Directorate for Education and Training's homepage,[3] cooperation between school and home is promoted because 'Parents and supervisors have the main responsibility for their own children, and they have a great influence on their motivation and learning outcomes'. Further, the increased role of parents within the educational system can also be understood as pertaining to the introduction of the citizen as client, brought about by the neoliberalisation of society (Bæck 2010b): parents are viewed as consumers with rights who expect the promised quality of the goods they are given (Bæck 2015; Breidenstein, Krüger, and Roch 2020).

Key concepts: the parent-school relationship and intensive parenting

We draw on two topics of research that are strongly interrelated: the parent-school relationship and ideas of intensive parenting. The first strand of scholarship discusses schools as places where hegemonic construction of what it means to be a good parent are constructed and played out, more or less explicitly. Research has indicated that the relationship between parents, particularly working-class and some minority-ethnic parents, and educational professionals is characterised less by equality (although termed 'partnership') and more by class background and an inequality of power in favour of the professionals (e.g. Lareau 1989; Vincent 1996, 2000, 113; Gillies 2005).

Studies in Norway show that parents, to a large degree, are satisfied with the home–school cooperation that they take part in (Nordahl and Skilbrei 2002), although some parents push this to the limit and confront the authority of teachers and school leaders, straining the parent-school relationship (Bæck 2010b). Further, Bæck (2010a) suggests that a specific category of parent, the more educated ones, are more inclined to participate and dominate the formalised settings in school and hence be more visible. Some parents engaged in public bodies in urban schools seek to represent the diversity of parents, aiming at social inclusion with various success (Danielsen and Bendixsen 2019). Notwithstanding, the voices of less resourceful groups (in economic and educational terms) are more seldom heard. Researchers have, therefore, questioned whether parental involvement in Norway and beyond is always a good thing (Reay 1998; Mcgrath and Kuriloff 1999; Crozier 2000; Vincent and Martin 2000; Hanafin and Lynch 2002; Bæck 2010a). Increased parental involvement risks expanding the differences between pupils from different socio-cultural backgrounds (Bæck 2010a).

The second strand of literature discusses intensive parenting as a hegemonic form, not only in schools but also in society more generally. Concerted cultivation or intensive parenting refers to how some parents (usually from the middle classes) intensively shape their child to take their place in society, for example, through paid-for extra-curricular activities or fostering particular styles of speaking within and outside the family that emphasise the ability to look people in the eye and present as a confident, engaged person ready to meet the world and its challenges (Lareau 2011). Globally, this child-centred, expert-guided parenting norm is common among the middle class (Hays 1996, 8) and is also identified in Norway (Bendixsen and Danielsen 2019). It is characterised by a prioritisation of the children's activities before all else (Vincent 2017) and involves shaping parenting as 'an educational project' of the parent; parenting has to be learnt and improved (Beck and Beck-Gernsheim 1995, 139; Vincent 2000).

The intensification of parenthood includes a process of parental determinism, namely a belief that all forms of parental behaviour will have direct consequences on the child's future (Lee et al. 2014). Such responsibilisation of parenting also encourages the privatisation and individuation of parenting (Lee et al. 2014) in that it becomes the parents' duty to ensure that their children have the best possible potentials for their current lives now as well as in order to have a good life (through good employment) later. In Norway, as in other European and North American countries characterised among other to be a 'risk society' (Beck and Beck-Gernsheim 1995), children are thought of as being in constant risk, and thus the 'good parenting' style of intensive parenting is also about 'risk management'. Risk, in this article, refers to a category of the emic discourse; it refers both to the subjective understanding of risk by the parents and the discourses about risk in society.

Methods: researching parents in Bergen

Our project, titled 'Parenting Cultures and Risk Management in Plural Norway', draws on fieldwork and interviews among parents, teachers and headmasters in Årstad, an urban borough in Bergen, the second largest city in Norway (300,000 inhabitants). It examines how migration and increased class differences reflect and contribute to generate differentiations in ideas of parenting. We have conducted fieldwork and interviews in three neighbourhoods in Årstad with staff at three different schools, and in conjunction with activities that involve parents, neighbourhood initiatives, and welfare state interactions. At all schools, we pursued observation during teacher-parent meetings at the beginning of the school year (first to sixth year) and at events in which parents were invited to the schools, such as end of school-year events, National Day celebrations (May 17), and particular events such as bike repair day and UN day. The particular demography of Årstad is marked by its clusters of very different socio-economic settings for its inhabitants: while one part is quite central to the city centre and largely made up of refugees and social assistance recipients who are provided municipal social housing, and a creative middle class in private owned houses (location of school B), another part is similarly made up of social assistance recipients with social housing and a middle class but situated further from the city centre (location of school C). The third area is a sought-after and expensive residential neighbourhood for upper middle class employees at the state hospital (location of school A). During the last couple of years, Bergen municipal and local actors have initiated projects and events in parts of the Årstad borough targeting parents and children specifically aimed at creating a 'safe environment' for children, particularly those areas characterised by a high concentration of child poverty.

A total of 45 interviews with parents (middle-class and working-class, non-migrant Norwegian and migrants) lasting between 1 and 3 hours each were conducted. These were informal, open-ended, digital recorded interviews, sometimes in their own homes, other times in a neutral place. In a few cases, we made use of interpreters. We recruited our informants through the meetings and activities at the schools we attended through the snowball method and through various free-time and neighbourhood activities where we met parents living in the area.

During the interviews, we asked about their parenting practices and ideals, including their relationship to their children's schooling, neighbourhood, their thoughts about free-time activities, and what it meant to them to be 'a good parent'. We also conducted more than 15 interviews with representatives of the municipality, teachers, and other professionals. We found differences in what the teachers and principals expected from the parents at the different schools (named here school A, B, and C), yet many of the parents' expectations were similar regardless of the school in which their children were enrolled. While acknowledging the differences that exist, in light of the main question of this article we have chosen to focus on the points of similarities and commonalities between these schools.

Many researchers have presented social class as the main variable in defining the relationship between teachers and parents (Lareau 1989; Vincent 1996; Reay 1998); however, parents with migrant and refugee backgrounds cannot be easily categorised into the working or middle classes. When we consider the differences among the 'migrant parents' we met, originating as they did from Iraq, Ethiopia, West Africa, and Somalia, we recognise a broad range of differences. Broad categories, such as 'migrants' and 'refugees', are not homogenous. Class differentiation, educational background, orientation towards a child's education (Irwin and Elley 2011), as well as place of origin, the number of years of residence in Norway, and the social networks available are all relevant forms of differentiations. Many migrants and refugees have a middle-class background in their country of origin, but in Norway, their occupational and economic positions belong to that of the working class. As we will show?, their middle-class family 'habitus' (dispositions, assumptions, and expectations) and the school's expectations of the parents' performance of a particular, middle-class habitus do not converge to the extent that is often expected by teachers. Yet, for the purposes of this study, we focus on the more general category of 'migrant parent' rather than their specific places of origin?, because, we found important aspects in common among these parents that are highly relevant to our consideration of the parent-school relationship. The similarity in practices and experiences evident among parents with a migration background from a non-Nordic country include the ways in which they understand the school's expectations and how the school approaches them, and, whether it is taken into account that they are parents in a country in which they did not grow up themselves. It also includes the fact that many have a relatively low level of Norwegian language competence, have been given municipal housing in an area that is considered to be socio-economically disadvantaged, and are included in categories that are frequently viewed by state officials (i.e. policy makers, teachers, child authorities) as potentially 'at risk' in terms of not providing their children with a 'correct' upbringing. Thus, while recognising the internal differences, and that the experiences of people with a migrant background should not be reduced to the social categories to which they are allocated, we would like to draw attention to some of the particular experiences of (and challenges in) the parent-school relationship that are shaped by simply being a migrant.

Great expectations from the schools: limiting risk?

At the beginning of every school year on a certain afternoon, teachers have parent meetings to which all parents are expected to attend. Teachers and principals consider these meetings to be an opportunity for the school to communicate directly what they expect of the parents. During our fieldwork and in the context of these meetings, most, if not all, of the teachers we encountered emphasised that a child's learning process occurs in a partnership between the school and the parents. One teacher at school A (with a rather homogeneous parent population and a high number of middle-class families in the area) put it like this when speaking to all of the parents:

> You cannot overstate how important it is to read with and to your children and to help them with homework. I will do my part, but you must help me. We must work together to ensure that the children learn what they should learn.

This exchange is one example of the ways in which teachers talk about the role of parents, conveying that the school is dependent on the parents' contribution to their child's learning if they are to achieve the learning goals as completely as possible. Some teachers showed the parents the specific learning objectives issued by the government for individual subjects, sometimes with the teachers saying that the learning objectives are extremely demanding and thus difficult to obtain with the few hours set aside for that particular learning goal. Several teachers asked parents to assist at home in correcting the children's mathematics, to memorise English vocabulary with them, or to contribute to the pupils' reaching the learning goals in swimming. Some of the parents we spoke with expressed surprise at how much children were expected to learn and showed anxiety about how this was supposed to happen.

At school B, where the number of pupils with migrant backgrounds was more than 50 per cent, we participated in a regular parent meeting for grade two. Around half of the parents present were of migrant background and during our conversations before and after the meeting, they gave the impression that they did not understand Norwegian to a significant degree. One teacher, Monica,[4] interpreted her messages into English at the request of some parents, however, only occasionally. This teacher initiated the meeting by pointing out the importance of parents coming to know one another and that this would help their children and improve the school's social environment. 'And you can help each other', Monica, the teacher, argued, and continued: 'Social training is very important for children – throw a party and so on'. She argued that they must talk nicely about school at home and that they can also use their native language.

Later during the meeting, Monica talked about different subjects and homework, saying: 'Give kids math skills in everyday life. Think math, talk about numbers'. She mentioned different math games that the parents could play with their children, some of them quite complex and some that we, as fieldworkers, did not understand. She stressed: 'We are dependent on having you folks with us'. As Monica continued discussing homework, she argued:

> It is you who must ensure that the child is doing his or her homework. You should not *do* their homework, but make procedures, facilitate. You should tell them that homework is important. But make a phone call to the teacher if it gets bad, your child should not be crying about homework. And read to your child, gladly in your mother tongue.

She reminded parents about the folder that the children bring home weekly and asked them to check it regularly – there might be signatures they need to give at short notice. Monica explained: 'We should do homework that includes reading every day and work with different sounds. Give feedback to the child. Make it into a cozy moment. For example, give them fruit. Give praise instead of criticism. It always works'. Monica suggested that the parents should time their child when reading and make it into a competition. One mother said that her son thought it was tiring to read and that is was difficult to make it into a fun situation.

After the talk about the parents' responsibility concerning homework, practical information was given. At this stage, Monica talked about cooperation with the school concerning behaviour, clothing, breakfast, and birthdays. The teacher urged the parents to go hiking in the nearby mountains and to attend their children's football matches to get to know other parents. Notably, during her talk, we observed that much of this information was not interpreted and how much of it was understood by the non-Norwegian-speaking parents was unclear.

In another parent-teacher meeting, in grade three in school C, there was an interpreter present. The interpreter translated: 'You have homework as a family. Every day you should practice English, writing. We hope to offer a homework group, do you want to volunteer?' A father asked about the homework, explaining that everyday life is busy in the afternoons and wondered if it would be possible to plan a little in advance with the homework. The teacher, Anita, answered that parents need to be in control: 'It will be your job to go through it'. The parents started to discuss how difficult it is to understand the children's homework. Anita responded that while she understood that it is complicated, the government has given learning goals that she must follow. Parents wondered about their role; how often should they write a mark on the lesson's overview: every single day or every single reading lesson? They were confused. The teacher responded that she considered this as feedback and she would reflect on it later. Meanwhile, the interpreter was unable to follow, and commented that he was unable to translate the whole discussion about homework. A father with a Polish background commented, somewhat humorously but also looking horrified, 'really?' (i.e. 'this is what is expected of us?') in relation to the discussion about homework.

In school C, there were 60 nationalities among the pupils attending and the principal emphasised: 'Parents should be engaged in the school'. At the time some groups of parents were not attending formal meetings, nor were they inclined to approach school staff about educational matters. The principal attributed this lack of contact to both language and culture and also unknown causes that the principal described as an *x-factor*. The school has tried a lot, he added,

> here and now, a lot is expected of parents' and he pointed out that not everyone could understand this. The school had initiated special programmes including hiring an extra advisor for parents and making extra homework groups, but still they did not come ...

In school B, where the number of pupils with migrant backgrounds was more than 50 per cent, one parent in the Parents' Council Working Committees (PCWC) initiated the idea of inviting another PCWC and their respective school leaders to discuss how to improve their efforts of reaching out to migrant families. During this meeting, the principal of the school said: 'the basic value of school is to develop competent people. We see opportunities in the diversity we have and we should help each other'. The principal made use of the keywords 'competence', 'curious', 'generous', 'open and inclusive', 'tolerant', and 'respectful'. He asked the following rhetorical question:

Are we representative? No. We are not good enough at inviting people in such a way that everyone feels it is equally natural to participate. (...) The conditions for good cooperation with parents are based on the ability to see the parents' significance in collaboration, and to create a sense of belonging for all.

During our interview with the principal of school B, she explained that in this particular school, when it comes to multi-language learners, they are invited to a 'welcome conversation' and to take advantage of home visits. Home visits are organised in order to get to know each other, the principal added, and 'some parents accept it and others don't want it. It is important that parents get to contribute on their own terms'. The principal implied that parents have different resources and starting point when meeting staff from the school. He self-critically stated that the school is not good enough at inviting parents in a way that would include everyone to participate in activities related to the school. He highlighted the following: 'We are good at meeting those who went to school in Norway. We need to think of new ways in order to include new parents as a resource'.

At this school, the principal was very concerned with the fact that children who attend the school had both highly educated parents and very poorly educated parents, as well as many single mothers, and parents who were drug addicts. Annually, he sent around 50 messages to the public child protection service due to violence, substance abuse, a failure to provide care, high absenteeism among students, as well as suspicions about child marriage and female circumcision. The principal worked actively to create a good public reputation for the school, and to ensure that the school results were above average in national tests in order to show that the area is an attractive place to live with children. In his work, he saw that some pupils had difficulties and high absenteeism, and many parents were not participating in the parent-teacher conferences. He believed that the school produced social inequality and thus he sought to strengthen the school-home relationship, among others measures, as one means of working to alleviate the social inequality.

One of the teachers at school C, Anne, believed it was her job to follow pupils and parents closely and to facilitate parental contact with her through informal conversations about 'how we together can make your child's school day as good as possible'. Talking to Anne, she explained her role: 'My goal is to get parents more involved. Parents are resources, they just need guidance. (...) We have to get parents to understand that they need to change their attitudes [towards the school]'. She was concerned that some parents were not following up on homework at home. She was leading a school initiated project which was targeting all pupils and parents who faced some difficulties; however, it was clear that the main target group, and the main group using the service, was made up of parents with migrant backgrounds outside of Europe and the US who were not performing what was expected of them as parents in the Norwegian school system. She also used time to explain what she considered to be the social and cultural codes and expectations in Norway to the parents, such as how to dress during winter, in addition to homework. Anne told us:

> Everyone must perform, so we must keep the parents with us. It takes time to change routines, to be able to follow up, do homework at a scheduled time, allow for the computer only after the homework has been done, get up on time, go to school even if they are a little sick. Having the right clothing, food, drink, maintain a few routines so that the children can manage school. One mother argued with me that she did not have the time to help her children do homework

because she had to keep the house clean, and I told her that it is more important to follow up on homework [than to keep the house clean].

She explicitly contrasted migrant and 'Norwegian' parents and their ways of following up on their children:

Norwegians follow their children very closely. People from other countries send their children alone to arrangements and gatherings at the school, so the school gets a lot of responsibility. Parents do not come to fetch their children after the May 17 national day parade in the city centre.

Anne sought not to be moralistic in her argumentation, but instead to get the parents to understand how important it is to follow up on their children and she wished to guide them in how to direct their children. She said: 'Many immigrant parents want their children to become a doctor. But they do not know what is needed to reach that aim'. She wanted to make explicit to immigrant parents the expectations that the school – and society – had towards them, to let them know what majority parents 'already know', and that they learn to follow up on their children very closely as 'Norwegians do'. Several of the teachers, like Anne, promoted parenthood constructed as a role defined by its significance for the future of individual children and society as a whole. Parents were considered as the main driving force behind fostering children that would behave as they should in school and thus be able to succeed later in life. We will now look at how these expectations were understood by migrant parents.

Great expectations from parents: doubt and hope

Parents expressed that the school had great expectations concerning their role as parents and many experienced it as demanding. They talked about the school's expectations as including an intense engagement with their child's education and in their daily interaction with their child. Simultaneously, the parents also expressed great expectations of their children's future – what their children would become or achieve – and for the future of the family.

When we asked more generally about how it is to be a parent in Norway today, many parents with a migrant background said that they found it difficult. Several struggled with following up on their children's schooling. They found it hard to understand the routines, the homework, the grades or lack of grades (in Norway, children are not graded before grade eight), and the information given by the school. Some of these difficulties derived in part from a lack of skills in the Norwegian language and, as we will see, an unfamiliarity with the Norwegian school system and especially the particular role given to parents in the educational system.

Among the parents with migrant backgrounds from Iraq, Ethiopia, Somalia, and Western Africa, we found great expectations for their children's educational success and later employment, which should ultimately lead to the whole family's social climb in Norway. We found both hope and fear concerning the future: a hope that their children would do well and a fear that their children (or they) would have to rely on welfare in the future. Education and work were ways to be included in society. One working-class migrant father said:

I hope that my children will not be a burden on society. I want them to contribute. I want them to get an education and good jobs. I want to move from this area because there are too many migrants right here. I want my children to interact more with Norwegians. I feel like I am half Somali, half Norwegian now, I am integrated. I want my children to be integrated.

The anxiety of not being included in the employment market, a fear of segregation, and that the neighbourhood constellation would adversely affect integration were mentioned by several parents with migrant backgrounds. Many stressed that the area where they had been given municipal housing was socially and economically challenging: too many non-Norwegian-speaking inhabitants could undermine the ability of their children to learn Norwegian well and put stress on the school as many pupils needed extra follow-up. It could also impede their children making enough 'Norwegian friends'. One Iraqi-Kurdish father said about his son's school: 'there are 36 nationalities that attend his school and most of them speak their own mother tongue at school and it affects the quality of the language (…). It affects integration negatively'.

The risk, as these parents considered it, was not related to their own engagement or involvement with their children's education, but that their children were growing up in an impoverished socio-cultural environment, which was detrimental to their Norwegian language abilities and limited their possibility of being included in Norwegian society. The way some migrant families dealt with this predicament was to move or by planning to do so when they had accumulated enough economic capital. Others wanted to stay in the area as it was central and they had a good social network in the area.

We found that many parents talked about feeling alone in their parenting simultaneously as they experienced the Norwegian state as scrutinising and judging their parenting practices:

> The parents here, especially migrants, have to follow a child to school, you have to pick up your child from school, you don't have relatives. But where I come from [Rwanda], if we are neighbours, I can collect your children from school, tomorrow you collect him … we make that arrangement. But here you have to do it on your own. And another issue I have seen, that the state, they decide a lot, they enter into private parenting activities … the people [working in Child Welfare Service] are manipulating the system and they steal children from migrants and they give them to Norwegian families … yes.

These parents experienced what we could call the privatisation of parenting in the context of a lack of shared responsibility for a child's activities compared to their home countries where they would involve more adults in sharing these time-consuming practices. Simultaneously, as the parents talked about the loneliness of parenthood compared to how they believed parenting would be pursued in their home country, the parents also expressed what it took to meet the high expectations placed on them as individual parents, particularly from the school when it came to their involvement in their children's education. They were also very concerned about 'the system', referring to the State and the Child Welfare Service's potential to intrude on their family. Not many of the parents were involved in the Parents' Council Working Committee. Some argued that they had no time, others felt that there were barriers to their involvement because of their language competence.

Many of the parents we interviewed expressed satisfaction with their children's school. They articulated no complaints about the teachers or the organisation of the school. One Palestinian father said: 'I don't mind the school, it is very good. Because, as I heard, they have very good competence, very good teachers'. Yet others voiced uncertainty about how the school conducted its education and the school system generally. One parent-couple from East Africa exclaimed that while they liked their children's school and had no complaints about the teachers, they did not understand the school system and, in particular, the expectation that they, as parents, should contribute to the teaching of their children. These parents had university degrees and had lived in Norway for ten years. The father expanded:

> They don't teach them well, they just say 'you go and your parents will help you'. So I don't know, I ask myself what they teach them ... homework ... some of it is complicated, I don't understand it, how they teach, so ... It's not like in Africa where the teachers teach everything, you work in class, if you fail, they correct you, but this one, even if you fail, there are no exams, and if you fail, nothing you can do ... (...) What if the parents don't know how to help? Like these people from Asia, they didn't go to school.

He explained that he finds that the schools in his home country in Africa were better because their children should not ask their parents to help them, but rather do the homework themselves. He was also not satisfied with the teacher not correcting the homework and that they, as parents, had also been told not to correct it: 'Even if they fail, the work is not good: you can't tell them ... they go ahead, they don't make corrections'.

The father's comment indicates the discrepant philosophies of learning and teaching between himself and the school staff. He was used to leaving education to those educated as teachers rather than being directly involved in his children's learning process. He and his wife expected that the school should correct the children, including their homework, grade them, and notify the children when they made mistakes in order for the children to improve. Parents with such a point of view thus had different expectations of the teachers and their own role as parents compared to what the school expected of them.

Other parents expressed that teachers had high expectations of them to become directly involved in their children's educational path. Sometimes, parents interpreted this expectation of parents' involvement as deriving from a lack of resources or competence on the part of the teachers. Additionally, how they were to engage with their children's education remained unclear to them, as neither the teachers nor they were to correct their children's mistakes, apparently. This made some parents confused and even irritated, as the parents consequently were without any means of letting their children know what they needed to improve or in which areas.

Discussion and conclusion

The title of this article, 'Great expectations', alludes to the school's expectations towards parents' participation in the cooperation between home and school, the parents' experience of this cooperation, the parents' expectations of what the school will do for their children, and their expectations for their children and their future. These expectations do not always correspond, complement, or facilitate each other and they are not necessarily directed towards the same goal or with similar ideas of how to fulfil the expectations.

Teachers' rhetoric and argumentation that emphasise the power of parenting drives the focus towards particular parenting skills and specific social characters and aspirations. The parents become the main determinants of their children's educational achievements and, ultimately, their future. The risks of a lack of success are presented as being the responsibility of individual parents. Parents' behaviour should help the child succeed, and some parent's behaviour (some more than others) towards their children is looked upon as a potential risk for the children's school performance. The focus remains on the individual parents, or the parents as part of a category ('immigrant parents') whose behaviour is culturalised ('they act like that because they are Muslims or from Kurdistan'). The expectations expressed during the parent-teacher meetings and the particular actions directed towards migrant parents promote, perhaps unconsciously, an intensive parenting style fronted as a way in which the success of the individual child can be enhanced. This depolitises the policies and school practices as regards the parents and the ways in which the school staff deal with their pupils.

A middle-class way of life comes to represent a norm against which everything is measured: it has become the civilising normality (also see Rugkåsa 2012). In this process, an intensive style of parenting becomes naturalised as the best for the child as a pupil and as a future citizen. It constructs the idea that the school can offer possibilities for all children in Norway, but in order for the child to become successful, and for the school to provide the pupils with the best potentials, parents must comply with a frame of teaching and education that embraces, expects, or even demands the intensive involvement and participation of the parents. The demands on the parents' involvement come across as responsibilitisation, accountability, and increased duties for the parents. These initiatives are also situated in a risk discourse in the sense that if the parents are not doing what they are supposed to be doing, it will have a negative impact on their child's education and the school as a whole. The initiatives might also be understood within the context of the Norwegian government's 'duty turn' and in terms of how it pursues its 'citizen-making', in which emphasis is placed on the activation of citizens. As in other EU/EEA states, the desired 'good citizen' should develop the respected civic dispositions that will make productive incorporation into society feasible, which is tied up with labour market participation and civic virtues, like learning the language and participating in civil society (Brochmann 2014). Through moralising and incentivising individual citizens, the Norwegian government has simultaneously contributed to individualising the task of contributing to social cohesion (cf. Soysal 2012; Brochmann 2014).

By expecting parents to be actively involved in the education of their children – an issue formerly held to be the responsibility of authorised governmental or private professional actors – education becomes an important part of parenting practices. The parents are required to take on an involved responsibility for these activities, both for getting them done and for their results. This obliges specific forms of behaviour and action and is a new form of 'responsibilisation'. Additionally, the schools' and teachers' expectations towards the children's parents are based on certain ideals and norms of intensive parenting as a way to alleviate the risk that a child will not 'make it'. While the principals and some of the teachers emphasised that they sought to use the different resources of all parents, their explicit and implicit expectations draw this into question. The great expectations from the teachers and principals towards the parents implicitly draw upon a specific ideology of parenting, in which some resources are considered as more valuable and relevant than others. The parenting approaches presented in the teacher-parent meetings implicitly evoke the idea that in order for a child to succeed in Norwegian society, both educationally and in future employment, the parents must strive to fulfil an ideal of intensive parenting.

While parent-school cooperation is structured in an individualised manner, with an emphasis on responsibilisation and self-discipline, the migrant parents are not, in large part, responding as expected by the school teachers and principals. The discrepancy between school expectations and that of the parents can be understood in light of the fact that many parents are uncertain as to what the school expects and how to fulfil those expectations. Some are also uncertain as to why the school is not meeting their expectations. Additionally, the lack of interpretation during meetings at various stages (i.e. when discussing birthdays and homework) which we experienced during our fieldwork, might contribute to the failure of the school to communicate appropriately and thus exascerbate the gap between parents' and schools' expectations. This state of affairs increases the loneliness of parenting, which is already prominent, partly because their relatives are far away and their ideas are linked to their own experiences growing up in a place where their nurturing was not only dependent on their particular parents.

Parents do not necessarily adapt an intensive parenting model as a response to these expectations. Many parents with a migrant background find the expectation that parents should engage with their children's education puzzling, which amplifies their distrust of the educational system ('do they not have enough or good enough teachers?'). It also causes uncertainty and doubt as to whether they, as parents, are capable of providing their children with the right kind of assistance in order for their children to progress towards the anticipated great future. In view of the fact that they have not gone through the Norwegian education system, or sometimes any educational system, and lack Norwegian language skills, many doubt whether they can provide what(ever) is expected of them for their children.

Several teachers and principals promoted a particular form of parent engagement with the indirect promise that this would contribute to their children's success in school. However, few of the parents we interviewed talked about a 'lack of cooperation' with the school or saw their own (lack of) involvement as a potential risk or major problem. Instead, they saw greatest risks to their great expectations for their children's education as being related to their neighbourhood's socio-economic constellation, as well as the perceptions and realities of a highly individualised parenthood. Difficulties in helping their children because of low Norwegian language skills and a lack of knowledge of the Norwegian system were also identified the struggle to be involved in their children's education, in a system that is highly unfamiliar t was a frequent topic of conversation. While the teachers focused on the individual parents and what they could do or were not doing, many of the parents were concerned about the socio-linguistic composition of the area, problematising the fact that there were too few children with Norwegian as their mother tongue in the area, which they saw as the greatest risk for their child's education and ultimately their future.

The new and great expectations of parents' involvement and engagement in their children's schooling in Norway shift the responsibilisation of equal education away from the state towards individual families. This form of responsibilisation on individual families for their child's education might reproduce social inequality in new ways. Migrant children's educational opportunities can be limited by their parents' unfamiliarity with the school's way of operationalising linguistic structures, systems of organisation, and models of learning, particularly if the school is not consciously working to counter such issues. There is an irony in that the focus on greater parent engagement with the school and the education of their child, brings along increased alienation of the parents most in need of teachers' professional assistance and guidance. While the great expectations towards parents should facilitate and produce upward mobility for the children, they are, though often not explicitly, an incursion of the home and act as a normative directive of how people should parent. Moreover, parents have different starting points to understand the expectations, as well as different resources and readiness to carry out this particular way of parenting. This lead to, on the one hand, frustrated teachers who blame the parents for not following up their child in the 'right way', and on the other hand, parents who doubt the school's capacity to provide their child with good education for the future. At the end of the day, this undermines the ideal of inclusive education and infringes on children's possibility of equal opportunity, a longstanding social ambition in Norwegian society.

Notes

1. The Regulations to the Education Act § 20-3 set the requirements for the content of the parent cooperation in primary and lower secondary schools.
2. See Ministry of Education and Research.
3. From https://www.udir.no/kvalitet-og-kompetanse/samarbeid/hjem-skole-samarbeid/, Accessed March 6, 2019.
4. All names in this paper have been anonymised.

Disclosure statement

No potential conflict of interest was reported by the author(s).

Funding

The work was supported by the Norwegian Research Council [grant number 236956].

References

Akselvoll, MØ. 2016. *Folkeskole, forældre, forskelle. Skole-hjem samarbejde og foreldreinvolvering i et klasseperspektiv*. Roskilde: PhD Roskilde University.
Bæck, U. K. 2010a. "Parental Involvement Practices in Formalized Home-School Cooperation." *Scandinavian Journal of Educational Research* 54 (6): 549–563.
Bæck, U. K. 2010b. "'We are the Professionals': A Study of Teachers' Views on Parental Involvement in School." *British Journal of Sociology of Education* 31 (3): 323–335.
Bæck, U. K. 2015. "Beyond the Fancy Cakes. Teachers' Relationship to Home-School Cooperation in a Study From Norway." *International Journal About Parents in Education* 9 (1): 37–46.
Beck, U., and E. Beck-Gernsheim. 1995. *Normal Chaos of Love*. Cambridge: Polity Press.
Bendixsen, S., M. B. Bringslid, and H. Vike. 2018. *Egalitarianism in Scandinavia: Historical and Contemporary Approaches*. London: Palgrave.
Bendixsen, S., and H. Danielsen. 2019. "Other People's Children. Inclusive Parenting in a Diverse Neighborhood." *Ethnic and Racial Studies* 42 (7): 1130–1148.

Breidenstein, G., J. O. Krüger, and A. Roch. 2020. "Parents as 'Customers'? The Perspective of the 'Providers' of School Education. A Case Study From Germany." *Comparative Education*, doi:10.1080/03050068.2020.1724485

Brison, K. J. 2011. "Producing 'Confident' Children: Negotiating Childhood in Fijian Kindergartens." *Anthropology and Education* 42 (3): 230–244.

Brochmann, G. 2014. "Scandinavia. Governing Immigration in Advanced Welfare States." In *Controlling Immigration. A Global Perspective*, edited by J. F. Hollifield, P. L. Martin, and P. M. Orrenius, 281–302. Standford: Stanford University Press.

Crozier, G. 1998. "Parents and Schools: Partnership or Surveillance?" *Journal of Education Policy* 13 (1): 125–136.

Crozier, G. 2000. *Parents and Schools: Partners or Protagonists?* Stoke-on-Trent: Trentham.

Crozier, G., and J. Davies. 2007. "Hard to Reach Parents or Hard to Reach Schools? A Discussion of Home–School Relations, with Particular Reference to Bangladeshi and Pakistani Parents." *British Educational Research Journal* 33 (3): 295–313. doi:10.1080/01411920701243578.

Danielsen, H., and S. Bendixsen. 2019. "Dealing with Diversity, Hoping for Inclusion. Parents' Involvement in Urban Schools in Norway." *Ethnicities* 19 (6): 1158–1180. doi:10.1177/1468796818822542.

Gillies, V. 2005. "Raising the 'Meritocracy': Parenting and the Individualization of Social Class." *Sociology* 39 (5): 835–853.

Hanafin, J., and A. Lynch. 2002. "Peripheral Voices: Parental Involvement, Social Class, and Educational Disadvantage." *British Journal of Sociology of Education* 23 (1): 35–49.

Hays, S. 1996. *The Cultural Contradictions of Motherhood*. New Haven, CT: Yale University Press.

Helgøy, I., and A. Homme. 2015. "Path-dependent Implementation of the European Qualifications Framework in Education. A Comparison of Norway, Germany and England." *Journal of Comparative Policy Analysis* 17 (2): 124–139.

Hornby, G., and R. Lafaele. 2011. "Barriers to Parental Involvement in Education: An Explanatory Model." *Educational Review* 63 (1): 37–52.

Irwin, S., and S. Elley. 2011. "Concerted Cultivation? Parenting Values, Education and Class Diversity." *Sociology* 45 (3): 480–495.

Lareau, A. 1989. "Family-School Relationships: A View From the Classrom." *Educational Policy* 3 (3): 245–259.

Lareau, A. 2011. *Unequal Childhoods: Class, Race, and Family Life*. Berkeley: University of California Press.

Lee, E., J. Bristow, C. Faircloth, and J. Macvarish, eds. 2014. *Parenting Culture Studies*. New York: Palgrave Macmillan.

Mcgrath, D. J., and P. J. Kuriloff. 1999. "'They're Going to Tear the Doors Off This Place': Upper-Middle-Class Parent School Involvement and the Educational Opportunities of Other People's Children." *Educational Policy* 13 (5): 603–662.

Ministry of Education and Research. *Report No. 16 to the Storting (2006–2007) Earl Intervention for Lifelong Learning*. Accessed May 21, 2019. https://www.regjeringen.no/en/dokumenter/report-no.-16-to-the-storting-2006-2007/id441395/.

Nordahl, T., and M. L. Skilbrei. 2002. *Det vanskelige samarbeidet : evaluering av et utviklingsprosjekt om samarbeidet mellom hjem og skole*. Oslo: Norsk insitutt for forskning om oppvekst, velferd og aldring.

Norwegian Ministry of Children, Equality and Social Inclusion. Meld.St. 6 (2012-2013). *En helhetlig integreringspolitikk – mangfold og fellesskap (White paper 2012–2013. A Comprehensive Integration Policy. Diversity and Community)*. 10–11. Accessed August 20, 2019. https://www.regjeringen.no/globalassets/upload/bld/ima/integreringsmelding_mangfold_eng.pdf.

Reay, D. 1998. *Class Work. Mothers' Involvement in Their Children's Primary Schooling*. London: UCL Press.

Rugkåsa, M. 2012. *Likhetens Dilemma*. Oslo: Gyldendal.

Soysal, Y. N. 2012. "Citizenship, Immigration, and the European Social Project: Rights and Obligations of Individuality." *The British Journal of Sociology* 63 (1): 1–21.

Turney, K., and G. Kao. 2009. "Barriers to School Involvement: Are Immigrant Parents Disadvantaged?" *The Journal of Educational Research* 102: 257–271.

Vincent, C. 1996. *Parents and Teachers, Power and Participation*. London: Falmer Press.
Vincent, C. 2000. *Including Parents? Education, Citizenship and Parental Agency*. Buckingham: Open University Press.
Vincent, C. 2017. "'The Children Have Only Got One Education and you Have to Make Sure It's a Good One': Parenting and Parent–School Relations in a Neoliberal Age." *Gender and Education* 29 (5): 541–557.
Vincent, C, and J. Martin. 2000. "School-based Parents' Groups – A Politics of Voice and Representation?" *Journal of Education Policy* 15 (5): 459–480.

What parents know: risk and responsibility in United States education policy and parents' responses

Amy Shuffelton

ABSTRACT
In this special issue exploring parents' responses to neoliberal policy changes, especially shifting notions of risk and responsibility, this article provides a historical account of local and national policy initiatives in the contemporary United States that have increased risk and placed responsibility for this risk on the shoulders of parents (as well as educators). The opening section of the paper reviews major recent policy documents and initiatives in the United States, from the landmark 1983 report 'A Nation at Risk' to the current age of test-based accountability. In the following sections, the paper explores what two Chicago parents themselves had to say about risk and responsibility in public schooling. What, in their views, were the actual risks? What did they think their responsibilities were, as parents? What did they do in response to the shifting policyscape?

Introduction

In this special issue exploring parents' responses to neoliberal policy changes, especially shifting notions of risk and responsibility, this article provides a historical account of local and national policy initiatives in the contemporary United States that have increased risk and placed responsibility for this risk on the shoulders of parents (as well as educators). The opening section of the paper reviews major recent policy documents and initiatives in the United States, from the landmark 1983 report 'A Nation at Risk' to the current age of test-based accountability. In the following sections, the paper explores what two Chicago parents themselves had to say about risk and responsibility in public schooling. What, in their views, were the actual risks? What did they think their responsibilities were, as parents? What did they do in response to the shifting policyscape? Chicago, as policy scholar Pauline Lipman has argued, is an excellent test case for analyses of contemporary education policy, because it has so often served as the incubator for ideas taken up at a national level, from housing reforms that affect the racial and socio-economic demographics of urban neighbourhoods, to mayoral control, to test-based accountability and the de-unionization of the teaching force. Parents with children in Chicago Public Schools, a system under-resourced, racially segregated, and subjected to neoliberal reform from the top down, therefore have an acute awareness of how policy changes put their children and their schools at risk, even as parents are asked to bear the responsibility for changes outside their control.

Risk and responsibility in the policyscape

'Risk' reconfigured the US landscape of educational policy – call it the policyscape – following the publication of *A Nation at Risk* (ANAR) in 1983. ANAR did not mince words. 'Our nation is at risk', it began.

> Our once unchallenged preeminence in commerce, industry, science, and technological innovation is being overtaken by competitors throughout the world. This report is concerned with only one of the many causes and dimensions of the problem, but it is the one that undergirds American prosperity, security, and civility. We report to the American people that while we can take justifiable pride in what our schools and colleges have historically accomplished and contributed to the United States and the well-being of its people, the educational foundations of our society are presently being eroded by a rising tide of mediocrity that threatens our very future as a Nation and a people (A Nation At Risk 2018).

From this opening declaration of the *risks* this 'rising tide of mediocrity' posed to the nation, the report turns in the second paragraph to the question of *responsibility:*

> If an unfriendly foreign power had attempted to impose on America the mediocre educational performance that exists today, we might well have viewed it as an act of war. As it stands, *we have allowed this to happen to ourselves*. We have even squandered the gains in student achievement made in the wake of the Sputnik challenge. Moreover, we have dismantled essential support systems which helped make those gains possible. We have, in effect, been committing an act of unthinking, unilateral educational disarmament.[1]

The three claims that preface the report are thus (1) That Americans were at *risk* of losing political and economic 'preeminence', (2) That *education* 'undergirds' the safeguards of the American way of life, and (3) That *we* bore full *responsibility* for this risk.

Historian Diane Ravitch, who helped create some of the neoliberal reform policies that ANAR spawned in the two decades after its publication before she subsequently became one of education reform's most outspoken critics, provides a useful synopsis of what ANAR did and did not propose as the appropriate course of action. Its collar-grabbing opening was widely read and cited, but 'in winning public attention', Ravitch says, 'the report dramatically overstated its conclusions' (2016, 28). Public schools were not in crisis; the economy, in a recession in 1983, soon rebounded; education was not wholly responsible for what political and economic problems the United States did have. Yet ANAR fostered a sense that schools were in need of a radical course-change. What was to be done? ANAR, Ravitch points out, notably did *not* call for the education reforms that followed. 'It did not refer to market-based competition and choice among schools; it did not suggest restructuring schools or school systems. It said nothing about closing schools, firing staff, promoting privatisation, or instituting any other heavy-handed forms of accountability'(Ravitch 2016, 28). Instead, ANAR proposed 'conventional remedies', such as stronger graduation requirements, more time on instruction and homework, and higher salaries for teachers. All the same, the language it used to declare a crisis laid the ideological groundwork for the embrace of risk and responsibilization that followed.

By 2002, ANAR's recommendations, as well as the teacher-designed national standards for school subjects that followed in the 1990s, were supplanted by a new reform plan for public schooling that relied heavily on market logic. The bipartisan No Child Left Behind act (NCLB) mandated that states use standardised tests to measure schools, relying on a mix of incentives and sanctions to reach the (unreachable) goal of ensuring that all children were proficient in literacy and mathematics skills by 2014. NCLB was a complicated policy, but its key provisions included mandatory annual standardised tests for children in third through eighth grade. Schools had to disaggregate scores by race, ethnicity, low-income status, disability status, and limited English language proficiency, and show annual progress for every subgroup. Schools that did not make adequate yearly progress faced a series of increasingly punitive sanctions that could end with the school being closed.

If ANAR introduced neoliberal *discourses* of risk and responsibility into educational policy, even as its recommendations were compatible with older notions of governmental provision of public schooling, NCLB injected actual risks into the bloodstream of American public schooling. Enacted in the wake of the 2001 terrorist attacks, at a moment when US citizens felt themselves at greater risk of harm from uncontrollable global forces than they had in decades, NCLB deliberately put every public school in the nation at risk of being closed. In doing so, it put administrators, staff, and teachers at risk of being fired. It put students and their families at risk of needing to make new arrangements for getting a K-12 education. Given the correlation between poverty and low performance on standardised tests, and the geographical concentration of extreme poverty in particular neighbourhoods and their schools, those families least able to find new housing, childcare, and employment in order to send children elsewhere to school were at the highest risk of needing to do so. Market logic shaped both the policy and its effects. Schools were redefined as corporate actors and their students as clients; self-interest replaced professionalism as the presumptive motivator of quality work; failure led to replacement (with for-profit charters and non-unionised teachers, in many cases) rather than repair. Risk itself, the policy presumed, would spur improvement, though with no evidence to back this up, the plan itself was a risky speculation.

As for responsibility, NCLB narrowed considerably the 'we' who were responsible for public schools' shortcomings. In its sweeping claim that 'we' were responsible for the national security risk posed by our schools, *A Nation at Risk* recognised the entire nation as bearing responsibility for educating future generations of Americans. NCLB, on the other hand, laid the blame on the shoulders of educators – and parents. Responsibility shifted from the public to individuals. In a nation that provided limited public health care, had recently restructured (and effectively reduced) welfare provisions for poor families, required all mothers to work full-time in order to receive benefits, guaranteed no maternity leave or sick leave, and mandated a minimum wage so low that a family could not live on it, NCLB's reconfiguration of education policy provided no accommodations for schools struggling to educate large numbers of impoverished children, even though hunger, untreated health conditions, and housing instability place extra hurdles in their educational pathways.[2] The US remains one of only 4 nations worldwide that does not guarantee maternity leave, which puts all mothers at an acute risk of job loss and poverty. It bears mentioning that United States policies keep approximately 20% of American children below the official poverty line; to meet basic living expenses, a family needs approximately double the poverty threshold income, and by that measure, the number of American children in poverty exceeds 40% (National Center for Children in Poverty 2018). Those numbers rose during the 'great recession' of 2008–2010. Yet there were no excuses for educators, parents, or children, politicians proclaimed. 'All children can learn' became the mantra of the era.

Education researchers have written extensively about how the responsibility to meet an impossible goal fell on teachers, as indeed it did. Less remarked is that it also fell on parents. NCLB includes multiple references to 'parents' and 'parental involvement', rhetorically positioning parents as responsibility-holders and choice-makers. In Title I, the section of the policy that directs the allotment of resources for students from low-income families, Part A Subpart 1 Section 1118, 'Parental Involvement', declares that to receive Title I funds, a local educational agency must implement 'programs, activities, and procedures for the involvement of parents in programs assisted under this part consistent with this section. Such programs, activities, and procedures shall be planned and implemented with meaningful consultation with parents of participating children'. NCLB was a rewrite of the 1965 Elementary and Secondary Education Act (ESEA), the law which first gave the federal government a major role in American schooling. Notably, ESEA does not use the word 'parent', or the gender-specific 'mother' or 'father'. It does include extensive references to 'families', especially to the 'low-income families' it was designed to aid. The rhetorical difference indicates a functional difference. 'Families' lumps together parents with children, and in ESEA it is families who are the objects of public concern. NCLB's use of 'parents', in contrast, distinguishes parents – framed now as agents who play a role in carrying out the policy – from children, who remain the policy's objects.

This rhetorical shift both reflects and enforces a shift from ESEA's social welfare interpretation of public schooling as national responsibility and families as rights-bearing units of citizens and future citizens to NCLB's configuration of school as a market option with parents and children as individualised consumers. Viewed in a positive light, NCLB treats parents as agents, whereas ESEA treated them as recipients of state support, which is to say, as objects. Yet in according parents agency in regards to children's schooling, while simultaneously saddling schools with unreasonable demands, parents were given responsibility for a now-much-riskier endeavour. A further twist is that NCLB shifted more real *power* over education, which is not the same as responsibility, to the federal government and away from the local and state authorities more responsive to (and, in the case of America's local school boards, often constituted of and by) parents. Thus, as risk and responsibility were handed to parents, as well as educators, their power directly to manage their schools was curtailed. 'Steer this ship', policymakers seemed to tell parents, 'while we attempt to scuttle it'.

Chicago was ground zero for many of the reforms that became national policy as NCLB and later, in NCLB's reenactment under President Obama, as Race to the Top. Chicago introduced test-based accountability measures in the 1990s, preceding the NCLB requirement that Illinois do so, started using them to close down public schools, and Chicago replaced democratic oversight of the city school system with a mayorally appointed CEO and school board. Chicago Public Schools' CEO in the early 2000s, Arne Duncan, took his market-driven reforms national when he was appointed Secretary of Education by President Obama in 2008. In Chicago, Duncan presided over the city's Renaissance 2010 plan, cooked up by Chicago's politicians and business leaders in 2003–04. Under Ren2010, Chicago Public Schools (CPS) planned to close 60 public schools and replace them with 100 new charter schools by 2010. Duncan's signature achievement as Secretary of Education, the reissuance of NCLB as Race to the Top, required states to include provisions for replacing public schools with charters in order to qualify for large federal grants. Chicago, in Pauline Lipman's words,

> is more than a rich example. It is incubator, test case, and model for the neoliberal urban education agenda. Chicago is where big city mayors go to see how to restructure their school systems. ... Chicago is also a prominent case of the transformation of the industrial, Keynesian, racially segregated, city to the entrepreneurial postwelfare city. (Lipman 2011, 9)

Chicago Public Schools, the nation's third largest school district, is therefore an excellent place to look at how parents are facing the risks and the responsibilities that have been foisted on them by neoliberal education reform policies in the past two decades. As Lipman documents, education reform has worked in tandem with other urban reforms, notably in housing, to shift resources from poor and middle class city residents to the pockets of real estate developers and business elites. When twentieth century housing projects that sheltered Chicago's poor were demolished and replaced in the first decade of the twenty-first century, the new mixed income housing did not include a comparable number of residences for low-income families. As a result, Chicago's (racialized – mostly African American) poor moved out of Chicago in large numbers. Predictably, the population of school aged children dropped in those neighbourhoods, and that drop became grounds for closing schools that were decreed 'underutilized' as well as 'failing'. Nonetheless, the (unelected) Board of Education approved charter schools in these same neighbourhoods, further draining students from the remaining public schools and increasing city expenses, though this money now went to chartering agencies rather than unionised teachers, reducing the Board's obligations to Chicago's workers (whose benefits and pensions had to be paid) in the long run.

Parents' responses

Curious to hear from Chicago parents how they perceived 'parental involvement' in the wake of these reforms, I interviewed parents whose children attended (or, in some cases, had attended but no longer did) Chicago Public Schools.[3] Interviewees were identified through their public involvement with a Chicago-based parent organisation that advocated for increased resources for CPS schools, and then through snowball sampling, with interviewees directing me to other parents they considered 'exceptionally involved' with public schools. Selections from 2 of those 10 interviews, in which parents spoke about risks that concerned them, are presented below. I did not prompt parents to talk about 'risk', and the parents did not use the word, but searching the interview transcripts for related affect words (e.g. worry, afraid) brought up instances of parents responding to risks that contemporary education policies have created. That search for affect-words related to risk led me to select the two interviews discussed in this article.

Because of methodological limitations, these parents' responses should not be considered representative. They are, however, informative. This project is meant to contribute to conversations about parents in political, social and ethical theory, insofar as such theory engages with empirical research – as I think it must. Its disciplinary grounds are those of philosophy of education with a particular twist, as I and other philosophers of education have argued that epistemological common grounds shared by philosophical inquiry and qualitative inquiry into education make cross-disciplinary research, of which this project is an example, both fruitful and methodologically legitimate.[4] I hope the following will enrich the literature about parental involvement by providing some of the parents' own rich accounts of their involvement with their children's educations. In enriching the theoretical conversations by engaging parents as interlocutors, I further hope to provide insights that empirical researchers can use in their work on parental involvement. All interviews were carried out by me. I asked interviewees for approximately half an hour of their time, and brought a list of questions, but in every case interviewees talked for longer, from approximately 45–90 min, and brought up what they thought was important for me to know, rather than sticking to my prompts. As the mother of two children in Chicago Public Schools myself, and a parent who shared many of my respondents' concerns about the direction of school policy, I found it easy to establish a rapport with other parents, which no doubt contributed to their responsiveness. This was most true of the middle-class and professional parents I interviewed, but it also helped establish rapport with low-income parents of colour. In Chicago (and perhaps more generally?), children's school experiences are what mothers frequently turn to as a conversation starter when they meet other mothers with school-aged children, a conversational convention that worked to my advantage in this research project. My position as a CPS parent influenced this study in many other ways as well, from the study's conception to my analysis of the interviews.

Before moving into the interview accounts, two other relevant factors of the policyscape merit mention, as they are as easy for international readers to overlook as for American readers to take for granted. The first has to do with responsibility. Public schooling in the United States has throughout its history been far more decentralised and subject to local control than in other industrialised nations. Public schooling has been supported primarily by local property taxes, and democratically elected school boards have had a great deal of oversight. Due to school boards, in fact, a significant percentage of American citizens hold elected office, and an even larger number attend public school board meetings. The diminishment of local control is thus, for all the problems with local control (especially racial segregation of schools), a blow to Americans' direct experiences with democratic self-governance. In her interview, Phuong expresses concern about this. The US education system can appear fragmented and incoherent; to its proponents, it represents democratic self-governance and the right of parents to determine the education of their own children.

The second reminder is about risk. Guns, keep in mind, are omnipresent in Chicago (as in the United States generally). Neoliberalism's replacement of social welfare ideology has coincided with the radicalisation of the National Rifle Association (NRA), which used to be a sportsman's association but has, in the past 50 years, become a major political influence, supporting the loosening of America's already liberal gun laws. At present, there are estimated to be more firearms in the United States than there are people. Addressing the material reality that guns create risks, furthermore, is complicated by gendered and racialized rhetoric, promulgated by the NRA, that casts *some* people (Black, Latino, youth) as 'risky' gun-bearers who make it necessary for *other* people (White, men, especially husbands and fathers) to own more guns. There are, in short, a lot of guns in Chicago, with gun violence concentrated more in some neighbourhoods than others, but requiring all parents to think about their children's risk of getting shot – and, as the reader can hear echoed in Angela's interview, about their children's safety as they grow into the less adult-supervised social life of adolescence. This gives risk, and parents' worry, a particularly American twist.

It is almost panic time: Phuong

Phuong described the neighbourhood school that her two daughters attended as a 'gem in the city'. A refugee when she came to the United States from Vietnam as a child, Phuong had earned an advanced degree in ethnobotany, which inspired her to develop a gardening programme with her neighbourhood school, where most of the students were Mexican American. Phuong was already planning the next year's gardening programme, which she took a few months leave from her job as co-owner of a small family business to carry out. Working with 17 teachers and approximately 280 schoolchildren, she taught practical 'garden lessons' about how to grow plants from seed to harvest but also

> really dug back into my ethnobotany and talked to the kids really about botany. Really 101 stuff, but trying to tie in these bigger global issues and also local issues of foods. Just trying to change our relationship with plants and food. And it was just so rewarding that I am like we have to do it!

In Phuong's view, the garden programme provided a means for immigrant children to stay connected to traditional, healthier foodways – 'that we used to – you would have to grow your own foods'. It was 'poignant', she said, to see children's excitement when their seeds sprouted.

Phuong took responsibility for the school; she also recognised risks it faced as a result of decisions made by the city and the state. In December 2015, when we spoke, Illinois had not passed its annual state budget (nor would it pass one until 2017), and although stopgap measures were passed so that schools could operate, CPS was severely short of funds. Meanwhile, in November 2015, CPS CEO Barbara Byrd Bennett had been indicted on corruption charges related to a kickback scheme, for which she would eventually be convicted and jailed. Phuong appreciated what her school's principal was doing in the face of constant financial pressure, but she thought a stronger response was called for. 'Even with all the burdens', Phuong said, 'this school continues to really try to meet the needs of the kids'. Recent events, however, seemed to her to be taking a toll on the principal's morale.

And for good reason – of course we all know why. But it has even gotten to where … the things she was saying [to parents at a recent holiday breakfast for volunteers] … it was very doomsday. Doomsday in the way that wasn't like 'hey we can do something about it. … I really wish she would be more, sort of, not a rebel, but even more of just like putting that out there. Even at LSC [Local School Council] meetings, this is my second year on the LSC, and I often felt like last year I would say things about opting out or really voicing my opinion about the park and I would just feel like, it's never like she would hush me, but it was this consensus that she just doesn't want to panic. Like cause panic in the teachers. Cause panic in the parents. And I am more like it's time to wake people up and actually cause them maybe not to panic, but we can strategize before we have to panic, because now it is almost panic time.

As her words make clear, Phuong had a nuanced understanding of the risks to parents, teachers, and communities. She, like many politically engaged Chicago parents, thought CPS was partly to blame for its fiscal woes (e.g. by hiring corrupt CEOs and opening new charter schools even as district enrolment was falling), and she recognised that the risks were handed down to individual schools as demands for achievement alongside reductions in resources. She recognised also that speaking out could be a risk, especially for parents who were not citizens. She responded to the risks facing her school by getting involved, in two distinct ways. She volunteered her time to the gardening programme. She also called for *political* involvement: through the elected Local School Councils, through collective testing opt-out, and through engagement with elected officials. Volunteering, which entailed forgoing paid employment for several months, and opting out of tests put Phuong at risk. But for Phuong, it was better to take those risks, in the hope of preventing other harms, than to let 'people in power … keep us where they want us'.

Phuong viewed the accountability measures imposed on schools as a waste of money the cash-strapped district could ill afford. She considered testing opt-out to be a means of forcing CPS listen to what parents wanted. 'For us it doesn't matter what the kids really score on their test', she told me. 'The fact that they are just so loved and nurtured [at their school] is huge for us'. In opting her children out of standardised testing, Phuong was part of a movement of American parents who oppose the tests. As Oren Pizmony-Levy and Nancy Green Saraisky report, based on their survey research, parents offer a range of reasons for opting their children out of standardised tests. Reasons stretch across the political spectrum, from libertarian objections to federal authority over local schools to progressive resistance to the tests' effective penalisation of schools serving children in poverty. Phuong objected because she saw the tests as a waste of resources, an inappropriate measure of school quality, and an unwarranted imposition by an unelected school board (Pizmony-Levy and Saraisky 2016).[5] Nor did her political speech stop there. 'To be honest', she wanted to tell her fellow parents at the breakfast,

> I don't think folks downtown [at CPS central office] really care about our building coming apart – like in the gym where we have the breakfast these wooden panels are literally coming off, and we have been trying to do a fundraiser for over a year and a half to get new curtains. The curtains that we have have been there since the Roosevelt administration, or something insane.

The morning of the breakfast, the neighbourhood's State Representative to the Illinois legislature was visiting the school's student council, and she urged parents to go talk to him.

To address the funding crisis hitting CPS schools like hers, Phuong thought parents needed to take collective action. 'I truly believe that small changes, just small little things, make big differences', she told me.

> When you drop anything in water that ripple goes and it's going to continue. And whether the change is going to happen, of course in my lifetime … I am like 'put that aside now'. I am like 'that's probably not going to happen'. But hopefully if it can happen, it might for my daughters, or their kids should they have kids or whatever, but just generations from now I feel like it is possible. The first step, I think, is just to really get the parents to be aware that they do have a voice.

Phuong recognised that in calling for immigrants to speak out, there was a 'sensitive line that we have to always be keeping in mind', but, she added,

> I also do feel for them, like, 'you know what, I do understand your concerns, but I also feel like that is just another fear. You know, that people in power do put on us. And that makes us, you know, it sort of does keep us where they want us.'

After addressing some of the objections to testing opt-out, and telling me how she came to be involved with the school. Phuong returned to the importance of political action. She turned to plants as a metaphor.

> Ahh, [gardening] has such an immediate sort of wakening effect. And I think in that principle of like you know, like I said earlier, I've been resigned to say change might not happen in my lifetime but if I can plant that seed … .

As long as you teach your child you don't have nothing to worry about: Angela

In Angela's account of her two children's schooling, immediate risks played a powerful role. Angela's children had attended three schools: a charter school, a neighbourhood elementary school, and a lottery-based magnet school. She moved her daughter from the charter to the neighbourhood school after second grade because the charter stopped providing bus service, making 'school choice' an unavailable choice. But she had other reasons as well.

> One of her kindergarten teachers when I was there told me that I should get her out of that school because the school wasn't good for her. And when I switched her over to [the neighborhood school] I found out that was true because my daughter was still at a first grade level. She was going to third grade and she wasn't nowhere near the third grade level. So they had to take my baby back and they found out that she had dyslexia. And [the charter school] knew something was wrong, but they wasn't trying to pay attention.[6]

Angela, who is Black, suspected that her daughter's neglect by the charter school was affected by race. Her new teachers

> worked really good with her compared to the charter school she went to, which was mostly Hispanic. And in [the charter school] they had my daughter, like it was a guy, it was a little child who did not know English so she had to sit by him and help him with his homework.

Angela, like Phuong, responded to her worries about school by getting involved, but differently. 'I did not like that idea. I told them to stop. So I decided to sit there and watch them, how they teach. I did not like the way they teach. I didn't like it at all'.

She kept up her vigilance at the neighbourhood school, and she thought all parents had a responsibility to do the same.

> Like they say, as long as you teach your child you don't have nothing to worry about. As long as you stay on your child and show them what behavior is, what's bad behavior, what's good behavior, you don't have nothing to worry about. And by me volunteering in the school I was always in the school, was always there every day, became a PAC [Parent Advisory Council] chair, was on the LSC, you know I built a lot of things with the school. So what I noticed is that when you are involved with your child in school, the teachers stay focused on your children because you are there. You see what is going on.[7]

Angela lamented that 'a lot of parents, especially in my race, don't have, don't do that'. Rather than blame parents, though, she took upon herself the responsibility for helping them work through problems with the school.

> We don't communicate with the teachers. Most of them are always fussing at the teacher, not trying to listen to each other about what's going on and how to help the child. But what I used to do as the PAC chair – every time a teacher had a problem with a parent I always sat there and listened to help the teacher out as well as the parent out. So if I

feel like the parent is wrong I would butt in and say no. This is this, and you need to do this, and they would listen to me.

For all her involvement with the neighbourhood school, Angela's children no longer attended it. She had moved them to a lottery-based magnet in a different neighbourhood because

> some of the neighborhood kids was horrible. I just didn't want my daughter to pick up their bad habits. It wasn't the teachers, it wasn't the principal, it was the children that I was afraid of for my child. That was it.

She worried even more about her son, whom she described as 'a follower'. She did not mention worrying that the neighbourhood school might be closed, though it was on the list of 54 schools CPS planned to close in 2013, but this may have been an additional consideration. At the magnet school, Angela was no longer serving on the PAC or the LSC, though she was present in the school, working as a custodian. She had taken that job when her son started attending, in first grade, so that she could keep an eye on him, which she felt she needed to do.

> I am in the school when he in the school. I am in the school from 6 to 2:30. He is there from 7:30–2:30, so I am there all day. I can go check on him when he's on lunch. I can go check on him when he's on recess. I can do all those things.

She wanted her children's lives in school not to repeat her own school experiences.

> I was bullied all the way from when I was a little kid … because I wore glasses and I didn't dress like everyone else. Like, glasses are popular now. Back in my days, it wasn't popular. No, you got teased, jumped, beat up. And I didn't dress like everyone else. So when I was in high school I couldn't take it. They was jumping me every day out of school.

She dropped out after her freshman year. Once she had children, however, she reflected back on conversations with her own mother, whose advice to stay in school Angela had dismissed because her mother had also dropped out.

> I used to be like 'you didn't stay in school how are you going to tell me?' So I went back to school, got my GED, and then I went to college and got my Associates degree. So my daughter she watched me through the process, she even cheered me on. I even let her make comments about my grades. Like I show her my grades, and she be like 'mom I don't like that C, you need to bring it up'. I'm like 'I'm gonna try, I do need to bring that up'. … So I let her voice an opinion about my grades, so that she can see how important it is when I get on her about her grades.

If in some respects Angela seems like a stereotypical 'helicopter parent', there are important differences. Angela intervened in response to risks that were real and imminent, like unaddressed dyslexia, rather than imaginary or distant in time. She also recognised that the example she set was one of her best means of influencing her children's decisions as they grew old enough to make them for themselves, and she shared authority by subjecting her school achievement to her daughter's judgment as well as her daughter's to hers.

Furthermore, Angela did not limit her attentiveness to her own children. When I asked her how parents at the neighbourhood school felt about her sitting in on their conferences with teachers, she told me they were willing to listen to her because the children love me. They all call me mama. And I fuss at them like they are my kids. I still do that, if I see them outside, most of them are in high school, if you walk with me they be like 'hey mom.' So. I treat all of them like they my kids. If I see them doing something I'll holler at them too.

Angela's name was suggested to me because the neighbourhood school her children had attended was designated for closure in 2012–13, and, like Phuong, Angela had connected with an organisation of parents mobilising to support public schooling in Chicago. Now that her children had moved to a magnet school, however, Angela no longer had a formal parent leadership role within the school.

> I am just cleaning and listening,' she told me. The principal at the magnet school, she said, 'wants people that clean to be out of the ... don't be in the open. The teachers are beautiful – they nice. I am always speaking to them. They open up. But the person that has the nerve to speak up, [for] leadership and commitment and teamwork, is not [treated by the principal as] a team player.

So she cleaned and listened, doing her best to ensure that her children got a solid education, certain that she, not professional educators or the system that employed them, had to take responsibility for that.

Angela's story speaks to obstacles in the path of a democratic approach to making school both excellent and equitable. Angela was thoughtful, disciplined, and seemed to have a knack for getting children, parents, and educators to work together. In a world that had protected her from the bullies and provided a high quality education to all students, she might have done great things with those abilities. In a world that failed her as a teenager but provided second chances through the GED and community colleges, she had become a leader within her school and neighbourhood. The systematic destabilisation of schools and neighbourhoods drove her out of the neighbourhood school where her leadership was appreciated, into a mixed-race school, where her involvement was not invited. Linn Posey Maddox has documented how the reengagement of white parents with urban schools has lifted the test scores and graduation rates of schools attended by white children but pushed Black parents out of those schools and neighbourhoods that had been, however imperfectly, theirs. Angela experienced this dynamic in two ways: as white families moved to the city, real estate value in her neighbourhood appreciated and the city had reason to close and sell school buildings, and when she moved her children to a mixed race school, her leadership abilities went unrecognised (Posey-Maddox 2014). In a democracy debilitated by racial inequality, Angela was left cleaning up the messes that others were making.

Technocratic solutions, however, have been no panacea either. While urging 'parental involvement' in public schools, CPS's Board of Education ignored the pleas of thousands of parents who turned out to beg CPS not to close their neighbourhood schools, assuring parents that children would receive a superior education under its plan. Five years after the 2013 closure of 49 CPS schools, a recent study shows that children whose schools were closed are faring no better. 'Did closing schools provide students with better educational opportunities and stronger academic outcomes?' the study asked (Gordon et al. 2018).[8] 'The evidence ... suggests that closing schools and moving students into designated welcoming schools to consolidate resources did not automatically expose them to better learning environments and result in greater academic gains'. According to the researchers, 'In this and other previous studies on the effects of school closures, we have seen that academic outcomes, on average, do not improve after students' schools were closed'. Furthermore, it created new problems, such as distrust and low morale among parents and teachers affected by the closures. As for solving other long term problems, the study noted that five years later the budget remains tight and enrolments continue to decline. The Board of Education, meanwhile, continues to open new charter schools, and after a five-year moratorium on school closures, in 2018 it closed all the remaining neighbourhood public schools, including the high school, in the Black neighbourhood of Englewood.

Technocracy or democracy?

The policies discussed in this paper, and the interviews that present two exceptionally engaged and thoughtful parents' responses to them, can be understood as part of an ongoing argument between American citizens who agree that federal authority over education, assigned to technocratic policy professionals, would fix longstanding problems of school quality and inequality and American citizens who believe that democratic control is a better path than technocratic fixes to achieving long-lasting solutions. To date, the technocrats have not fixed the problems; whether democracy could do better remains an open question.

Test-based accountability regimes, and the reconstitution of a public system as a market system by means of school closures and charter schools, are technocratic approaches to the extraordinarily complex problem of educating children. Their legitimacy rests on the premise that mastery of information, nearly all of it quantitative, will enable master technicians – namely policy makers at the district, state, and federal levels – to tinker with the implementation of programmes in order to bring about desired results. This premise is profoundly apolitical. It harkens back to a debate between Walter Lippman and John Dewey in the 1920s, a time when the United States was also struggling to address the massification of social services, an influx of recent immigrants, and a changing international role. Lippman argued, in his influential book *Public Opinion*, that since the foundation of the United States as a republic in the eighteenth century, technological changes to work, communications, and daily life had rendered the affairs of the government sufficiently complicated that the founders' premises of an 'omnicompetent citizen' were no longer plausible. Lippman doubted that the Jeffersonian premise that citizens were ever qualified to vote on all matters had ever held, but in any case, he argued, the modern complexity of problems and the wealth of extant information made it less credible than ever. Government, Lippman argued, should be in the hands of experts.

John Dewey reviewed both *Public Opinion* and Lippman's subsequent book about voter apathy, *The Phantom Public* favourably in the *New Republic*, but although Dewey thought Lippman had accurately diagnosed a significant problem, he disagreed with Lippman's solution (Dewey 1983, 340).[9] Publics, Dewey argues, form as members of a community come to recognised the '[i]ndirect, extensive, enduring and serious consequences of conjoint and interacting behavior' (1983, 110). Called into existence by this shared recognition of consequences, publics have 'a common interest in controlling these consequences' (Dewey 1983, 110). Dewey agreed with Lippman that the machine age has so enormously expanded, multiplied, intensified and complicated the scope of the indirect consequences, has formed such immense and consolidated unions in action on an impersonal rather than a community basis, that the resultant public cannot identify and distinguish itself (1983, 110).

Yet experts will never be able to solve political problems without the input of citizens, Dewey argues, because those affected by a problem are those best positioned to identify what, precisely, the problem is. Too removed from the consequences – those frayed curtains from the Roosevelt era, those charter schools that neglect a Black first grader's dyslexia, those White principals who even as they claim to advocate for racial equity prefer that Black cleaning staff stay out of sight – experts are unable to grasp the consequences as only the public can. In Dewey's words, 'the man who wears the shoe knows best that it pinches and where it pinches, even if the expert shoemaker is the best judge of how the trouble is to be remedied'. The problem, for Dewey, is that a 'class of experts'[10] – e.g. technocratic education policy makers – 'is inevitably so removed from common interests as to become a class with private interests and private knowledge, which in social matters is not knowledge at all'(1983, 154). For Dewey, there is a role for expertise *and* an essential role for publics that come together around shared problems.

Phuong's and Angela's responses to educational policy in Chicago, from test-based accountability to school closures, represent the kind of public involvement that Dewey recognised as essential. They were involved parents, participants in what Dewey would recognise as a public that formed around a conjoint recognition of consquences, but not in precisely the mode that NCLB, state and Chicago Public Schools recognises and mandates. In Phuong's case, parental involvement included resistance to official policy as well as cooperation with her local school. In Angela's case, parental involvement was valued by a mostly Black school that ultimately faced closure and then devalued by a mixed-race school praised as one of the city's best. Their stories suggest the limitations of policy solutions that fail to attend to parents' own experiences of risk and responsibility within public schooling. Phuong's and Angela's insights suggest also the need to engage the wider public, including but not limited to parents and teachers, in taking responsibility as citizens for the real risks facing America's schoolchildren. Dewey would recognise their knowledge about the problems facing their schools as the kind of social knowledge more relevant to public problems than policy-makers' quantified knowledge that, insofar as it is removed from what parents, teachers and students know, is no knowledge at all. In sharing their words with the wider audience reading this journal, I hope to have given their knowledge the place at the table it deserves.

Notes

1. Emphasis added
2. On welfare-to-workfare reforms of the 1990s and their effect on parents and children, see Hays (2003); DeParle (2005).
3. The interviews were transcribed by my graduate assistant, Samantha Deane, for whose help I am grateful. All names of interviewees are pseudonyms. I have edited speakers' words slightly for sake of clarity by trimming filler words but have otherwise quoted them directly.
4. See especially Shuffelton (2014).; c.f. other articles in that issue. See also *Educational Theory* 65 (2) 2015, especially Michele Moses's introduction on non-ideal theory in philosophy of education.

5. I have written more about parents and testing opt out in 'Opting Out or Opting In? Test Boycott and Parental Engagement in American Public Education,' forthcoming *Educational Theory*.
6. Not only was her daughter's dyslexia ignored for several years by the charter school, CPS has been no model for upholding special education law. In May 2018, its special education programme was put in state hands, after an investigation uncovered systematic delay and denial of services to students. Although Angela was satisfied with the services her daughter received (prior to 2016, when policy changes created the problems identified by the state investigation), it is important to recognise that her vigilance was not paranoia. Parent complaints about the effects of the new policies on their children drove the media reports that drove state action.
7. PAC stands for Parental Advisory Committee. These committees were established in Chicago Public Schools in response to the requirements in NCLB, cited above.
8. Cf. Ewing's (2018).
9. I have discussed this at greater length in Shuffelton, Amy. "The Chicago Teachers Strike and Its Public". Education and Culture, 30 no 2 (October 2014): 21–33.
10. Dewey, John. The Public and its Problems. Ohio University Press, Athens OH, 2016 p.224.

Disclosure statement

No potential conflict of interest was reported by the author(s).

References

DeParle, Jason. 2005. *American Dream*. New York: Penguin.
Dewey, John. 1983. "Public Opinion." In *The Middle Works of John Dewey*, edited by Jo Ann Boydston, vol. 13, 1921–1922, 340. Carbondale: Southern Illinois University Press.
Ewing's, Eve. 2018. *Ghosts in the Schoolyard: Racism and School Closings on Chicago's South Side*. Chicago: University of Chicago Press.
Gordon, Molly, Marisa de la Torre, Jennifer R. Cowhy, Paul T. Moore, Lauren Sartain, and David Knight. 2018. *School Closings in Chicago*. Chicago: University of Chicago Consortium on School Research.
Hays, Sharon. 2003. *Flat Broke with Children*. New York: Oxford University Press.
Lipman, Pauline. 2011. *The New Political Economy of Urban Education*, 19. New York: Routledge.
Moses, Michele. 2015. "Introduction on non-Ideal Theory in Philosophy of Education." *Educational Theory* 65 (2): 170–110.
National Center for Children in Poverty Website. Accessed May 14, 2018. http://www.nccp.org/topics/childpoverty.html.
A Nation at Risk. 1983, April. Accessed June 5, 2018 at https://www2.ed.gov/pubs/NatAtRisk/risk.html
Pizmony-Levy, Oren, and Nancy Green Saraisky. 2016. "Who Opts Out and Why?" New York, Teachers College.
Posey-Maddox, Linn. 2014. *When Middle-Class Parents Choose Urban Schools: Class, Race, and the Challenge of Equity in Public Education*. Chicago: University of Chicago Press.
Ravitch, Diane. 2016. *The Death and Life of the Great American School System*, 28. New York: Basic Books.
Shuffelton, A. 2014. "Estranged Familiars." *Studies in Philosophy of Education* 33 (3): 137–147.

Parents as a problem: on the marginalisation of democratic parental involvement in Swedish school policy

Susanne Dodillet and Ditte Storck Christensen

ABSTRACT
This article proposes that the scope for parental involvement is limited in the current Swedish school system, despite its claim to the highest level of democracy and its extensive marketisation and juridification. In order to define this deficit, we introduce the notion of democratic parental involvement. We further trace the history of the pronounced reluctance towards parents seeking to influence the education of their children in Swedish education policy since the 1940s. Three characteristic ideas in this policy are highlighted: (1) its concept of 'democratic education', (2) the idea of 'the best interest of the child' and (3) the concept of 'the professional teacher'. We argue that these strands together make the idea of democratic parental involvement being a positive force in education virtually inconceivable.

Introduction

This article emanates from our observations as parents trying to influence the education of our children in the Swedish school system. In Sweden, school attendance is compulsory for children aged 6–15 and cannot be replaced by other forms of education, e.g. homeschooling. In other words, parents are prohibited from taking overall responsibility for the education of their children. In view of the fact that Sweden is a democracy, stressing the importance of active citizen participation, this school system of coercion might be expected to be offset by comprehensive forms of parental involvement. Accordingly, we expected to be involved in discussions on, and even to define strategies for educational questions concerning, learning targets, teaching methods, classroom climate, homework rules, the use of mobile phones and excursions. However, our requests to have a say in the education of our children were routinely overruled. Instead of being accepted as competent collaborators, we were told about fixed rules at parents' evenings, and were expected to comply with them.

Our experiences inspired us to investigate what is meant by having responsibilities as a guardian of a child subject to compulsory schooling in Sweden. The aim of this article is to identify the background to what we experienced as an attitude of ignorance and occasionally distrust of parental involvement in Swedish school policy.

The sceptical attitude towards parental involvement that we experienced is not unique to Sweden. While parental involvement in early education seems to be welcomed more in other countries (Janssen & Vandenbroeck 2018, 821), other school jurisdictions concerning older children also seem reluctant about parental involvement (e.g. Breidenstein, Krüger & Roch forthcoming; Bendixsen & Danielsen forthcoming). With reference to the Anglo-American world, sociologist Frank Furedi identified the idea of 'the best interest of the child' and teachers' expertise as central arguments to exclude parents from decisions concerning the education of their children (Furedi 2009). Similar arguments are mobilised by opponents of home-schooling in many countries (Myers & Bhopal 2018; Pearlman-Avnion & Grayevsky 2017; Torres 2016; Barbosa 2016). We, therefore, expect our analysis of the Swedish case to be germane to understanding the limitations of parental involvement in other countries too.

Democratic parental involvement – a blind spot in earlier research

The form of parental involvement that we found lacking in Sweden differs from the concepts usually referred to in research about parents and schools. Current research on the influence of Swedish parents typically frames parental involvement in relation to the school reforms that have transformed the Swedish school system since the 1990s (Dahlstedt 2009; Englund 2011b; Novak 2017). Particular emphasis has been put on two shifts in school policy. Firstly, *marketisation* is said to have given increased power to individual parents by choosing a school for their children. Since the 1990s the formerly state-governed Swedish education system, has been transformed in a neo-liberal direction, including decentralisation, the introduction of free school choice, school vouchers and publicly funded private schools (Lundahl, Arreman, Holm and Lundström 2013). Englund describes this trend in terms of 'the increased impact of the rights of parents' (Englund 2011b, 8).

Increased power of parents is also identified with reference to *juridification*, viz. the increasingly formal regulation of what schools must and must not do, combined with equally formal procedures for 'reporting' schools and teachers that fail to comply with policy (Arneback and Bergh 2016). One obvious object of study regarding this trend is the Swedish Education Act (2010:800), which was gradually transformed from detailed regulation of schools' obligations to more indirect (but no less constraining) framework legislation, specifying children's right to education (Novak 2017). As a consequence, a rapidly growing number of parents report schools and teachers to the Swedish Schools Inspectorate, a governmental agency founded in 2008 to monitor schools and to hold them accountable for their failings.

While some researchers interpret parents' discretionary powers with regard to their children as a too far-reaching shift in the relationship between the family and schools, and as a danger to educational equity (Englund 2011b), others describe parents' influence as ultimately decided by economic and legal rationalities and thus as limited (Novak 2017). In line with recent international research on the *responsibilisation* of parents (Halse, Hartung and Wright 2017), Dahlstedt interprets the increasing emphasis on parental involvement in Swedish education policy as a strategy to turn parents into ideal partnering subjects, 'willing to engage in partnering on the conditions that apply for the partnership in question' (Dahlstedt 2009, 799). According to this interpretation, parents are not encouraged to introduce their own thoughts about the aims and practice of schooling, but to comply with current education policy and its paradigm of success and achievement.

Even though earlier research differs in its judgement regarding whether parents have received too much, or merely a limited amount of influence, researchers relating parents' activism to marketisation, juridification and responsibilisation portray parental activities as generally complying with policy makers' intentions. They tell the story of parents who are encouraged or even manipulated into realising a policy that supports the logic of New Public Management. Parents are thus assigned the role of agents of economic and legal regimes not only by policy makers but also by educational research. Parents trying to influence the education of their children irrespective of the logics of marketisation, juridification and responsibilisation risk being marginalised. This is true not only for the Swedish examples referred to above, but also for the view of parents as resources for increased goal achievement gaining prominence in policy (Helgøy & Homme 2017; Oelkers 2018) and research (Hornby and Blackwell 2018, 2011; Wilder 2014; Hill & Taylor 2004) elsewhere.

The form of parental involvement that we found lacking as parents of children in the Swedish school system, and that we also find underrepresented in research on parent-school relationships, differs from the ideas of compliance and effective parental involvement. Our expectations concerning our role as parents were not limited to being used as tools to fulfil official school policies. Instead, we expected to be involved in discussions about how to plug the gaps that these policies leave. We expected our ideas and objections to be considered, and to thus be taken seriously as competent, collaborative partners in the education of our children. We wanted to identify shortcomings in existing policies and thus to contribute to better solutions for the future. We could also imagine participating in or even organising protests against existing school policies in order to improve the working conditions of our children and their teachers. Gofen and Blomqvist call the more extreme form of this type of parenthood 'proactive'. Proactive parenthood 'embodies a refusal to take familiar arrangements for granted and questions fundamental assumptions about what is considered to be possible' (Gofen and Blomqvist 2014, 548). Proactive parents wish to take responsibility for the educational system, and to thus 'act as a social force which promotes the public good' (Gofen and Blomqvist 2014, 548). The question we aim to answer in this article is why these forms of *democratic parental involvement* were neither expected from us nor welcomed.

Material and approach

Sweden has an exceptionally well-developed culture of public inquiry, and even after the decentralisation reforms of the 1990s a proliferation of governmental policy documents. It is on this set of documents, e.g. government inquiries, government bills and school regulations, that we built our analysis. These documents do not just regulate the day-to-day activity of schools, we read them as representations of prevalent attitudes and mindsets that underscore the passive role of parents with respect to school matters.

Approaching our question, we collected both official policy documents regulating parental involvement and documents in which decisive arguments in more or less direct support of parental involvement are articulated. An example of such documents are the

Swedish government bills to implement the UN Convention of the Right of the Child, in which it is clearly stated that the interest of the child takes precedence over the interests of parents (Govt Bill 2009/10:165; Govt Bill 2017/18:186).

In an initial stage of our analysis of these documents, we formed the idea of three strands in the history of the Swedish education system, which together make it difficult to conceive of *democratic parental involvement* as a positive and constructive force in education. These three strands are: (1) the idea of 'education for democracy', (2) the concept of 'the best interest of the child' and (3) the idea of 'professionalism and science-based teaching'. These three strands guided our research from that point on.

We start our presentation with a short overview of the historical roots of our themes, before we outline them one by one and discuss their impact on the scope for parents' involvement with schools.

The margins of parental involvement

In Sweden, the state's influence over the education and upbringing of children increased steadily in the twentieth century. This trend was nurtured by the breakthrough of the Social Democrats in 1932, and the 44 years of Social Democratic government that followed, but it has been continued by other political groupings up to the present day. The process of educational reform that was initiated in the 1940s and led to the Swedish model of a nine-year compulsory comprehensive school was shaped by the perception that the family lacks the capacity to shape the democratic, collectively well-functioning citizen that could guarantee peace and welfare in the future.[1] The family was further depicted as weakened by societal developments following industrialisation and disoriented in a world characterised by constant change (SOU 1946:31, 23f). In the 1960s policy-makers stated that the family 'no longer occupies the central position of earlier times, in the upbringing of children and youth' (SOU 1961:30, 104). It appeared necessary for the state to step in and take increased responsibility.

Through an extension of compulsory school, where children from all parts of society should meet to be raised together, policy makers aimed to guarantee the *democratic education* of all children. On the one hand, the school should be coherent and convey a common base for all. At the same time, post-war education policy was characterised by a high degree of confidence in scientific progressive education and pragmatic thinking that put the individual at the centre. The school should, on the other hand, be differentiated and individualised. *The individual child*, 'the perception of the student's human worth, his personality and self-esteem', should be at the heart of the educational system (SOU 1961: 30, 145). The idea of public responsibility for the education of each individual child became a central argument to expand the access of the education system to apply to the whole child, including the social environments in which children spend time. For example, schools were encouraged to collect information on children's private life and family conditions in order to ensure individual child support.

Scientific paedagogy has also paved the way for the *professionalisation* of education. In Sweden, teachers have been assigned the role of 'social engineers' who, with the help of science, were expected to realise the vision of school policy. In this regard, parents appear as laymen in need of help. The emphasis on science and rationality further conveys the vision of Sweden as a modern country without ideological contradictions, like in the following quote from the government inquiry that led to the introduction of the Swedish model of a school for all in the 1960s.

> In our country, where class contradictions are levelled out and where ideological contradictions exist in an atmosphere of objectivity and tolerance, one does not need to cope with the difficulties that, for example, certain other countries face, where the struggle between the confessions constitutes obstacles for agreement on the norms of education. (SOU 1961: 30, 239)

In this context parents who did not cooperate with the school system as intended, but had a negative or indifferent attitude towards this educational project, appeared to be in need of consciousness-raising (SOU 1961: 30).

The Swedish concept of education for democracy

Swedish compulsory school aims to provide democratic education to all children. There are at least two ways to perceive of this aim, which can both be found in the history behind the K-9 Swedish compulsory school. Firstly, education for democracy can be understood as a project aiming to shape enlightened *individuals* able to take responsibility for and shape their still unknown future. Secondly, it can be understood as a social project, shaping *citizens* of a predefined 'democratic society'. In Swedish education policy, the first of these concepts has gradually been sacrificed to the benefit of the second (Dodillet 2019). As we will argue, the idea of education as a means to shape a specific 'democratic society' claims parents' compliance with this policy and prevents them from formulating alternative teaching methods and targets.

Crucially for the introduction of the Swedish model of a school for all in the 1960s, schooling was described both as a social and as an individual project. Public education is 'an important instrument for the nation: by means of education, a nation seeks to clarify and determine the kind of knowledge and the ideals that are to be instilled in young people', a school commission emphasised in 1946, but not without adding:

> However, it should not be forgotten that people do not only live for society and the state, but also for themselves, for their own personal development, for their relatives, for their home. (SOU 1946: 31, 21)

The School Commission emphasised that the individual could have different interests than society and the state. People were not defined as one collective unity, but through their individual personalities and capacities as creating and entering into different social contexts and relationships worth upholding. The school should not 'take a particular, set organisation of society as its point of departure', but 'create conditions for social development based on the insights and will of the citizens' (SOU 1946:31, 17-18). As these quotes show, Swedish school policy aimed at the enlightenment and development of individuals to become independent adults rather than members of a specific model of society, in the years after the Second World War.

In the 1960s policy makers were no longer satisfied with democracy and ethics being taught about in school, and demanded that pupils actually embrace and act out these norms. In the first curriculum for the comprehensive school from 1962, this was expressed in formulations such as the responsibility of the school to 'build a foundation for, and develop such capacities in the children that [...] can carry and strengthen the democratic principles of tolerance, cooperation and equality between the sexes, nations and ethnicities' (Lgr62, 18). By instructing the school to not only inform about, but also influence students to embrace, these democratic principles, decision makers disregarded the warnings that Swedish policy makers had expressed in the 1940s when they emphasised that: 'Teaching must not be authoritarian, which it would be if it was put in the service of a particular political doctrine, even if this doctrine was that of democracy' (SOU 1948: 27, 3). Individual freedom and enlightenment were now subordinated to collective values, as can be read in the 1969 curriculum:

> Collective life in the democratic society must be shaped by free and independent individuals. But liberty and independence must not be ends in themselves. They must be the basis for collaboration and cooperation. [...] It is of importance that pupils become accustomed to helpfulness towards and collaboration with all people. (Lgr 69, 14)

Here, liberty is conditioned by the readiness to cooperate, not only with friends or colleagues but 'with all people'. Cooperativeness and solidarity with the whole community, not the individual's right to represent her convictions, even when they contain particular self-interests, thus became two of the most important features of democracy.

The norm of cooperation does not only apply to pupils but is regarded as a pillar of Swedish society at large, and thus also concerns adults. According to the curriculum from 1980, schools can 'expect [...] that even parents accept and seek to promote the principles and rules of democracy.' (Lgr 80, 19) If parents shared the same view of democracy as the school, students could 'experience that the home and the school are part of the same world' (Lgr 80, 19). A common value base or consensus regarding core norms appears here as the hallmark of the societal vision of education policy. The educationalist Tomas Englund thus characterised the curriculum Lgr 80 through its view of the school as 'an active institutional force in a collective will formation' (Englund 1999, 26).

The idea of schooling as a common national interest has also been highlighted in policy documents on the role of parents in the education system. *School for Participation* is a government inquiry that forms part of the so-called Democracy Committee, which in the mid-1980s was commissioned to develop a system for citizen participation and influence. There, it is described as self-evident that parents should be excluded from decisions concerning school:

> School is a matter for the whole of society and should be governed in the same way as other societal operations, viz. through politically elected bodies. (SOU 1985: 30, 28)

> A clear boundary between citizen influence and political democracy is needed. (SOU 1985: 30, 31)

Although the Swedish Parliament regularly emphasised the value of increased citizen influence, parents did not gain any significant influence on public education (see Lindbom 1995, 143; Erikson 2004, 296-299; Börjesson 2016, 122). In the 1980s the most radical provision regarding parental involvement was the introduction of a consultation obligation for head teachers, who were instructed to continuously inform and consult parents on 'certain issues' at school conferences (Govt Bill 1979/80:182). Even after this reform, however, parents remained excluded from decision-making. School was not considered an institution in the service of parents, and school policy was not considered a concern primarily for those directly involved, but the responsibility of the whole of society. In the late 80s, the Social Democratic education minister Bengt Göransson stressed that parents' interests were personal in character and 'should not be represented in bodies representing general citizens' interests' (Govt Bill 1988/89:4). Parents were expected to embrace policy objectives, determined by the collective will as represented by the Parliament. In connection with the decentralisation of school responsibility during the 1990s, the compulsory school conferences were also deregulated. Parental involvement in the school now again lacked support in the Education Act (Börjesson 2016, 151; Lindbom 1995, 139 f.).

The idea of the school as an institution for the realisation of a common social vision continued to constitute the base line of Swedish educational policies after the neoliberal reforms of the 1990s. Between 1997 and 2000, a government inquiry on democracy chaired by Bengt Göransson gathered 45 reports that formed the basis for the continued dialogue on forms of citizen representation in Sweden. The societal ideal presented in these reports is, in many ways, similar to the vision of solidarity and cooperation already expressed in the 1960s curricula. In the inquiry's main report, this ideal is refined as a 'participatory democracy with deliberative qualities' (SOU 2000: 1, 23). Accordingly, parents' involvement in school activities should take the form of deliberative conversations, i.e. conversations where different arguments are weighed against each other with 'an ambition that the individual takes a stand him-/herself by listening, considering, seeking arguments and evaluating them, at the same time as there is a collective ambition to find values and norms that everyone can agree on' (Skolverket 2000, 6; Englund 2000a).

The deliberative approach became prevalent both as a didactic concept in school education and as a strategy for citizen participation in the late 1990s. The main aim of this approach was not to meet the individual's right to represent and even adhere to her beliefs, but rather to improve the individual's understanding for and compliance with collective decision-making (Englund 2000b, 2011a). The Swedish version of participatory democracy can be understood as an educational project aimed at increasing the citizens' spirit of compromise and cooperation. In this context, people who hold on to their individual convictions and represent different values than the collective appear as undemocratic and primitive. In the inquiry on democracy mentioned above, this was expressed as follows:

> Through participation, citizens develop fundamental qualities in society. Citizens who mutually respect each other generate great human and social capital that all spheres in society benefit from. Those who do not receive comparable training in creating trust by being tolerant towards dissidents miss out on the schooling and refinement of their more primitive instincts. Those who practise cooperation, criticism and tolerance become an asset both for themselves and for society, both the private and the public sphere. (SOU 2000:1, 33)

Swedish policy equates schooling with learning to tolerate the beliefs of others and developing a readiness to subordinate individual interests to the collective with the aim of finding a common solution for the best interests of society. Not only passive parents, but also parents who defend their interests as parents rather than citizens, threaten this idea of common social interest.

Children's versus Parents' rights

Besides the notion of school as a societal affair, the idea of public education as a concern for children rather than families is a factor behind the marginalisation of parents in the

Swedish school system. One example of this perspective is Sweden's handling of the UN Declaration of Human Rights from 1948. This agreement aims at ensuring parents 'a prior right to choose the kind of education that shall be given to their children' (Article 26(3)). In a similar way, Article 2 of the Additional Protocol to the European Convention on Human Rights states that the state shall 'respect the right of parents to ensure such education and teaching in conformity with their own religious and philosophical convictions'. In the discussion that preceded the European Convention, parents were described as children's 'natural protectors' (Wahlström 2011, 37). The Swedish government had reservations about these formulations of parental rights. While these conventions were devised as a means of protecting the individual from state abuse, they were perceived as a threat to the right to equal education for all children in Sweden (Quennerstedt 2011, 192). It was not until 1995 that the European Convention was incorporated into Swedish education policy. At that time Sweden had reformed its formerly centralised public school system and introduced state-funded private schools. Now parents had the opportunity to choose between public and private school options for their children. This reform became the Swedish way of meeting parents' right to decide on their children's education (Wahlström 2011). However, this reform did not mean a revaluation of parental involvement.

Parents continued to be viewed as a latent threat to the interest of the child, while the state was regarded as protecting children's rights and interests. This order was motivated with reference to the Convention on the Rights of the Child that Sweden ratified in 1990. This was the starting point for a long series of reforms that step by step capacitated children at the expense of their parents.

One first result of the ratification was the creation of a new authority: the Children's Ombudsman, which was established in 1993 with the task of representing children and young people's rights and interests vis-à-vis legislators, other authorities and in public debate. In other words, the state created an agency that competed against the family as an interpreter and administrator of the interest of the child (Quennerstedt 2011, 171ff).

Sweden's work on implementing the convention was intensified in 1997, following the 'Child Committee', an inquiry commissioned by the government to ensure that Swedish law and government practices were in accordance with the Children's Rights Convention. The report published by this committee was entitled *The best of the child comes first* (SOU 1997:116), and criticised the emphasis on parents' rights in earlier policies.

> [A]lthough the right to education has a long history in international documents, it is only in the Children's Rights Convention that the child *itself* is given the right to its own education. The child has been seen as a passive recipient of education and, according to the previous conventions, the true right to the child's education was granted to the parents. (SOU 1997:116, 280)

The Children's Rights Convention was interpreted as a request to the state to distinguish between children's rights and parents' views on their children's education, and as a call to engage directly with the children. In its report, the Child Committee declared that the older parent-centred conventions had been drawn up against the background of the abuse of the German education system by the Nazis: 'By giving parents the right to influence education, a counterweight to the power of the state over the content of education should be created.' (SOU 1997:116, 280) The Swedish Child Committee did not dwell on this problem, but maintained that the welfare state should function as the provider of an educational system that guarantees equality, democracy, prosperity and thus is also in the best interest of the child.

In the 2000s the children's rights perspective was further extended. In the 1990s, policy makers had assumed that it was possible to implement the policy of children's rights by means of information campaigns for children and adults. The Children's Committee had devoted several pages of its report to telling the story of teachers who, after a 5-week course on the Children's Rights Convention, had succeeded in transforming a school with severe problems into a pleasant and successful knowledge environment with the child at the centre (SOU 1997:116, 308-311). Ten years later, however, this policy seemed powerless and confidence in legal tools grew. The Swedish 'Child Policy', which was introduced in 2002 as its own policy area (Skr 2001/02:166) was replaced by a more explicit 'Children's Rights Policy' in 2008 (Govt Bill 2017/18:186).

In 2010, the government bill *Strategy for Strengthening the Rights of the Child in Sweden* clarified that all legislation relating to children should be designed in accordance with the Convention on the Rights of the Child (Govt Bill 2009/10:232). The appropriate changes in the Swedish Education Act were implemented in 2011. Since then, the concept of 'The best interests of the child' has been introduced as a thread in all Swedish education policy. This concept is clarified in the following way:

> In order to take the best interests of the child into account, the child must be able to speak and express his or her opinions on all matters concerning him or her. This right applies regardless of the age or maturity of the child. The child's opinions shall be taken into account in relation to his or her age or maturity. (Govt Bill. 2009/10:165 231)

As explained below, the influence of the child is explicitly given priority over the view of the parents:

> For children and pupils, influence is a part of their right to influence the organisation where they live and act every day. This is important in order to anchor decisions and actions in the organisation. Therefore, it is reasonable to formulate the regulations on children's and pupils' influence in a stronger way than concerning the parents. (Govt Bill 2009/10:165, 638)

In her study of policy documents concerning the relationship between parents and school, Ann Quennerstedt stated that 'references to parental rights [are] very sparse' (Quennerstedt 2011, 179).

The downgrading of parents' influence is also reflected in the fact that schools are depicted as institutions in the service of children, not parents, by Swedish policy makers. Accordingly, the government explained in its bill for a new Education Act in 2010:

> Children and students are the actual users, and with increasing age and maturity, they should have influence over both the structure of the daily activities and their own learning. (Govt Bill 2009/2010:165)

In Sweden, it is not the parents or the family who use the services of the education system. Instead, school policy is aimed directly at the child. It could also be said that it is the child, rather than the parent, who is subject to responsibilisation in the Swedish education system. New legislative proposals to incorporate the UN Convention on the Rights of the Child into Swedish law indicate that the child's perspective will remain central to Swedish education policy in the future. According to the incorporation of the UN Convention into Swedish law, the Swedish Government clarified in 2018:

that the child's right to express his/her views and have them taken into account is an essential part of the assessment of the best interests of the child. Another important issue to note is the question of how the decision-making rights of the guardian relate to the right of the child to make himself/herself heard. Regulations containing restrictions or reservations regarding the right of the child to express his/her views should be reviewed. (Prop 2017/18:186)

As long ago as 2011 Quennerstedt stated that the Swedish policy has 'a more powerful language and concretisation of content' and thus goes beyond the Convention's original requirements (Quennerstedt 2011, 188). Her assessment also seems valid today.

Science-based professionals versus laypeople

A third way to understand the resistance against parents' involvement in the educational system is through the strong belief in objectivity and rational planning that is characteristic of Swedish education policy. The introduction of the comprehensive school system in the 1960s was closely connected to the belief that it is possible to control the development of the society by means of science.

In the first post-war decades, the idea of a science-based education policy concerned the educational system at large, as a tool for social development. By means of research, Swedish policy makers tried to achieve 'a rational allocation of students' (SOU 1948:27, 69). The scientific base for this policy included Torsten Husén's theory of the 'talent pool', the then new research field of *economics of education,* and human capital theory (e.g. SOU 1963:42, 74f & 169).

Due to the disappointing results of these post-war policies Swedish policy makers shifted their focus from the general structure of the educational system and students' career paths to the paedagogical activities in the classrooms in the mid-1970s. Now, policy makers came up with precise, science-based instructions concerning teachers' working methods (Govt Bill 1975/76:39). The rationalist and technocratic ambitions of that time were connected to a strong state and central governance. In this conceptual world, private and local initiatives such as single or groups of parents lacked the overview necessary for rational decision-making (Lindbom 1995, 62f).

The belief in predicting and planning the economic and social development of the society by means of state regulations weakened during the second half of the 1970s. The system was not only expensive, it also failed to realise the policy goals of social justice and knowledge development. Decentralisation should become the proposed solution to these problems.

In Sweden, decentralisation did not mean that the state retreated from its position as provider of quality guidelines for the education system, defining both its objectives and scope. What happened, however, was that municipalities became responsible for the implementation of these provisions. For those municipalities that lacked own school authorities and experiences concerning school development, decentralisation in practice meant a responsibilisation of individual schools and teachers with regard to the realisation of the political intentions of the state. In 1992, a centre-right government summed up this situation with the following words:

> The political governance of the school is focused on decisions on goals and resources. However, the executive responsibility for achieving these goals lies with the professional staff at the school. (Govt Bill 1991/92:75, 6)

The government bill for a teacher education reform, from which this quote is taken, is an example of the idea of teaching as a profession, which became of increasing importance for Swedish education policy in the 1990s. According to this idea, inspired by sociological theory, professions distinguish themselves from other occupations through their scientific knowledge base. Thomas Brante, probably the most influential Swedish theorist concerning professionalism, describes professionals as 'heroes', who with the aid of their expert knowledge and a mixture between technology and routine can in principle solve any societal problem (Brante 2009, 27).

In order to shape such heroes, able to guarantee high educational standards, Swedish policy makers started to focus on teachers' education. Between 1988 and 2011 they launched three large teacher education reforms, in order to equip teachers with an adequate scientific base (Govt Bill 1984/85:122; Govt Bill 1999/2000:135; Govt Bill 2009/10:89). In order to improve the scientific base of teachers who have already qualified, two new school authorities were installed, the purpose of which was to provide research reviews, evidence-based guidelines and examples of best practices: the Agency for School Development (*Myndigheten för skolutveckling*) in 2003[2] and in 2015, the Swedish Institute for Educational Research (*Skolforskningsinstitutet*). As well as considering the recommendations of these agencies, Swedish teachers are encouraged to conduct their own practice-centred research (*praktiknära forskning*) and to thus contribute actively to the scientific knowledge base that education is supposed to be built on in Sweden (SOU 2018:19, 24f).

We share the assessment of educational researcher Lars Erikson who argues that the idea of teachers' professionalism has widened the distance between teachers and parents in the Swedish educational system. According to him, the shift in responsibility from the state to individual teachers can 'be interpreted as a mark of a fundamental difference between home and school, a difference that highlights the professional teacher as an expert in school knowledge and learning.' (Erikson 2011, 213) At the same time as parents are considered capable of improving the educational system by identifying the best school for their children and to thus oust the inferior or force them to improve, their influence on the individual school is limited by a professional discourse where they are represented as laymen. This marginalisation is also expressed in the proposal for the latest revision of the Education Act, where a centre-right government explained under the heading 'Parents' Influence':

> In relation to the parents too, it is further self-evident that it is the educational staff who, on the basis of their profession, are responsible for how the teaching is planned, realised and evaluated together with the children and pupils. (Govt Bill 2009/2010:165, 313)

In 2010, the idea of science-based professionalism, and thus the dividing line between teachers and parents, was formalised in a new provision in the Education Act according to which school must 'rest on a scientific base and on approved experience' (Chapter 1, Section 5, 2010:800). The legislators explained that this provision should apply to both the content and methods of teaching (Govt Bill 2009/2010:165, 224). Almost 10 years after its introduction, policy makers still describe this regulation as 'unique, in an international perspective' as it shows that 'the Swedish educational system [...] is to be developed through the application of relevant research results and approved experience' (SOU 2018:19, 21).

The Education Act does not define in detail what should be meant by 'a scientific base'. The authorities commissioned to support teachers' professionalism, however, do provide such a definition. According to the Swedish Institute for Educational Research, which is quoted by the government inquiry *Research together – collaboration for learning and improvement* that was set up to propose measures to improve the cooperation between universities and schools, the concept of teachers' scientific base must not be confused with a general scientific approach or critical way of thinking. While a general scientific or critical approach is described as a way of thinking that people develop by themselves (SOU 2018:19, 25), teachers' scientific base stands for 'teaching that is based on the results of scientific studies, both concerning contents and how someone teaches' (SOU 2018:19, 25). According to this idea of a science-based professionalism, even well-informed and reasoning parents are not qualified to influence school work as they lack access to teachers' professional knowledge base.

Concluding remarks

The aim of this article was to identify the background of what we experienced as an attitude of ignorance of, and occasionally distrust of, parental involvement in Swedish school policy. Analysing policy documents as representations of prevalent attitudes and mindsets, we have shown how this scepticism can be explained by patterns of thought concerning the appropriate relationship between parents and schools. Firstly, these patterns concern how the education system is supposed to be governed democratically in Sweden. In contrast to conceiving democracy as the possibility for teachers and parents, as citizens, to influence their own educational activities directly and locally, democracy in Sweden is interpreted as the central governance, by elected officials, of education as a national project. This idea prevents teachers and parents from promoting what in this perspective appear to be their idiosyncratic agendas. Secondly, we have discussed the special importance that is assigned in Sweden to the rights of children. In contrast to an understanding of education as a concern for adult citizens, it is characteristic of Swedish policy to conceive it as a concern for the individual children. Given the conception of democracy just described, this means that school, with its teachers, is positioned as a mediator, between the state and the child, leaving the parents with little or no positive role to play, except as a supporting character. The third component of our story, concerns how teachers, as instruments for the realisation of state policy, have been conceptualised as *strengthened by science*. The teaching profession is basically conceived of as a scientific instrument, a means, for effective realisation of policy. It is not difficult to see how this attempted elevation of the status of the professional teacher further works for the exclusion of parents from democratic involvement in the education of their children.

Notes

1. In 2018, compulsory school was extended to 10 years.
2. The Agency for School Development was closed and its tasks were integrated into the National Agency for Education in 2008.

Disclosure statement

No potential conflict of interest was reported by the author(s).

ORCID

Susanne Dodillet http://orcid.org/0000-0002-0899-5909

References

Arneback, Emma, and Andreas Bergh. 2016. "Tema: Juridifieringen av skolan." *Utbildning & Demokrati* 25 (1): 3–9.
Barbosa, Luciane Muniz Ribeiro. 2016. "An Overview of the Homeschooling in Brazil: Analysis of Its Principles and Attempts of Legalization." *Open Journal of Social Sciences* 4 (4): 203–211.
Bendixsen, Synnøve, and Hilde Danielsen. forthcoming. "Great Expectations: Migrant Parents and Parent-School Cooperation in Norway."
Börjesson, Mattias. 2016. *Från likvärdighet till marknad: En studie av offentligt och privat inflytande över skolans styrning i svensk utbildningspolitik 1969-1999*. Örebro: Örebro University.
Brante, Thomas. 2009. "Vad är en profession? Teoretiska ansatser och definitioner." In *Vetenskap för profession*, edited by Maria Lindh, 15–34. Borås: Högskolan i Borås.
Breidenstein, Georg, Oliver Krüger, and Anna Roch. forthcoming. 'Parents as 'Customers'? The Perspective of the 'Providers' of School Education. A Case Study from Germany'.
Dahlstedt, Magnus. 2009. "Governing by Partnerships: Dilemmas in Swedish Education Policy at the Turn of the Millennium." *Journal of Education Policy* 24 (6): 787–801.
Dodillet, Susanne. 2019. 'En skola i samhällets tjänst eller för individen? Om relationen mellan politik och pedagogik i skolans styrdokument sedan 1940-talet.' *Statsvetenskaplig tidskrift*.
Englund, Tomas. 1999. "Den svenka skolan och demokratin." In *Det Unga Folkstyret*, edited by Jan Carle, and Erik Amnå, 13–50. Stockholm: Fakta info direkt.
Englund, Tomas. 2000a. *Deliberativa samtal som värdegrund — Historiska perspektiv och aktuella förutsättningar*. Stockholm: Skolverket.
Englund, Tomas. 2000b. "Rethinking Democracy and Education: Towards an Education of Deliberative Citizens." *Journal of Curriculum Studies* 32 (2): 305–313.
Englund, Tomas. 2011a. "The Potential of Education for Creating Mutual Trust: Schools as Sites for Deliberation." *Educational Philosophy and Theory* 43 (3): 236–248.
Englund, Tomas. 2011b. "Utbildning som vems rättighet?" In *Utbildning som medborgerlig rättighet*, edited by Tomas Englund, 7–10. Göteborg: Daidalos.
Erikson, Lars. 2004. *Föräldrar och skola*. Örebro: Örebro Universitet.
Erikson, Lars. 2011. "Vad betyder föräldrarätten i relation till olika principer för relationen mellan föräldrar och skola?" In *Utbildning som medborgerlig rättighet*, edited by Tomas Englund, 211–240. Göteborg: Daidalos.
Furedi, Frank. 2009. *Socialisation as Behaviour Management and the Ascendancy of Expert Authority*. Vossiuspers UvA: Amsterdam.
Gofen, Anat, and Paula Blomqvist. 2014. ". 'Parental Entrepreneurship in Public Education. A Social Force or a Policy Problem?" *Journal of Education Policy* 29 (4): 546–569.

Govt Bill 1975/76:39. *Om skolans inre arbete m.m.* Stockholm: Riksdagen.
Govt Bill 1979/80:182. *Om elevers och föräldrars medinflytande i skolan.* Stockholm: Riksdagen.
Govt Bill 1984/85:122. *Om lärarutbildning för grundskolan m.m.* Stockholm: Riksdagen.
Govt Bill 1988/89:4. *Om skolans utveckling och styrning.* Stockholm: Riksdagen.
Govt Bill 1991/92:75. *Om lärarutbildning m.m.* Stockholm: Riksdagen.
Govt Bill 1999/00:135. *En förnyad lärarutbildning.* Stockholm: Riksdagen.
Govt Bill 2009/10:165. *Den nya skollagen - för kunskap, valfrihet och trygghet.* Stockholm: Riksdagen.
Govt Bill 2009/10:232. *Strategi för att stärka barnets rättigheter i Sverige.* Stockholm: Riksdagen.
Govt Bill 2009/10:89. *Bäst i klassen - en ny lärarutbildning.* Stockholm: Riksdagen.
Govt Bill 2017/18:186. *Inkorporering av FN:s konvention om barnets rättigheter.* Stockholm: Riksdagen.
Halse, Christine, Catherine Hartung, and Jan Wright. 2017. "Responsibility and Responsibilisation in Education." *Discourse: Studies in the Cultural Politics of Education* 38 (1): 1.
Helgøy, Ingrid, and Anne Homme. 2017. "Increasing Parental Participation at School Level." *Nordic Journal of Studies in Education Policy* 3 (2): 144–154.
Hill, Nancy E, and Lorraine C. Taylor. 2004. "'Parental School Involvement and Children's Academic Achievement. Pragmatics and Issues.'." *Current Directions in Psychological Science* 13 (4): 161–164.
Hornby, Garry. 2011. *Parental Involvement in Childhood Education: Building Effective School-Family Partnerships.* New York: Springer Science.
Hornby, Garry, and Ian Blackwell. 2018. "Barriers to Parental Involvement: An Update." *Educational Review* 70 (1): 109–119.
Janssen, Jeroen, and Michel Vandenbroeck. 2018. "(De)Constructing Parental Involvement in Early Childhood Curricular Frameworks." *European Early Childhood Education Research Journal* 26 (6): 813–832.
Lgr 69. *Läroplan för Grundskolan.* Stockholm: Utbildningsförlaget.
Lgr 80. *Läroplan för Grundskolan.* Stockholm: Utbildningsförlaget.
Lindbom, Anders. 1995. *Medborgarskapet i välfärdsstaten: Föräldrainflytande i skandinavisk grundskola.* Uppsala: Almqvist & Wiksell.
Lundahl, Lisbeth, Inger Erixon Arreman, Ann-Sofie Holm, and Ulf Lundström. 2013. "Educational Marketization the Swedish Way." *Education Inquiry* 4 (3): 497–517.
Myers, Martin, and Kalwant Bhopal. 2018. "Muslims, Home Education and Risk in British Society." *British Journal of Sociology of Education* 39 (2): 212–226.
Novak, Judit. 2017. "Juridification of Educational Spheres: The Case of Sweden." *Educational Philosophy and Theory*, doi:10.1080/00131857.2017.1401464.
Oelkers, Nina. 2018. "Kindeswohl. Aktivierung von Eltern(-verantwortung) in sozialinvestiver Perspektive." In *Elternschaft zwischen Projekt und Projektion*, edited by Kerstin Jergus, Jens Oliver Krüger, and Anna Roch, 103–120. Wiesbaden: Springer.
Pearlman-Avnion, Shiri, and Mor Grayevsky. 2017. "Homeschooling, Civics, and Socialization: The Case of Israel." *Education and Urban Society* 51 (7): 970–988.
Quennerstedt, Ann. 2011. "Relationen mellan barns och föräldrars rättigheter gällande utbildning i den svenska barnrättspolitiken." In *Utbildning som medborgerlig rättighet*, edited by Tomas Englund, 169–195. Göteborg: Daidalos.
Skolverket. 2000. *En fördjupad studie om värdegrunden.* Stockholm: Skolverket.
Skr 2001/02:166. *Barnpolitiken – arbetet med strategin för att förverkliga FN:s konvention om barnets rättigheter.* Stockholm: Riksdagen.
SOU 1946:31. *1940 års skolutrednings betänkanden och utredningar.* Stockholm: Riksdagen.
SOU 1948:27. *1946 års skolkommissions betänkande.* Stockholm: Riksdagen.
SOU 1961:30. *1957 års skolberedning.* Stockholm: Riksdagen.
SOU 1963:42. *1960 års gymnasieutredning.* Stockholm: Riksdagen.
SOU 1985:30. *Skola för delaktighet: Betänkande från en arbetsgrupp inom 1983 års demokratiberedning.* Stockholm: Riksdagen.
SOU 1997:116. *Barnets bästa i främsta rummet: FN:s konvention om barnets rättigheter förverkligas i Sverige.* Stockholm: Riksdagen.
SOU 2000:1. *En uthållig demokrati! Politik för folkstyrelse på 2000-talet.* Stockholm: Riksdagen.
SOU 2018:19. *Forska tillsammans: Samverkan för lärande och förbättring.* Stockholm: Riksdagen.

Torres, Ana Llano. 2016. "Homeschooling Regulation vis-à-vis Democratic Demands of Pluralism, Integration, and Freedom in Spain." In *Homeschooling in New View*, edited by Bruce Cooper, Frances R. Spielhagen, and Carlo Ricci, 203–223. Charlotte: Information Age Publishing.

Wahlström, Ninni. 2011. "Internationella konventioner och debatten om fristående skolor i Sverige." In *Utbildning som medborgerlig rättighet*, edited by Tomas Englund, 87–127. Göteborg: Daidalos.

Wilder, Sandra. 2014. "Effects of Parental Involvement on Academic Achievement." *Educational Review* 66 (3): 377–397.

Building trust: how low-income parents navigate neoliberalism in Singapore's education system

Charleen Chiong and Clive Dimmock

ABSTRACT
Singapore is described as a hybrid neoliberal-developmental state. While politicians have, since the city-state's independence, exercised 'strong' ideological leadership over Singapore's economy and society, including education – there are simultaneously aspects of 'neoliberal' logics in Singapore's education system: extensive school choice and streaming, academic competition and the self-responsibilising meritocratic ethos. Literature on the nature and effects of neoliberalism typically depicts rising inequalities and families' growing anxieties, due to competition and self-responsibilisation. Drawing on in-depth interviews, this article explores how a group of low-income Malay parents navigate two aspects of institutionalised neoliberalism: (1) responsibilisation of young people within a meritocratic regime, (2) responsibilisation of parents as stakeholders in an increasingly complex education landscape. We find that while families internalise responsibilisation – profound trust in the state remains. Empirical particularities are drawn upon to understand how a socio-politically-constituted 'architecture of trust' between state and low-income parents is built, and its implications on families' lives.

Introduction

This paper examines how low-income Singaporean parents endeavour to support their children in negotiating a successful future within the hyper-competitive Singapore education system, characterised by various neoliberal institutional practices. To understand this, we draw on the conceptual apparatus of an 'architecture of trust'. We note that 'trust', while sometimes implied or theorised as the underlying roots of social behaviour and interactions (Misztal 1996; Blind 2007), is rarely foregrounded in studies of parents' pedagogic practices and beliefs. Yet, our analysis of interview data suggests that conceptualising parents' pedagogic work in terms of 'trust' – specifically, 'political trust' – is important, particularly in the 'strong' Singaporean state (Lim 2016) which actively mediates everyday life in Singapore.

Political trust – or trust in government institutions – is not entirely an *a priori* virtue, depending on whether it is justified or not (Field 2008). Nonetheless, it is generally theorised as beneficial in myriad ways: it is vital to regime stability and to citizens' support of policy reform (Wong, Wan, and Hsiao 2011); it also lubricates social life, facilitating both the government's daily functioning in providing services, and its ability to act decisively in moments of crisis (Ho 2018). However, 'neoliberal' institutional practices have been linked to the weakening of political trust and other forms of interpersonal trust. 'Neoliberal' practices are understood as creating feelings of distance, disenfranchisement and distrust, particularly between state institutions and ethnic minority, low-income groups (Ule, Živoder, and du Bois-Reymond 2015; Güemes 2017), who are especially vulnerable to the inequalities generated through neoliberal policy reform.

'Neoliberalism' is a term that is often used, yet often unclearly demarcated. In this paper, we define it on two levels (Flew 2014). At the 'ideas' level, it is the entrenchment of the 'mercantile society' (Foucault 1979, 194) where knowledges and practices are legitimated within a 'pragmatics of optimization [sic]' (Ball, 2013, 33). At the 'institutions' level, neoliberal governing prioritises the market form, commodification, capital accumulation, skills and profits over ideals (Shamir 2008) and other social goals (Flew 2014) – which generally leads to detrimental equity effects. While this delineates the term's conceptual parameters, we agree with Ong (2007, 3) that 'neoliberalism' is a 'mobile technology'; thus, contexts such as Singapore offer 'a rich empirical context for illuminating how neoliberal logic is inveigled into constellations of authoritarian politics and cultural ethics'.

Yet, insufficient empirical research has explored the relationship between neoliberal education policies and families' pedagogic practices, particularly in Asian socio-political and educational contexts. Research on the expansion of school choice in Australia points to feelings of anxiety, powerlessness and frustration with institutions, rather than trust (e.g. Campbell, Proctor, and Sherington 2009). The responsibilisation of parents and increasing anxiety related to 'intensive' parenting in response to neoliberal imperatives, has been described in largely European-American contexts (e.g. Vincent and Maxwell 2016). Moreover, research suggests the relation between living within a neoliberal political-economic regime and families' pedagogic practices is likely classed and raced. For instance, research often portrays relations between low-income, ethnic minority families and schools as strained (Lareau 2003; Vincent and Ball 2007; Watkins and Noble 2013), due to home-school mismatches in cultural values, role expectations, communication styles and child-rearing approaches. However, little is known about low-income families' pedagogic work, and its relations with neoliberalism and trust, particularly in Asia.

Against this backdrop, the Singapore context is an apposite site for inquiry. The Republic of Singapore is a city–state of 5.6 million people (75% 'Chinese', 13% 'Malay-Muslim', 8% 'Indian'), that has transitioned rapidly from a backwater fishing village at the time of independence in 1965, to a bustling cosmopolitan city. It is a city–state widely viewed as a 'success' story, with a world-renowned education system (Dimmock and Tan 2015; Deng and Gopinathan 2016) and high levels of political trust, compared to other states in Asia (Quah, 2010; Wong et al. 2011) and globally (Edelman 2018).

In this paper, we explore two instances of institutionalised neoliberalism, from the perspectives of low-income parents in Singapore: (1) responsibilisation of young people within a competitive, meritocratic regime, (2) responsibilisation of parents in an increasingly diverse education landscape. We then reflect on the co-construction of an 'architecture of trust' between state, schools and families – which enables, and makes plausible the devolution of responsibility to parents and children.

Raising children in 'neoliberal-developmental' Singapore

We begin by outlining features of Singapore's socio-political and educational context that are pertinent in understanding families' pedagogic practices and beliefs. Singapore is described as a hybrid 'neoliberal-developmental' state (Liow 2011, 241), combining governing logics that both invites dependence on itself ('developmental' logics), and devolves responsibility to individuals and families ('neoliberal' logics).

On the one hand, the 'developmental' Singapore state has long exercised ideological leadership – even 'soft authoritarianism' – over economy and society, including its education system (Gopinathan 2007). The 'developmental' state seeks political legitimacy through active interventions to boost economic performance (ibid). Historically, according to Singaporean politicians, this interventionist approach was necessary to ensure social stability and optimal human capital development under conditions of 'crisis' and vulnerability. Furthermore, the Singapore state espouses a 'pastoral' function to take care of its citizens, unlike the chiefly 'procedural' function of politically liberal states (Lim and Apple 2016). For instance, there exists a highly-developed, 'social democratic' programme of largely state-owned, well-resourced, highly-subsidised public education and housing (Chua 2017, 7).

Furthermore, while Singapore's Ministry of Education (MOE) has over time devolved some autonomy to schools (particularly to high-performing, prestigious schools) – it closely oversees many aspects of its largely-centralised education system, including the prescribing of curricula, textbook use, administration of national examinations, the hiring and firing of teachers and their professional development and training (centralised in the MOE's National Institute of Education) (Deng and Gopinathan 2016). The vast majority of Singaporean students attend schools that, though diversified, remain closely regulated by the MOE.

On the other hand, market logics are clear in Singaporean governance; politicians from the People's Action Party (hereon, PAP) – Singapore's ruling party from independence until the present-day – have long advanced a forceful anti-welfarist ideology (Teo 2013; Chua 2017). The PAP explicitly describes Singapore as a 'meritocracy'; this self-responsibilising, individualistic ethos is underlaid by the assumption that anyone with talent and effort can achieve educational and life success. Distancing itself from affirmative action policies adopted by Malaysia, 'meritocracy' was adopted as a fundamental organising principle of the Singapore state, since independence. 'Meritocracy' was framed as a fair, efficient way to allocate resources, to reward talented, hardworking individuals and protect against complacency and nepotism – and to select the most meritorious (in the Singapore context, *academic* results are the main arbiter of merit) to occupy high-ranking jobs for optimal political leadership and economic efficiency (Tan 2008).

Singaporean 'meritocracy' translates to a highly-diverse education system, characterised by a growing diversity of school types and extensive streaming (justified politically as catering to students' different abilities and interests) and high-stakes examinations. Following the Primary School Leaving Examinations, extensive streaming takes place – each stream has different curricula, and is associated with different educational and life outcomes (Anderson 2015). After Secondary school, students can enrol in Junior College (the academically most competitive post-Secondary institution), or one of the two major vocational institutions: Polytechnic, or the Institute of Technical Education (the least academically competitive). Overall, principles of competition, diversification, human capital development, and individual and familial responsibility for success, pervade Singapore's education system.

In light of these neoliberal institutional practices, it is unsurprising that class and ethnic-based social and educational inequalities exist (Ng 2014). For instance, a disproportionately large group of upper-middle-class Chinese students obtain prestigious scholarships and attend elite schools (Lim 2013). Moreover, emerging research on middle-class parenting problematises the rise in academic competition, and '*kiasuism*' (a Singaporean colloquialism referring to the intense anxiety and fear of losing out) and 'tiger' parenting (e.g. Bach and Christensen 2017). Commentators have described an effective shift from 'meritocracy' to 'parentocracy' (Ong 2014), as middle and upper-class parents cope with academic competition through investing in private tuition and extracurricular activities, and extensive strategising in school admissions enrolment. School choice is constrained by catchment areas, where students are likelier to gain entry to schools within a specific radius of where they live. Consequently, many wealthy parents have bought homes near to good schools (Koh 2014), producing 'wealthy enclaves' (Gee 2012, 4–5). Furthermore, large-scale quantitative analysis suggests a persistent gap between the Malay minority group and their Chinese counterparts, not only in earnings (Moore 2000), but in educational attainment and opportunities (Barr and Skrbis 2008; Senin and Ng 2012).

Thus, families' pedagogic work takes place within a socio-political context comprising governing logics that both invite *dependence* on the state, yet devolve *responsibility* to individuals and families. Within this complex context, the concept of political trust helps us understand families' pedagogic work.

Political trust, the state-citizen compact and neoliberal fractures

Recent growth in social scientific literature on 'trust' has occurred, out of the recognition that trust levels are generally declining in European-American contexts (Levi and Stoker 2000). Surveys (e.g. Edelman 2018) and theoretical analyses (e.g. Misztal 1996), attribute such decline partly to trends of individualisation and responsibilisation that are connected to neoliberalism and neoliberal policy reform that fragment and atomise (Barbalet 2019).

This study explores how political trust exists, rather than becomes negated by, neoliberal self-responsibilisation. Broadly, political trust refers to citizens' evaluative orientation in appraising the government and its institutions as responsive, and able and willing to do what is right, even in the absence of constant monitoring (Hetherington 1998; Levi and Stoker 2000). This study, in line with relevant literature, views 'political trust' as follows. Firstly, political trust operates through dispositions, beliefs and affects experienced by the trust-giver (Misztal 1996) and thus has an individual dimension, even if the 'recipient' of trust is an abstract, collective entity, such as the state. In Singapore, the 'recipient' of political trust is the state (specifically, the PAP, which has been the only political party to rule Singapore since independence) and state institutions (such as schools), although both tend to be conflated in interviewees' perspectives, in the 'strong' state of Singapore. Secondly, political trust always involves an element of risk-taking and vulnerability (Levi and Stoker 2000) – at its core is 'something other than knowledge or uncertainty' (Barbalet 2019, 87).

Thirdly, political trust tends to be self-reinforcing – although ruptures of trust also commonly occur (and even when they do, relationships between state and citizens might still continue – for instance, due to fear of state reprisal) (Barbalet 2019). Fourthly, political trust is not unconditional; perceptions of institutional performance is crucial in forming political trust. Institutional performance can be subdivided into economic performance (e.g. securing satisfactory standards of living) and political performance (e.g. the state's transparency, lack of corruption, and protection of human rights) (Levi and Stoker 2000; Mishler and Rose 2001). Furthermore, cultural values such as deference to authority, and socio-demographic variables (age, occupation, education level) can influence political trust by shaping perceptions of institutional performance (Mishler and Rose 2001). Fifthly, political trust brings various benefits, but is not always desirable; some degree of *mis*trust is healthy in a well-functioning democracy (Field 2008). Hence, social capital and trust (including political trust) should be viewed as conceptually distinct (Field 2008). The former is conceptualised as bringing unequivocal benefits to individual and society, while the latter may or may not, depending on whether the trust is misplaced, built on 'cruel optimism' or unlikely fantasies of social mobility within 'compromised conditions of possibility' (such as an economy in austerity) (Berlant 2011, 4).

A growing literature on political trust in authoritarian Asian states, such as China (Wang 2005; Tao et al. 2014), suggests that political trust tends to rise with economic growth and living standards. However, these authors also point to a likely decline in political trust as more educated, 'critical citizens' emerge who are more assertive and less deferential to authority (Wang 2005). In Singapore, state-citizen relations have followed a 'prosperity-loyalty' state-citizen compact (Gopinathan 2007), where the state provides the conditions for material flourishing (high-quality public infrastructure, steady economic growth, social stability and a low crime rate) in exchange for citizens' loyalty to the government and its ideals of a disciplined workforce (Gopinathan 2007). While for decades the PAP has secured economic growth and upward social mobility, commentators suggest that the state-citizen compact has come under increasing pressure from the growing dissatisfaction of a more critical, assertive populace – over the increasing cost of living, slowing social mobility, immigration and the precarities of globalisation, and growing educational and job competition (Gopinathan 2012; Rodan 2016). Despite reaching a historic low in popularity in the General Elections of 2011, following the PAP's concerted efforts at social spending boosts, the results of the subsequent 2015 General Elections (Rodan 2016), and large-scale surveys (Edelman 2018), suggest that Singaporeans continue to exhibit high levels of trust in their government.

Singapore's 'prosperity-loyalty' compact may seem a limited, instrumental state-citizen relationship. However, richer ideological forces structure this compact – including neo-Confucianism, which Singapore's Chinese-majority political elite have drawn on from the city-state's early days (Chua 2017). According to Confucian ideology, deep morally-based exchanges of trust exist between those who rule and those who are ruled; 'trustworthiness' must be earned by the political elite, to secure the trust of the masses – after which, the state has a moral charge to take care of its citizens (Lim 2016). Such socio-political arrangements have implications for how both citizens and those in authority are to act in relation to one another. Political trust, then, has a 'thicker', moral texture to it in Singapore (compared to political-liberal conceptions of 'trust') – although the PAP is likely to draw on a mixture of both ideological traditions (Chua 2017).

Overall, political trust, generated through cultural reasons and (perceptions of) institutional performance, appear to deeply structure the lived experience of the state-citizen compact in Singapore. However, what is the constitutive nature of these trust relations, and to what extent, and how, do these relations reconfigure families' pedagogic work? This question is suitably unpacked through empirical qualitative inquiry.

Method

This study draws on a subset of findings from a larger project. It focuses on in-depth, semi-structured interviews with parents (six mothers, three fathers) from low-income, Malay families. The aim of this small-scale study is not statistical generalisability, but to provide preliminary analytic insights into an under-researched area: how low-income families negotiate educational opportunities, within the Singaporean socio-political context. All parents in this study self-identified as 'Malay'. While we recognise that social class is racialised in complex ways in Singapore, we do not make generalisations in this paper concerning how participants' ethnic background relates to their narratives (further scholarship might foreground this). This is because firstly, the purpose of this paper is to sketch families' pedagogic work and the processes and challenges they identify as important; secondly, to avoid racial stereotyping; thirdly, social class divisions are described as more salient than racial divisions in Singapore (Teo 2018) – and seemed to be so, from families' interviews.

Interviews took place with participants' voluntary, informed consent and with promise of anonymity, and were typically conducted in participants' homes. While the aim was to interview both parents in each family, due to irregular working (shift) hours, divorce and linguistic barriers, this was not always possible. As there is no detailed mapping of 'social class' structure in Singapore, a conceptualisation of indicators of household economic disadvantage was constructed – derived from a combination of Tan's (2004) work on inequality in Singapore, Lareau's (2003) work on working and middle-class families in the U.S., and the Singapore Department of Statistics (2016) report:

(1) Monthly household income per household member of SGD$1100 and below (bottom 20% of population)
(2) Parental education – typically attainment of secondary school qualification at most
(3) Parental occupation – typically either unemployed or working in the lowest-earning occupation categories in Singapore (Sales/Service Workers; Plant and Machine Operators/Assemblers; Cleaners, Labourers and Related workers)

Furthermore, we focused on parents with children at the Secondary Four level in mainstream government schools (attended by the majority of Singaporean students), as young people in this group are at the cusp of making decisions about which post-Secondary institutions to attend. As such, Secondary Four is an apposite time to understand families' perceptions of the entanglement of opportunities and constraints in Singapore's education system. A local community organisation facilitated contact with families.

Semi-structured interviews allowed a balance between pre-prepared questions, and participants' expression of perspectives on their own terms. Two rounds of semi-structured interview (each lasting 60–120 min) were conducted with each parent. First-round interview questions invited parents to expand on their general imaginary and worldview concerning education and child-rearing (e.g. 'what is the purpose of education?', 'who is most responsible for a child's success – the child, the parents or the school?'). Second-round questions focused specifically on the social and educational policies and services parents use, and the meanings they attach to these policies and services (e.g. 'What do you like/dislike about your child's school?', 'How often do you meet your child's teachers? What are those meetings like?'). The interviews were transcribed, coded and analysed thematically (Braun and Clarke 2006), drawing on an understanding of Singapore's socio-political and educational context, developed through speaking to academic and policy experts, and reading policy documents, speeches, news articles and academic literature. We have edited interview quotes lightly to help non-Southeast Asian readers understand these quotes.

Discussion

In understanding how parents endeavour to negotiate a successful future for their children, the notion of political trust co-existing with, rather than becoming negated by, neoliberal responsibilisation of children and parents – emerged as a key theme. To explore this, we discuss how parents negotiate two key instances of institutionalised neoliberalism: (1) responsibilisation of the child, (2) responsibilisation of parents within a complex, diverse education landscape. Through this, we elucidate reasons why responsibilisation might coexist with political trust – and then elaborate on these reasons as building-blocks of an 'architecture of trust'. The word 'architecture' highlights the socially constructed nature of 'trust' in this study, and thus does not preclude the notion that 'trust' may be a product of state-craft. Yet, to read parents' expressions of political trust wholly as a product of state manipulation is to see parents less as autonomous agents and more as dupes, and to advance an overly pessimistic view of Singaporean parents' agency. As such, it is more valuable to delve deeply into the empirical elements comprising the construction of political trust.

Reproducing meritocracy: responsibilising the child

A key form of neoliberal institutional practice in Singapore is the *responsibilisation* of families and individuals. This responsibilisation is inculcated through a highly diverse, high-stakes education system; Singapore's '[diversity] metaphor is deeply connected to policy construction and the legitimation of neo-liberalism and individual/social responsibility' (Talib and Fitzgerald 2015, 449). Responsibilisation is a technique of government that constructs in its citizenry a sense of 'moral agency', a 'reflexive subjectivity' and certain dispositions and actions – in order to partake in self-government and authority, and bear the consequences for one's actions (Shamir 2008, 4).

All interviewed parents seemed to internalise meritocratic responsibilisation, holding *young people* to be the most crucial actors in achieving educational (and thus, life) success. 'The government', 'schools' and 'parents' were typically depicted as playing subsidiary roles in achieving successful outcomes. One mother, Izzati, remarked: '[E]ven though the school gives them [everything] – if they don't try to work it out in their heart to want to study, they won't get it. There won't be any changes in their life, actually'.

Many parents perceived that education stakeholders (parents, school, society) play a facilitative role, while young people themselves are most responsible. Parents often discussed their children's heavy workload and insufficient time for rest, yet nevertheless ultimately seemed to accept that the child was most responsible for their own success (and conversely, to be blamed if they failed). Furthermore, crucially, it seemed that parents' negative emotions regarding workload and stress, and acceptance of responsibilisation, were mediated by a respect for, and trust in, the competence of the Singapore state that *enabled* this responsibilisation.

Parents' reasons for trust can be placed in two categories: (1) generous, high-quality material provision of education-related services, (2) belief in the efficacy of the Singaporean education system and of Singacccporean meritocracy. Firstly, despite espousing an 'anti-welfarist' (Teo 2013, 387) ideology, the Singapore government invests heavily in the widespread provision of quality education, including vocational training, as it does for other collective-consumption goods and services, such as public transport and housing (Chua 2017). Parents cited the speed of the government's processing of requests for financial help for anything education-related, such as school books and shoes (relative to anything non-education-related), because they understood education to be a national priority in Singapore. Interviewed parents largely agreed that the state had provided the conditions for prosperity (their part to play, in the state-citizen compact), particularly through providing the means for high-quality, highly-subsidised schooling.

Furthermore, parents were convinced of the quality of Singaporean public education, reinforced by its international reputation. Through what we call ideational-comparative reasoning, parents compared education in Singapore with that of countries where many of their extended family reside (generally, Malaysia and Indonesia). Singapore's political leaders had, in their view, effectively consolidated the education system, re-moulding it to be highly professional and effective. They felt their views were legitimised through the results of international ranking tests, such as PISA, that positioned Singapore as the 'top' and 'best' in the world – narratives of global recognition that parents read or heard about via (largely state-regulated) media channels in Singapore.

Thus, overall, in a context where there is a strong values orientation towards the importance of academic achievement, typical of majority-Chinese and Confucian societies (Tan 2018) – *education* (defined by parents mainly as basic skills of literacy and numeracy, and qualifications) was seen as a protective shield against life's perils. Moreover, it is *precisely* because of the state's generous provision of education and education-related activities (through government schools and free or highly-subsidised tuition through welfare organisations) that parents deeply trusted the state. The state, in parents' views, has already 'done its best'; it is now up to the child to work hard, and it is also the child's fault if they fail.

Secondly, due to the state's careful, interventionist management of the 'tight coupling' between education and economy (Dimmock and Tan 2015), parents could draw on anecdotal evidence of the successful operation of the meritocratic mechanism in the lives of friends and extended family members, who achieved high academic qualifications and subsequently succeeded in attaining well-paid jobs. One mother, Naadia, stated:

> Whenever we go out, I tell [my son], I'm not trying to say the other people are so good. [But] I say, 'You see baby -' we call him 'baby' […] cos he's the younger one so he's like a baby to us.

So I say, 'Baby, you see ... I get to know from my cousin the son pass his Poly' [...] I say: 'You see he pass his Poly, he go NS [National Service], the moment he finish NS, he go university and now he can find a better job. Don't you like to be like him?'

Parents evidenced deeply-rooted confidence in the teleological, inevitable linearity of meritocratic logic (i.e. get-good-grades so you can get-good-jobs). One father, Khairul, noted that getting good grades 'can help you become minister, can become doctor, can become all these, you need to study also. You don't [study], you cannot go anywhere'.

Thus, the coalescence of neoliberal and developmental state logics likely structure pedagogic beliefs whereby parents *both* trust the state *and* believe their children should shoulder individual responsibility for their futures, even if they feel the overall academic stressfulness of the system should be reduced. Overall, in light of the material and ideational-comparative reasons above, deep trust co-exists with (rather than becomes negated by) self-responsibilisation, in the 'strong' state of Singapore. Notwithstanding parents' confidence in the Singapore state, there were glimpses of disillusionment with the heavy workload children shouldered. Most parents accepted the harshness of meritocracy with a stoic pragmatism, seeing this as a way of life in Singapore, where they are at least provided with a roof overhead and a globally respected education system, which they trusted would secure their children a better future.

Parents as stakeholders: responsibilising parents

Increasingly, convergent with broader shifts towards the responsibilisation of parents (Forsey, Davies and Walford, 2008), the MOE describes parents as 'stakeholders' or 'partners' in helping their children negotiate Singaporean education (Khong and Ng 2005). For instance, schools expect parents to supervise their children's homework, and help them with school selection. Within an increasingly complex education landscape, how do low-income parents in Singapore navigate their roles as 'stakeholders' in education?

Generally, parents hold the *family* as responsible for educational and life success, in a context of perceived government competence and its normative orientation towards fairness and doing good. For instance, one mother, Dania, cited the 'low self-esteem' of parents, as the reason for why 'low-income families' cannot rise beyond their circumstances:

> Some of them, they are not very confident, or they are not brave enough to come out and step up, you see? So for me, I know that the government is doing their best to get every child the same education [...] It's just that the parents have to step up, they cannot just keep quiet and let their children suffer.

While some parents seemed self-conscious over their limitations in providing any 'specific' help with schoolwork and decision-making (particularly as, they felt, they were 'uneducated'), all parents took seriously their role as stakeholders in their child's education. Parents saw their role as 'getting behind' their children to 'push them' to attain the highest academic qualifications they can attain, as one mother, Juriffah, described. 'Getting behind' involved advising, encouraging, filling in complicated forms to apply for state subsidies, monitoring their children's academic progress, even checking school bags to ensure children had completed homework, and above all, nagging their children to 'study hard'. They played by the rules of the meritocratic game, in the belief that such an approach would help their children acquire future success.

Parents' belief in the normative orientation of the state towards doing good, is remarkable particularly in Singapore, where the intensification of parenting (and the stratified nature of this intensification) is increasingly apparent. At least two parents described having no concrete 'strategy' for their child's academic success. Most interviewed parents did not seem fully aware of, and were somewhat nonchalant about, the spectrum of 'parentocratic' strategies wealthier parents deploy. The two parents who *were* aware, recognised that while they would *like* to send their children for private tuition and enrichment classes, they could not compete financially with their wealthier counterparts. However, these parents also simultaneously felt that 'extra' programmes were not particularly desirable, given schooling hours often lasted until late afternoon and early evening, usually due to 'remedial classes' (after-school classes geared towards examination preparation). After remedial classes, young people often attended tuition run by state-initiated local community organisations for additional educational support. Parents were conscious of their children's physical and mental limitations; they felt that between formal schooling and tuition (which often ran from 7 to 9 pm on certain weekdays, and on Saturday mornings), their children were adequately supported. 'Studying hard', within limits, they felt, was sufficient for life success. All were contented with their level of participation in their children's educational lives. As such, while wealthy parents are described as holding increasing power in 'parentocratic' Singapore, most families interviewed in this study did not seem aware or very bothered by it, placing trust in the dependability of the 'strong' state.

Crucially, parents' belief in the state's orientation towards doing good, was mainly constructed through everyday pedagogic practices of close, warm and often informal collaboration with schools. In coping with the pressures and complexity of the education system, parents generally felt they were working 'hand-in-hand' with teachers (as one mother, Dania, described) – to help their child reach their full potential. Instead of home-school relationships characterised by distance and disenfranchisement (Lareau 2003), parents portrayed their relationships with teachers in positive terms, emphasising teachers' nurturing attitudes towards students and their frequent communication with parents via phone calls and WhatsApp. As some parents worked shift hours, making attendance at parent-teacher meetings difficult, they appreciated teachers updating them in these ways. Communication between parents and teachers was, for at least two families, two-way – parents would update teachers on difficulties at home or in their children's personal lives that they felt teachers should know about (e.g. divorce and school bullying), while teachers provided parents with advice on how their children could study more effectively. Teachers were consulted by parents and young people alike on appropriate post-secondary institutions to attend; parents encouraged their children to seek advice from 'educated teachers' whom they felt, 'know better' than they did – although some families saw the collaboration as more equal, with families and schools both required to help young people develop holistically.

Notably, while critical of the stress in Singapore's education system, families collaborated with schools to monitor children, and if necessary, punish them. While young people were responsibilised (as argued earlier) in adult-like ways to bear responsibility for their success and failure, they were also viewed as requiring surveillance by the seemingly true 'adults'. For example, one mother, Hannah, shared:

> I think sometimes it's the influence from the friends ... [my son] started to do the funny things, so the teacher spoke to me. I really whack him. And then the teacher told me yesterday, 'Hey, really, after I complained to you, he really improved in his studies, he really focuses now.' I said, 'Yeah it's a good thing you tell me earlier, rather than too late!' So, if let's say, the teacher gives feedback earlier, so, we can also can take action.

In the case of most parents, collaboration with schools also helped to compensate for their perceived inadequacies as relatively less-educated parents. Parents drew on another comparative imaginary: their own knowledge and ability, vis-à-vis the state and teachers' knowledge and ability, in a very high-level and challenging education system. As a low-income group with few credentials valorised within Singapore's financial and cultural systems, it is unsurprising that parents had strong perceptions of their own helplessness, which they connected to their low educational and professional standing.

In spite of the responsibilisation of parents in Singapore, parents simultaneously deeply trusted the state – a trust rooted in an affectively-charged belief in the state's overall orientation towards doing good, rather than harm. This is most clearly seen in families' close, personal relationships with teachers. Teachers were commonly viewed by parents as representatives of the state, particularly as education is viewed as part of the state's benefaction. As teachers were viewed as knowledgeable, professional and caring, parents' positive relationships with teachers reinforced their positive view of, and trust in, the state.

Towards an 'architecture of trust'

This analysis suggests that neoliberalism, trust and responsibilisation simultaneously exist and interrelate in Singapore – though, it seems, not in ways typically conveyed in Anglo-American literature (e.g. Güemes 2017). We have demonstrated several ways in which the out-workings of these logics in the paternalistic 'strong' state of Singapore are unique to Singapore's socio-political context. In particular, we argue that the co-existence of 'self-responsibilisation' and 'trust' is bridged through an 'architecture of trust'. Moreover, rather than dismissing this 'architecture' as pure 'state-craft', it seems sociologically more meaningful to examine the empirical elements that comprise this 'architecture'.

Interview data suggests that the building-blocks of this 'architecture of trust' include: (1) material provision of education and education-related services in a context where parents deeply value qualifications, (2) belief in the efficacy of the Singapore education system (particularly compared to other countries) and in Singaporean meritocracy, (3) friendly, warm relations with school personnel, characterised by close communication and consultation, which powerfully strengthens families' belief in the Singapore state's normative inclination towards doing good, rather than harm.

Although a small-scale study, this research highlights how the dynamics of political trust work in relation to education, amongst low-income families – and underline why the perceived performance of the state and its education system, as well as the ethical orientation of the state towards citizens, are key reasons why families trust the state.

On the one hand, this co-existence of responsibilisation and trust can potentially pry open possibilities for families to optimistically and proactively participate in negotiating better educational and socio-economic opportunities for their children. However, living entirely within an 'architecture of trust' can also normalise the harshness of meritocracy and responsibilisation (particularly of young people), consolidate the ruling party's dominance, and limit the developing of alternative visions of a good life and ways to achieve it. Insofar as an 'architecture of trust' limits critical questioning and the possibility of critical distance from itself, it can exacerbate inequalities, reducing resistance even as middle and upper-class families continue to deploy material resources and cultural capital to leverage their comparative advantage and acquire valorised forms of 'merit'. This analysis suggests that most (though not all) low-income parents generally tend to be unaware of the full extent of the shift from 'meritocracy' to 'parentocracy' precipitated by wealthier families. Moreover, while academic qualifications are viewed as a buffer against future perils – most parents seem unaware of emerging social realities of credential inflation and graduate unemployment. Thus, while political trust can '[oil] the wheels of a variety of ... transactions' (Field 2008, 70), it can also lubricate the mechanisms of the affective machinery of 'cruel optimism' (Berlant 2011).

Finally, this 'architecture' is co-constructed by multiple actors – notably, the 'strong' state, schools, parents and children. As such, the foundations of this 'architecture' – the underpinning power/knowledge relations – warrant interrogation. Notably, are the above-mentioned building-blocks under-laid by a foundation of fear of state reprisal, which may have hindered parents from articulating more pointed critiques during interviews? Interview data provides important, yet partial, windows into how fear and trust interrelate. Ultimately, in understanding how 'neoliberalism' is recontextualised (within the Singapore context or elsewhere), the politics of an 'architecture of trust' must be a subject of simultaneous study. While this study has elucidated what we view as key aspects of families' pedagogic work, one way future scholarship might mitigate methodological problems related to the politics of expression, is through longer-term ethnographic work to grasp the pervasiveness of dynamics of trust and responsibility.

Conclusion

Overall, the notion of an 'architecture of trust' charts a way of understanding how low-income parents navigate the coalescence of neoliberal-developmental logics in Singapore's education system. It opens up the possibility that self-responsibilisation *can* and *does* co-exist with trust, in the 'strong' neoliberal Singaporean state. However, whether this co-existence continues, and whether this will lead to greater equity, is contingent on whether the Singaporean state can, through its incrasing incorporation of education policy measures towards greater equity (Lim 2013), provide sufficient support for low-income groups that enable fair competition – and in so doing, deliver on the 'prosperity-loyalty' compact for all Singaporeans. As theorists (e.g. Mishler and Rose 2001) point out, political trust is closely-wedded to perceptions of effective performance, politically and economically.

While our analysis is specific to the Singapore context, it demonstrates possibilities of how neoliberal practices in a 'strong' state can dynamically interact (in ways often not captured in European-American theorisations), and shape everyday lives. It also highlights the methodological value of foregrounding the perspectives of families as an important prism through which state logics are inflected, and through which we might trace the effects of state logics. As such, families' perspectives, contextualised within the socio-political regime in which they live, remains deeply valuable, in understanding the entanglement of opportunities and constraints embedded in putatively 'successful' Singapore.

Acknowledgments
The authors gratefully acknowledge the help of the families who participated in this study. This work was financially supported by the Cambridge Trust.

Disclosure statement
No potential conflict of interest was reported by the author(s).

ORCID
Charleen Chiong http://orcid.org/0000-0001-9246-5187

References

Anderson, Kate T. 2015. "The Discursive Construction of Lower-tracked Students: Ideologies of Meritocracy and the Politics of Education." *Education Policy Analysis Archives* 23 (110): 1–30.

Bach, Dil, and Søren Christensen. 2017. "Battling the Tiger Mother: Pre-school Reform and Conflicting Norms of Parenthood in Singapore." *Children and Society* 31 (2): 134–143.

Ball, Stephen J. 2013. *Global Education Inc: New Policy Networks and the Neo-Liberal Imaginary*. New York & Abingdon.

Barbalet, Jack. 2019. "Trust: Condition of Action or Condition of Appraisal." *International Sociology* 34 (1): 83–98.

Barr, M., and Z. Skrbis. 2008. *Constructing Singapore: Elitism, Ethnicity and the Nation-building Project*. Copenhagen: NIAS Press.

Berlant, Lauren. 2011. *Cruel Optimism*. Durham and London: Duke University Press.

Blind, Peri K. 2007. "Building Trust in Government in the Twenty-first Century: Review of Literature and Emerging Issues." 7th Global Forum on Reinventing Government Building Trust in Government. http://unpan1.un.org/intradoc/groups/public/documents/UN/UNPAN025062.pdf.

Braun, Virginia, and Victoria Clarke. 2006. "Using Thematic Analysis in Psychology." *Qualitative Research in Psychology* 3 (2): 77–101.

Campbell, Craig, Helen Proctor, and Geoffrey Sherington. 2009. *School Choice: How Parents Negotiate the New School Market in Australia*. Sydney: Allen and Unwin.

Chua, Beng Huat. 2017. *Liberalism Disavowed: Communitarianism and State Capitalism in Singapore*. Ithaca & London: Cornell University Press.

Deng, Zongyi, and Saravanan Gopinathan. 2016. "PISA and High-performing Education Systems: Explaining Singapore's Education Success." *Comparative Education* 52 (4): 449–472.

Dimmock, Clive, and Cheng Yong Tan. 2015. "Explaining the Success of the World's Leading Education Systems: The Case of Singapore." *British Journal of Educational Studies* 64 (2): 1–24.

Edelman. 2018. "2018 Edelman Trust Barometer: Global Report." 2018. https://www.slideshare.net/EdelmanAPAC/2018-edelman-trust-barometer-singapore.

Field, John. 2008. *Social Capital*. 2nd ed. New York: Routledge.

Flew, Terry. 2014. "Six Theories of Neoliberalism." *Thesis Eleven* 122 (1): 49–71. doi:10.1177/0725513614535965.

Forsey, Martin, Scott Davies, and Geoffrey Walford. 2008. *The Globalisation of School Choice?*. Oxford: Symposium Books.

Foucault, Michel. 1979. *Discipline and Punish: The birth of the prison*. New York: Vintage Books.

Gee, Christopher. 2012. "The Educational 'Arms Race': All for One, Loss for All." 20. Singapore: Institute of Policy Studies.

Gopinathan, Saravanan. 2007. "Globalisation, the Singapore Developmental State and Education Policy: A Thesis Revisited." *Globalisation, Societies and Education* 5 (1): 53–70. doi:10.1080/14767720601133405.

Gopinathan, Saravanan. 2012. "Are We All Global Citizens Now? Reflections on Citizenship and Citizenship Education in a Globalising World (With Special Reference to Singapore)." Hong Kong: Centre for Governance and Citizenship, The Hong Kong Institute of Education.

Güemes, Cecilia. 2017. "Neoliberal Welfare Policy Reforms and Trust: Connecting the Dots." *Journal of Iberian and Latin American Research* 23 (1): 18–33. doi:10.1080/13260219.2017.1298825.

Hetherington, Marc J. 1998. "The Political Relevance of Political Trust." *The American Political Science Review* 92 (4): 791–808.

Ho, Peter. 2018. "The Evolution of Public Trust in Singapore and the Impact of Technology." In *Public Trust in Singapore*, edited by David Chan, 3–16. Singapore: World Scientific.

Khong, Lana Yiu Lan, and Pak Tee Ng. 2005. "School-parent Partnerships in Singapore." *Educational Research for Policy and Practice* 4 (1): 1–11.

Koh, Aaron. 2014. "Doing Class Analysis in Singapore's Elite Education: Unravelling the Smokescreen of 'Meritocratic Talk'." *Globalisation, Societies and Education* 12 (2): 196–210.

Lareau, Annette. 2003. *Unequal Childhoods: Class, Race and Family Life*. Berkeley: University of California Press.

Levi, Margaret, and Laura Stoker. 2000. "Political Trust and Trustworthiness." *Annual Review of Political Science* 3: 475–507.

Lim, Leonel. 2013. "Meritocracy, Elitism, and Egalitarianism: A Preliminary and Provisional Assessment of Singapore's Primary Education Review." *Asia Pacific Journal of Education* 33 (1): 1–14. doi:10.1080/02188791.2012.711294.

Lim, L. 2016. "Globalization, the Strong State and Education Policy: The Politics of Policy in Asia." *Journal of Education Policy* 31 (6): 711–726.

Lim, Leonel, and Michael W. Apple. 2016. "Introducing the Strong State and Curriculum Reform in Asia." In *The Strong State and Curriculum Reform: Assessing the Politics and Possibilities of Educational Change in Asia*, edited by Leonel Lim and Michael Apple, 1–20. Abingdon: Routledge.

Liow, Eugene Dili. 2011. "The Neoliberal-developmental State: Singapore as Case Study." *Critical Sociology* 38 (2): 241–264.

Mishler, William, and Richard Rose. 2001. "What Are the Origins of Political Trust? : Testing Institutional and Cultural Theories in Post-communist Societies." *Comparative Political Studies* 34 (1): 30–62.

Misztal, Barbara A. 1996. *Trust in Modern Societies*. Malden: Blackwell.

Moore, R. Quinn. 2000. "Multiracialism and Meritocracy: Singapore's Approach to Race and Inequality." *Review of Social Economy* 58 (3): 339–360.

Ng, Irene Y.H. 2014. "Education and Intergenerational Mobility in Singapore." *Educational Review* 66 (3): 362–376. doi:10.1080/00131911.2013.780008.

Ong, Aihwa. 2007. "Boundary Crossings: Neoliberalism as a Mobile Technology." *Transactions of the Institute of British Geographers* 32: 3–8. doi:10.1111/j.1475-5661.2007.00234.x.

Ong, Andrea. 2014. "Beware Growing 'Parentocracy': NIE Don." *The Straits Times*, March 30. https://www.straitstimes.com/singapore/beware-growing-parentocracy-nie-don.

Quah, Jon, S. T. 2010. "Trust and Governance in the Philippines and Singapore: A Comparative Analysis." *International Public Management Review* 11 (2): 4–37.

Rodan, Garry. 2016. "Capitalism, Inequality and Ideology in Singapore: New Challenges for the Ruling Party." *Asian Studies Review* 40 (2): 211–230. doi:10.1080/10357823.2016.1155536.

Senin, Nursila, and Irene Y. H. Ng. 2012. "Educational Aspirations of Malay Youths from Low-income Families in Singapore." *Asia Pacific Journal of Social Work and Development* 22 (4): 253–265.

Shamir, Ronen. 2008. "The Age of Responsibilization: On Market-embedded Morality." *Economy and Society* 37 (1): 1–19. doi:10.1080/03085140701760833.

Singapore Department of Statistics. 2016. "General Household Survey 2015." 2016. https://www.singstat.gov.sg/publications/ghs/ghs2015.

Talib, Nadira, and Richard Fitzgerald. 2015. "Inequality As Meritocracy." *Critical Discourse Studies* 12 (4): 445–462.

Tan, Ern Ser. 2004. *Does Class Matter: Social Stratification and Orientations in Singapore*. Singapore: World Scientific.

Tan, Kenneth Paul. 2008. "Meritocracy and Elitism in a Global City: Ideological Shifts in Singapore." *International Political Science Review* 29 (1): 7–27. doi:10.1177/0192512107083445.

Tan, Charlene. 2018. "Parental Responses to Education Reform in Singapore, Shanghai and Hong Kong." *Asia Pacific Education Review* 20 (1). doi:10.1007/s12564-018-9571-4.

Tao, Ran, Dali L. Yang, Ming Li, and Xi Lu. 2014. "How Does Political Trust Affect Social Trust? An Analysis of Survey Data From Rural China Using an Instrumental Variables Approach." *International Political Science Review* 35 (2): 237–253. doi:10.1177/0192512113492599.

Teo, Youyenn. 2013. "Support for Deserving Families: Inventing the Anti-welfare Familialist State in Singapore." *Social Politics: International Studies in Gender, State & Society* 20 (3): 387–406.

Teo, Youyenn. 2018. *This Is What Inequality Looks Like*. Singapore: Ethos Books.

Ule, Mirjana, Andreja Živoder, and Manuela du Bois-Reymond. 2015. "'Simply the Best for My Children': Patterns of Parental Involvement in Education." *International Journal of Qualitative Studies in Education* 28 (3): 329–348.

Vincent, Carol, and Stephen J. Ball. 2007. "'Making up' the Middle-class Child: Families, Activities and Class Dispositions." *Sociology* 41 (6): 1061–1077. doi:10.1177/0038038507082315.

Vincent, Carol, and Claire Maxwell. 2016. "Parenting Priorities and Pressures: Furthering Understanding of 'Concerted Cultivation'." *Discourse* 37 (2): 269–281. doi:10.1080/01596306.2015.1014880.

Wang, Zhengxu. 2005. "Before the Emergence of Critical Citizens: Economic Development and Political Trust in China." *International Review of Sociology* 15 (1): 155–171. doi:10.1080/03906700500038876.

Watkins, Megan, and Greg Noble. 2013. *Disposed to Learn: Schooling, Ethnicity and the Scholarly Habitus*. London: Bloomsbury.

Wong, Timothy Ka-ying, Po-san Wan, and Michael Hsiao. 2011. "The Bases of Political Trust in Six Asian Societies: Institutional and Cultural Explanations Compared." *International Political Science Review* 32 (3): 263–281. doi:10.1177/0192512110378657.

Parents as 'customers'? The perspective of the 'providers' of school education. A case study from Germany

Georg Breidenstein, Jens Oliver Krüger and Anna Roch

ABSTRACT
The global establishing of school choice has often and convincingly been criticised in terms of social inequality because parents have very different access to resources to enforce their expectations and demands as 'costumers'. What is less discussed in the literature is the perspective of the 'providers': Do schools have to give up their position of predominance towards parents, when the single school becomes dependent on the parents' choice and decisions? The contribution explores the viewpoint of providers of primary school education in Germany. This may be particularly instructive as school choice is a rather new phenomenon in Germany. By focusing on a selection of three contrasting interviews with school leaders, representing different positions on the educational 'market', we show that only in a very fragmented and precarious sense reference is made to the concept of parents as 'customers'.

Increasing school choice activities in many parts of the world (see Forsey, Davies, and Walford 2008) can be seen as part of the marketisation of education: parents take the role of 'customers' and schools take the role of 'providers' of education. This development has often and convincingly been criticised in terms of social inequality because parents (as 'customers') have very different access to resources like information or money (Ball, Bowe, and Gewirtz 2006). The 'customer role' in an 'education market' is by no means equally taken up – and cannot be taken up – by all parents. Parents have very unequal resources to enforce their expectations and demands: This applies not only to financial resources, but also to sources of information, social contacts and time. Against this background, the concept of 'parentocracy' (Zymek and Richter 2007; Brown 1990; Waldow 2014) is proposed to mark that a (albeit highly imperfect) distribution of educational opportunities, according to the meritocratic model, is now being replaced by the dominance of those parents who are oriented towards an involvement in school matters.

What is less discussed in the literature on school choice is the perspective of 'providers': What does school choice mean for the single school? Does the power of parents increase towards schools, if parents are conceived as 'customers'? The ideal of the 'market' would suggest that the power of customers and the pressure of competition leads to enhancing quality overall: 'market competition forces schools to continuously improve their standards in order to attract parent customers of the educational "product" they are offering' (Angus 2015, 395). But this logic would presuppose informed and rational acting customers. Can parents be regarded as this kind of customers? And, furthermore, can schools regard them as such? How do school principals describe the new parental power? And how do they position themselves?

School choice is supposed to change the relationship between families and schools in a fundamental way. Since the institutionalisation of compulsory schooling in the nineteenth century, a complementary relationship between private and public responsibility for children has been assumed – one in which family and school complement each other as independent areas (cf. Casale 2012). The parental role was largely naturalised and understood in terms of supervision and emotional care. The school's task, on the other hand, was professionalised and seen as conveying universally valid knowledge as well as socially positioning children and youth within a horizon of performance and talent. Traditionally it has been assumed a superior position for the school in relation to parents. An 'adaptation' of the family to the school's demands was claimed (Tyrell 1987), and it was stated that parents were in a weaker position compared to schools (Busse and Helsper 2007). With the logics of school choice, this seems to change significantly: Schools become dependent on the parents' choice and decision – do they have to give up their position of predominance towards parents?

Our contribution explores the relationship between parents and schools under the conditions of school choice in primary education in Germany, from the viewpoint of schooling providers. For purpose of comparison, the German context may be particularly interesting as school choice is a rather new phenomenon, especially in the German primary school sector and it is embedded in public discourse and educational politics in a specific way. Thus the shape of the transformations in the relationship between parents and schools can be observed and analysed *in statu nascendi*.

In this paper, we first introduce our research project and take a closer look at the specific conditions of the German educational system, in which school choice is currently establishing. We then consider the perspective of 'providers' of school education by focusing on a selection of three contrasting interviews with school leaders, representing different positions on the educational 'market'. Case-by-case, we explore how each protagonist represents her or his own position in relation to parental expectations and demands toward schools. We use these different cases to show that only in a very fragmented and precarious sense reference is made to the concept of parents as 'customers'. From the perspective of schools, a one-sided shift of power in favour of parents is threatening. As we will show, the parent-as-customer raises for professionals the urgent question of how autonomy can be maintained when dealing with parental involvement.

1. Exploring German primary school choice

The case-study is part of a larger, long-term research project on school-choice in primary education in Germany.[1] We interviewed overall 33 parents as well as 8 school principals. We conducted ethnographic fieldwork in two German cities, took part in schools' 'open day' presentations, in meetings of school funders and we analysed school homepages as well as one exemplary online portal dealing with school choice activities from abroad

(Breidenstein et al. 2017; Forsey et al. 2015). Our analysis of the school choice discourse shows the ways in which parents come to see the enrolment in primary schools as a choice and how, at the same time, different private and public schools become actual *options* in the education landscape and what this means for the relation between schools and parents (see Krüger, Roch, and Breidenstein 2020).

We explore how schools are advertising themselves by means of 'school fairs' or 'open days'. An emerging phenomenon is the school homepage which is growing in importance for representing the school on the new 'marketplace'. In these advertisements, parents of school-aged children are addressed as if they were 'customers' who have to decide between various educational 'offerings'. School choice guidebooks use headers such as: 'What parents should know when exploring the "school market"' (Bönsch 1994, our translation).[2] These are phenomena which are, of course, by no means exclusive to Germany, but the German context may be particularly interesting and instructive as school choice opportunities are still not self-evident and are accompanied by heightened levels of distrust and public debate, when compared with nations in which the notion of school choice has been taken for granted (Ball, Bowe, and Gewirtz 2006; Forsey, Davies, and Walford 2008; Campbell, Proctor, and Sherington 2009).

This is especially true for Primary education in Germany. After Primary education, in Germany pupils are distributed to different streams of Secondary education. As education is the responsibility of the federal states in Germany, the educational system differs a bit from state to state. What is common is that Primary education only lasts four years (except for Berlin and Brandenburg where it is six years) and that the Gymnasium (year 5 to 12 or 13) as the favoured path to university only takes between 40 and 50% of a cohort. Access to Gymnasium after year 4 depends on the grades of Primary school and the decision of parents as well. Therefore, the ideology of distribution according to meritocratic principles in Secondary schooling very much depends on the assumption of an egalitarian Primary education with equal chances offered for all children (see Bröckling and Peter 2014). Underpinning this egalitarian ideal, school enrolment is in most municipalities governed by catchment areas. The address of the school-child determines his or her school, so officially there is no school choice in Primary education in most parts of Germany.

However, fundamental transformations have been taking place in the educational system of Germany over the past 20 years or so (see Radtke 2019). The results of the first iteration of the OECD's Programme for Student Assessment (PISA) in 2000 caused ructions in approaches to student performance throughout the nation, triggering a wide debate within education circles as well as in the public discourse (see Baumert 2001). The trust in the educational system and especially the public schools (run by the municipality) has arguably been eroded. Parental engagement and responsibility concerning the school education of their children have become an imperative in a new way (see Henry-Huthmacher 2008; Lange 2010; Betz and Bischoff 2015; Lange and Thiessen 2018).

On the side of the state, the implementation of a new education politics referring to 'Bildungsstandards' and 'output-orientation' took place; the performance orientation of the Anglophone world was something of a role model. Even though there is no publication of comparative performance data of schools in Germany, promises of improving school quality led to devolutionary reforms and principles of school autonomy, competition and parental participation (see Bellmann 2008; Bellmann and Weiß 2009; Höhne 2015). Thus, options beyond the designated school catchment area are provided through, for example, the political call for developing specialised school programmes in the public sector (Flitner 2007; Altrichter, Heinrich, and Soukup-Altrichter 2011; Koinzer et al. 2018). At the same time, some middle-class parents resist enrolling their children in schools the state requires them to attend because of features of the school they perceive as undesirable or detrimental to their children's education. In some cases 'school choice' can mean moving – or pretending to move – to a preferred school catchment area (Baur 2013; SVR 2013).

Furthermore, there is an expanding range of private schools, which is in international comparison still small with 10.2% of the total educational system (Kraul 2015, 9), and which is characterised by relatively low school fees (100-300 Euro per month) (see Ulrich and Strunck 2012; Koinzer and Mayer 2015). Only several bilingual schools, run by educational companies, are rather expensive (on average between 300 and 1000 Euro per month) and have thus been especially criticised as 'places of exclusive closure' (Gibson and Helsper 2012, 240).

From the assemblage of different school choice options which are currently coexisting, we have selected for this exploration of the perspective of 'providers' of school education three contrasting interviews, representing different versions of 'marketisation'. These are: an interview with the school principal of a public primary school to which the enrolment is organised by catchment area, but which some middle class parents try to avoid (school A); an interview with the school principal of a private primary school with a good reputation and moderate school fees (school B); and an interview with the representative of an educational company offering bilingual profiled private schools for comparatively high school fees (case C).

2. Speaking with school leaders

We read our interviews from a discourse analytical perspective which means that we do not so much try to 'understand' the point of view of the interviewee but try to capture the conditions, possibilities and restrictions of speaking. Our analysis focuses on the connection between the self-positioning of the speaker (the school principal) towards the parents and his or her way of speaking about those parents. By choosing three contrasting interviews we show that the perceptions of the (new) parental power differs to some degree according to the relative position of the school on the educational 'market'. The three school leaders configure (their) parents in three different ways.

2.1. Parents as 'amateurs'

School A is a state school located in a district inhabited by a population with a weak socio-economic background. According to its principal, school A does not have a good reputation and middle class parents often try to avoid the school. Even though all parents are required to visit school A during the process of school registration, in the end, the ambitious families tend to decide against it. The principal of primary school A can nevertheless rely upon a stable number of students at his school, due to the educational planning at the district level as in most places in Germany. Insofar, as he sees little chance of certain parents choosing his school, but is not dependent on them either, he is able to express his frustration in a very explicit manner.

First, he characterises a performance-oriented group of parents:

> The attitude of the [...] parents is, my child already has Chinese and Japanese, and in the afternoon piano, and this, and this, and this, and my child is now in the first grade and is, in any case, highly gifted – don't you see that Mr. Principal? And I would like my child to also have this, and this, and this, and your mission statement is ridiculous. I've already written you a new one.

The image created of the parents in this passage of the interview is clearly overstated. Within the dynamics of the interview, such exaggerations are appropriate for challenging complacency of those conducting the interview. Exaggerations legitimise one's own indignant position in a humorous vein. This indignation does not refer to a lack of cooperation on the part of the parents but rather to their tendency to be overbearing. The principal describes a situation in which his pedagogical competence in the assessment of the child's performance is vehemently called into question. Even the mission statement, as a key document of school self-description, is not safe from parental interference, which is communicated by means of taking up the speaker position – in terms of a caricature – of the parents being criticised ('your school programme is ridiculous'). The school position depicted in these remarks is weak, because it is made clear that no core school business is safe from parental pretensions. But the exaggeration and outraged gesture in which the principal presents this puts him in a position in which he is able to emphasise not only the excessive interference of parents but also their lack of qualification for doing so.

A second criticism of parents concerns their safety-orientation. Again, the school initially appears to be in a weak position insofar as it cannot convince parents that it is able to protect children from the (imagined) dangers in their environment. This problem is staged through the use of anecdote during the course of the interview:

> And the parents have a lot of time on their hands, so the parents are constantly out and about and watching what's going on here. And then you have situations, where a first-grader, after eight weeks of school, stubbornly stays out in the yard. I'm not going in with you guys; I don't want any of this, and she cries a little. But the mother is then called by another mother via mobile phone. Hey, your child is standing in the schoolyard and is crying, alone. And then things take off from there, as you can imagine. Mama immediately swoops in and then things really get out of hand. And we had such a situation last autumn, too; it was just this kind of mother [...], and it was something where she felt that the supervisory duty had been violated, and so she told everyone about it [...] we really had to fight hard until we were able to straighten things out.

A panoptic scenario is sketched in which the school is (at least potentially) permanently under observation. You can never be certain which parent is spending their time 'watching what's going on'. Once again, the image of a weak school position is sketched; one in which, through no fault of one's own, gossip and rumours are spread, and one has to 'fight' to correct a distorted picture of the school. At the same time, however, the principal emphasises his own professionalism and criticises pedagogical deficits on the part of the parents.

Finally, the interview invokes a third group of parents, ironically referred to as 'biodynamic organic muesli parents':

> The biodynamic parents who live here [...] are pretty alternative. Extreme – yes. And it is also quite exhausting to deal with such parents. They complain because someone has a glue thing containing solvents, for example, in the classroom. That can't be.

Here, too, a school position is represented in which parental interference is to be expected. Here, the use of a 'glue thing' (probably a glue stick) can quickly develop into a fundamental problem.

In summary, the interview with the school administration of school A sketches a supposedly weak school position: He complains about parents' unwillingness to cooperate, improper interference and a lack of trust. However, the supposed inferiority of the school is masterfully reversed, not least through the consistent use of polemical exaggerations. Compared to the parental articulations outlined above, one sees oneself in the right. As the principal of a public school with a stable number of students, he can afford to be very critical of those parents who claim a 'customer's power' for themselves and to distance himself from them as persons lacking appropriate qualification or knowledge to participate; they are positioned as 'amateurs'.

2.2. Parents as 'clients'

The private primary school B enjoys a good reputation. Despite its rather remote location and school fee (though moderate), right at the beginning of the interview, the school administration emphasises that the demand for school places regularly exceeds the supply.

Parents' demands are initially interpreted in the interview as a sign of quality – at least if parents are satisfied. The principal proudly reports, for example, that parents value the school as a well-protected space:

> There are always parents who say they are happy to be here, because they can go about their hard work with a truly clear conscience, because they know their child is doing well here – it is not parked somewhere; but instead, they have an absolutely clear conscience, it is nice here, the child is happy and doesn't have the desire to want to go home early. So, I think there's a really large group here who really say, that's a good thing.

At first glance, a harmonious relationship between school and home is presented. Rhetorical support words such as 'real' or 'absolute' preventively parry any doubt about the legitimacy of the parental appreciation of the school's offerings. As the interview proceeds, however, the picture of a harmonious relationship between parental home and school starts to develop small cracks. It becomes clear that, as a general rule, parental claims cannot be rejected as easily as they can in public school A:

> Then there are those within this group who say: yes, um, I really don't want to do anything anymore and if I pick up the child, then all is done and I don't have to worry, you've done it all, that's what you promised me […] But there are also things I think that belong in the family home, that don't belong in a school.

Even if the performance of the school and its ability to meet the parents' demands is not called into question, it is implied, however, that individual parents rely too heavily on the school and shift the responsibility of 'things' that belong in the context of the parental home to the school. From the principal's point of view, such a far-reaching utilisation of the school is also questionable from an educational point of view:

> We open at six and close at six, and we always talk to the parents – like in mining, twelve-hour shifts, we always try to counter this, not because we want to get rid of the children, but because we say, well, it can't be the standard that your child is with us for twelve hours.

This report on the struggle against the parental practice of sending children to school for up to twelve hours is used in the principal's narrative to take up an advocate position for the child and, in this sense, to signal pedagogical professionalism. Furthermore, the ability to solve this problem by communication is assumed.

The relation to parents is particularly sensitive when discussions about school fees open up:

> Yes, and then we have the special ones, that's how I call them […] who try in this way 'after all we are paying', perhaps to demand some or the other thing, because they pay – whether it's the Gymnasium [admission to the university-track programme] or about getting higher grades, things like that. But that's not the bulk, one simply must say, that's not the bulk, but of course these are the things that stick.

When parental desire for good marks for their children is linked to arguments involving payment, then a structural problem becomes strikingly acute. From the perspective of a school that needs to justify the awarding of educational qualifications by meritocracy, parental claims to the certification of student achievements on the basis of payment represent an absolute taboo. While situations involving a violation of this taboo are characterised as exceptional, such incidents somehow 'stick'. The conviction that such claims must be rejected seems so self-evident that it is not even reported.

As a rule, however, one could also negotiate with parents about their excessive demands. A possible criticism of the parental demands remains restrained; the need to remain in dialogue with the parents is emphasised above all, since these parents require a kind of attention that exhibits pedagogical traits:

> [There are parents] who expect a lot, expect far too much, and we always say that the child is robbed a little bit of his childhood, because it has a lot to do – it has to do this and this and that, and preferably piano as well and even this, and, uh, where we say: you know, you don't work fourteen hours a day, yet you expect that of your child, and then the child should also be cheerful and sleep at night, yes. That's what we always try to discuss. […] they already have a life plan in mind for the child and it is really all planned out, how the later life has to unfold, and yet the child is forgotten a little bit, and we continually try in all conversations to move the child back into the centre and say: First of all, we are talking about a child. And yes, on the other hand, the expectations the parents have of their child are sometimes their own unfulfilled expectations.

The school presents itself in a position in which it not only stands up for the child as an advocate, but can also act to care for the parents – and even challenge them. The parental demands placed on the school and on the children are reinterpreted in a psychologising manner. Within the context of such an interpretation, parental expectations on the children's educational success can be analysed as a transfer of the failed self-expectations on the part of the parents. In the course of this psychological interpretation, the relation between parental home and school is conceived as one between laypersons and professionals. In the case of the private primary school, however, parental claims cannot simply be rejected, but rather must be taken very seriously. Thus the school is confronted with the requirement to work not only with the children, but also comprehensively with their parents.

> It's sometimes difficult to ease the fear of the parents. […] Sometimes we act as relaxation therapists for the parents, and we really say that everyone should just relax. Relax and everything will be fine, it's primary school.

By laying claim to a therapeutic position, the school principal can also reconfigure the demanding attitude of the parents: Customers become clients who can and must be professionally counselled. This school cannot ignore the demands of its parents, but for various reasons, it cannot meet them either. Against this background, the representative of the school sketches the relationship to the parents as a pedagogical-therapeutic one, which harbours a chance to deal with what are, from the school's point of view, problematic and unsuitable demands of the parents which, if necessary, the school attempts to defuse.

2.3. Parents as 'customers'

A third version of talking about parents can be found in an interview with a representative of an educational company responsible for the running of a chain of private schools in different German cities. Each of these schools having a locally specific profile but all follow the company's key standards and logics of brand establishment. Tuition fees are related to the parents' income, but can be several hundred Euros per month even for primary school (which is an exceptionally high fee in the German context).

In this interview, the meaning of offering a school programme like a 'product' that has to comply with certain customer requirements if wishing to succeed in the 'market' becomes tangible at some points. However, it also shows the precariousness of this perspective and the ambivalences connected to it.

The following representative's explanations answer the interviewer's question regarding parents' expectations of the school:

> Well, generally the expectations are, and that is very hard to comply with in the higher school years, that really everything in school should be working and no homework has to be done at home and really everything is done here at school, and then our time is also, because we too work according to the state curriculum, so our time, it is tight, it doesn't quite work like that. Well, the first three years it's okay, but after that it just gets, because of increase in the timetable it gets difficult for us. For most of them it is extremely important to have a the small classes, this maximum of twenty-two children, even though by now it is more or less like that at public schools, too. Then, the fact that we have native speakers, mainly for English. For many parents, this is very important and also that we generally have a teacher and an assistant teacher in the first school years, who are responsible for the class and the care of the children. And this, for most of the parents, these are the most important points. Well, they also really want their children to learn English from someone who speaks English as their mother tongue. Though we have German colleagues who speak English very well and everything, but still for many parents this is really the sticking point.

Similar to the principal of school B, this representative to mentions parents' demands concerning (her) school that she sees as far too wide-ranging and to which she first answers referring to time restrictions. However, the school representative does not discuss parents' expectations in general or with reference to their own pedagogical responsibility but in relation to external regulations (curriculum) and restricting conditions (time available). Doing so, she does position herself as a service provider potentially trying to comply with the parents' expectations. Nevertheless, at the same time, she claims a professional expertise in opposition to the (assumed) parents' views. Here, the expertise refers not so much to pedagogics as to the organisational conditions framing school – and that escape the parents' view.

Mentioning 'small classes', our interview partner introduces a second widely spread expectation from parents. However, concerning this criterion, she has to admit it is unable to distinguish her offer from other primary schools in the city, as they have similar class sizes 'by now'. It becomes clear that the representative of the educational company, asked about parents' expectations, (implicitly) reflects on the criteria that played a part in parents' decisions in favour of her offer. Other criteria are English classes with 'native speakers' and a continuous double care arrangement in the first school years.

If 'expectations' of this kind are being understood as criteria of 'demand', they gain a certain power – even if they are contrary to the own perception and convictions. This becomes evident when the school representative, after finishing her list, comes back to the criterion of 'native speakers'. Against this, she holds German colleagues 'who speak English very well and everything'. Nevertheless, even without articulating it, implicitly it becomes clear that the school's offers have to comply with the demand for 'native speakers' as this seems to be 'really the sticking point' for many parents. The choice may be made by one 'sticking point'. That is why she cannot risk leaving this demand unfulfilled, even if she is not quite convinced of it.

At a later point, the interviewer again specifically asks about parents' demands that might possibly be justified pointing to the payment of tuition fees. This would concern mostly how to deal with parents whose children already attend the school and not the criteria of parents in the choosing process. Here too the representative's statement is instructive.

> I: Are there parents that make certain claims, well, I can imagine that it can be different at such a private school than it is at a state school, that they make certain claims, because, after all we are paying for it or we give//
> S: /Exactly, exactly/ You have to learn how to deal with those, too (laughing)
> I: That exists?
> S: Yes, yes, yes, yes. Well, that is, partly I find that by this way to, well the way they also treat the teachers and educators, well where such situations develop, where we really have to ask again, because it is really this, yes it is really this attitude and also often this in school, everything has to work, well that they don`t even understand when we say, yes but things like reading and reading out loud and stuff like that, that should actually happen at home. Or like cooking with the child and just things like that, that somehow belong to the whole picture of course, developing mathematical comprehension and stuff like that, I can't take care of that at school, can't even take care of that in all-day-schooling. I cannot cook with every single child. These are things that should happen at home, and there are, sometimes, two worlds are crashing there.

As the interviewer cautiously draws a picture of parents who 'make certain claims' because of tuition fee payment, he is being interrupted by his interview partner enthusiastically approving. She responds to the subject as if she had been waiting for it. Apparently, she sees significant problems in the 'the way they [not even naming anymore: the parents] also treat the teachers and educators'. She does not further describe the criticised parents' interaction with educators and school but returns to the already mentioned demand (now called 'attitude') that 'in school, everything has to work'. Again, she gives practical reasons ('I cannot cook with every single child') for her refusal of too encompassing educational demands of parents towards the school. But then it becomes clear that more is at stake: 'sometimes two worlds are crashing there'. What kinds of worlds are these? The nature of these worlds is not further specified. However, this school representative states basic differences between parents and school rather than invoke the idea of a harmonious 'educational partnership'.

This passage shows the representative of the educational company caught in a dilemma: she cannot fully confront the (paying) school's parents but also cannot fulfil all of their wishes – for a variety of pragmatic and systematic reasons. To some extent, she chooses strategically which demands the school can fulfil (native speakers) and which she has to refuse (learning to cook). The representative does so, unlike school B, not so much referring to a professional advocacy for the child but to the pragmatic limits of schooling. Out of such a position, parents appear to a lesser extent as clients potentially in need of pedagogical therapeutic advice but as a powerful counterpart that requires the school to make strategic concessions at some points and to be aware of the limits at other points.

3. Conclusion: contested educational responsibilities

Economic logics cannot be transferred to the education sector without some cracks showing. As a consequence, shifts occur in the relation between parents and schools. In Germany, the effects of the marketisation of education on the relationship between schools and parents probably have a specific shape. Compared to some parts of the Anglophone world parents (and schools) lack information concerning the measured performance of schools. There are no websites providing standardised data about schools like 'MySchool' (in Australia) or 'compare-school-performance' (in England) which can be considered a 'choice machine' (Forsey and Brown 2019) organising the market in certain way. But as soon as parents (and schools) *take* school enrolment as a choice this choice seems to be regarded as highly relevant by middle-class parents in Germany. They are very aware that pupils are sent along hierarchically structured tracks at the early age of ten years. So the tensions arising out of contesting views of educational responsibility between parents and schools may be especially intensive in Germany, but we assume that conflicting relations between parents and schools are related to the marketisation of educational systems and the connected mobilising policies in general: Seemingly solid structures of responsibility are now in need of being reshaped and contested in practice. Parents formulate new demands placed on schools, whereas schools try to maintain their autonomy towards parents' demands.

Our analysis has shown that in the view of school leaders the majority of parental demands – whether they are lifestyle-oriented, safety-oriented or in the most cases performance-oriented – seem to be challenging and at least an expression of deficient educational responsibility. At the same time the school leaders' positions differ, depending on their position at the 'educational market':

At the public school A, the school administrator (unlike in the other two interviews) can afford to speak polemically and downright disparagingly about certain parents. Due to the binding catchment area, there is no need to accommodate parents or entertain their special wishes. However, according to the school principal and his bitter-sarcastic mourning, the school sometimes is affected by parental wishes and demands that challenge his own position as a professional.

The interview with the principal of the private primary school B shows the dilemma that she cannot completely ignore the demands and wishes of the parents. The school administrator's response to increased parental customer wishes consists in shifting the relation to the parents to a therapeutic one, ascribing them a need for psychological care. In this view, the problematic expectations of parents need to be responded to and, if possible, modified by the school.

Dilemmas of not being able to ignore the wishes of the (choosing) parents because of economic reasons are even more clearly articulated in the interview with the representative of an educational company. In this setting parents' wishes and demands (e.g. native speakers as English teachers) become effective as criteria of school choice and decision-making. They have to be considered in the creation of the school's offers. At the same time, there are certain demands that cannot be fulfilled by the school for practical and professional reasons. To differentiate between those wishes that can be fulfilled and those that cannot, appears as a strategic problem the school has to deal with.

Though the three versions of describing the relation to parents seem to represent very different approaches – distancing parents' wishes in a sarcastic way, treating them in a therapeutic frame and regarding them as much as possible – they prove to be three facets of a broader constellation: Despite the differences, there seems to be a consensus across the interviews that the concept of parents as 'customers' in an 'educational market' is ultimately unacceptable from the perspective of a professional. Otherwise, the professional self-image and the fate of one's own educational offering would be subject to an incalculable 'voting by feet'. The judgement about the pedagogical quality of the own school cannot be given over to the demands of those whom one does not consider qualified to make a judgement in the complex field of school education. The parents' choice of school can hardly be considered a fully informed decision; instead, it is determined by the always partial perspective of parents focused on their own child. Upon closer inspection of the fragility and ambivalence of positioning parents as 'customers' in an education market, the idea of increasing the educational quality of schools through 'competition' becomes highly problematic overall (cf. Weiß 2001). Against this background, further research on the conflicting relation between logics of school choice and discourses of teacher professionalism would be instructive.

Furthermore, it becomes clear that the 'market power' of parents is not only reflected in the choice of school, but also in the internal relation of the institutions: Educational 'providers' must at least tend to focus on parental 'customer satisfaction' – however precarious this relationship may remain. The widespread rhetoric of 'partnership' and parental 'participation' in schools (see Stange 2012) does not solve this problem. Recent educational policy and programmes in many national contexts have increasingly focused on parental participation in schools (Crozier and Reay 2005; Richter and Andresen 2012; Franklin, Popkewitz, and Bloch 2013). It became obvious, that 'parent-school relationships are a key component of national reforms intended to educational standards across the board' (Nawrotzki 2012, 69). Parents are activated in various ways to become more involved in their child's school matters, and at the same time schools are asked to be open for dealing with parental requests.

Both sides – schools as well as parents – are made responsible, and are engaged in the regime of 'singularities' (cf. Reckwitz 2018) within the neoliberal era. Childhood, and the own child, have become a 'project' which challenges the traditional way of perceiving the relationship between school and parents: Schools are asked to develop specialised programmes and 'programs' which compete with each other – and parents are asked to take the responsibility of choice. But – what is not always seen clearly enough – parents and schools stay on different sides of the relationship and the tensions between the two sides probably will not vanish, they may even intensify. School education is not a 'product' which can be shaped according to the wishes of (certain) parents but, instead, school education has to insist on professional standards which cannot be subordinated to 'customers' preferences.

Note

1. The research project 'Excellence in Primary Education. The 'Best School' as a Matter of Negotiation in the Discourse of School Choice', was funded (2011–2018) by the German Research Foundation (DFG), https://www.zsb.uni-halle.de/forschungsprojekte/2503071_2617909/exzellenz_im_primarbereich/.

Disclosure statement

No potential conflict of interest was reported by the author(s).

References

Altrichter, H., M. Heinrich, and K. Soukup-Altrichter. 2011. *Schulentwicklung durch Schulprofilierung? Zur Veränderung von Koordinationsmechanismen im Schulsystem*. Wiesbaden: Springer VS.
Angus, L. 2015. "School Choice: Neoliberal Education Policy and Imagined Futures." *British Journal of Sociology of Education* 36 (3): 395–413.
Ball, S. J., R. Bowe, and S. Gewirtz. 2006. "School Choice, Social Class and Distinction: The Realization of Social Advantage in Education." *Journal of Education Policy* 11 (1): 89–112.
Baumert, J. 2001. *PISA 2000. Basiskompetenzen von Schülerinnen und Schülern im internationalen Vergleich*. Wiesbaden: Springer VS.

Baur, C. H. 2013. *Schule, Stadtteil, Bildungschancen. Wie ethnische und soziale Segregation Schüler/-innen mit Migrationshintergrund benachteiligt*. Bielefeld: Transcript.

Bellmann, J. 2008. "Choice Policies – Selektion, Segregation und Distinktion im Rahmen von Bildungsmärkten." In *Begabtenförderung an Gymnasien. Entwicklungen, Befunde, Perspektiven*, edited by H. Ullrich and S. Strunck, 249–270. Wiesbaden: VS.

Bellmann, J., and M. Weiß. 2009. "Risiken und Nebenwirkungen Neuer Steuerung im Schulsystem. Theoretische Konzeptualisierung und Erklärungsmodelle." *Zeitschrift für Pädagogik* 55 (2): 286–308.

Betz, T., and S. Bischoff. 2015. "Denn Bildung und Erziehung der Kinder sind in erster Linie auf die Unterstützung der Eltern angewiesen. Eine diskursanalytische Rekonstruktion legitimer Vorstellungen guter Elternschaft in politischen Dokumenten." In *Erziehungswissenschaftliche Diskursforschung. Empirische Analysen zu Bildungs- und Erziehungsverhältnissen*, edited by S. Fegter, F. Kessl, A. Langer, M. Ott, D. Rothe, and D. Wrana, 263–282. Wiesbaden: Springer VS.

Bönsch, M. 1994. *Die beste Schule für mein Kind. Was Eltern wissen sollten, wenn sie sich auf dem "Schulmarkt" umsehen*. Freiburg im Breisgau: Herder Verlag.

Breidenstein, G., M. Forsey, F. La Gro, J. O. Krüger, and A. Roch. 2017. "Choosing International. A Case Study of Globally Mobile Parents." In *Elite Education and Internationalisation. From the Early Years to Higher Education*, edited by C. Maxwell, U. Deppe, H.-H. Krüger, and W. Helsper, 161–180. Houndmills: Palgrave Macmillan.

Bröckling, U., and T. Peter. 2014. "Mobilisieren und Optimieren." *Exzellenz und Egalität als hegemoniale Diskurse im Erziehungssystem. Zeitschrift für Erziehungswissenschaft* 17 (3): 129–147. Elite und Exzellenz im Bildungssystem: Nationale und internationale Perspektiven.

Brown, P. 1990. ": The 'Third Wave': Education and the Ideology of Parentocracy." *British Journal of Sociology of Education* 11 (1): 65–85.

Busse, S., and W. Helsper. 2007. "Familie und Schule." In *Handbuch Familie*, edited by J. Ecarius, 321–341. Wiesbaden: Springer VS.

Campbell, C., H. Proctor, and G. Sherington. 2009. *School Choice. How Parents Negotiate the New School Market in Australia*. Sydney: Allen & Unwin.

Casale, R. 2012. "Verstaatlichung von Erziehung und Entstaatlichung von Bildung. Anmerkungen zur Krise der Komplementarität von Staat und Familie." In *Positionierungen. Zum Verhältnis von Wissenschaft, Pädagogik und Politik*, edited by C. Aubry, M. Geiss, V. Magyar-Haas, and D. Miller, 128–139. Weinheim: Beltz Juventa.

Crozier, Gill, and Diane Reay, eds. 2005. *Activating Participation: Parents and Teachers Working Towards Partnership*. Stoke on Trent. Sterling: Trentham Books.

Flitner, E. 2007. "Schöne Schulprofile. Zur Dynamik ethnischer Segregationsprozesse am Beispiel der Entwicklung exklusiver Angebote im Berliner öffentlichen Schulsystem." In *Bildung und Öffentlichkeit*, edited by R. Casale and R. Horlacher, 44–59. Weinheim: Beltz.

Forsey, M., G. Breidenstein, A. Roch, and J. O. Krüger. 2015. "Ethnography at a Distance? Globally Mobile Parents and School Choice in a Textual Community." *International Journal of Qualitative Studies in Education* 28 (9): 1112–1128.

Forsey, M., and G. Brown. 2019. "Inside the School Choice Machine: The Public Display of National Testing Data and its Stratificatory Consequences." *Zeitschrift für Pädagogik* 65: 124–143.

Forsey, M., S. Davies, and G. Walford, eds. 2008. *The Globalisation of School Choice? Oxford Studies in Comparative Education*. Vol. 19, No. 2. Oxford: Symposium Books.

Franklin, Barry M., Thomas S. Popkewitz, and Marianne N. Bloch, eds. 2013. *Educational Partnerships and the State: The Paradoxes of Governing Schools, Children, and Families*. New York: Palgrave Macmillan.

Gibson, A., and W. Helsper. 2012. "Erziehung und Bildung der "Auserwählten" - Privatschulen und deren "Elite"-Anspruch." In *Private Schulen in Deutschland. Entwicklungen - Profile - Kontroversen*, edited by H. Ulrich and S. Strunck, 225–246. Wiesbaden: Springer VS.

Henry-Huthmacher, C. 2008. "Zusammenfassung der wichtigsten Ergebnisse der Studie." In *Eltern unter Druck. Selbstverständnisse, Befindlichkeiten und Bedürfnisse von Eltern in verschiedenen Lebenswelten*, edited by C. Henry-Hutmacher and M. Borchard, 1–24. Stuttgart: Lucius & Lucius.

Höhne, T. H. 2015. *Ökonomisierung und Bildung. Zu den Formen ökonomischer Rationalisierung im Feld der Bildung*. Wiesbaden: Springer VS.

Koinzer, T. H., S. Gruehn, C. Habeck, and J. Schwarz. 2018. "Welche Schule passt zu meinem Kind? – Elterliche Schulwahlentscheidungen und die Frage der Passung im öffentlichen und privaten Grundschulwesen." *Zeitschrift für Pädagogik* 64 (5): 612–634.

Koinzer, T., and T. Mayer. 2015. "Private Schulen - Entwicklung und empirische Befunde unter besonderer Berücksichtigung des Grundschulwesens." *Zeitschrift für Grundschulforschung* 8 (2): 28–41.

Kraul, M. 2015. *Private Schulen*. Wiesbaden: Springer VS.

Krüger, J. O., A. Roch, and G. Breidenstein. 2020. *Szenarien der Grundschulwahl. Eine Untersuchung von Entscheidungsdiskursen am Übergang zum Primarbereich*. Wiesbaden: Springer VS.

Lange, A. 2010. "Bildung ist für alle da oder die Kolonisierung des Kinder- und Familienlebens durch ein ambivalentes Dispositiv." In *Kindheit zwischen fürsorglichem Zugriff und gesellschaftlicher Teilhabe*, edited by D. Bühler-Niederberger, J. Mierendorff, and A. Lange, 89–114. Wiesbaden: Springer VS.

Lange, A., and B. Thiessen. 2018. "Eltern als Bildungscoaches? Kritische Anmerkungen aus intersektionalen Perspektiven." In *Elternschaft zwischen Projekt und Projektion. Aktuelle Perspektiven der Elternforschung*, edited by K. Jergus, J. O. Krüger, and A. Roch, 273–294. Wiesbaden: VS.

Nawrotzki, Kristen. 2012. "Parent-School Relations in England and the USA: Partnership, Problematized." In *The Politicization of Parenthood. Shifting Private and Public Responsibilities in Education and Child Rearing*, edited by Sabine Andresen, Martina Richter, and Martina Dordrecht, 69–83. Wiesbaden: Springer VS.

Radtke, F.-O. 2019. "Erziehungsdienstleister und ihre Kunden." *Zeitschrift für Pädagogik* 65: 299–315.

Reckwitz, A. 2018. *Die Gesellschaft der Singularitäten. Zum Strukturwandel der Moderne*. Berlin: Suhrkamp.

Richter, M., and S. Andresen, eds. 2012. *The Politicization of Parenthood. Shifting Private and Public Responsibilities in Education and Childrearing*. Dordrecht: Springer.

Stange, W. 2012. "Erziehungs- und Bildungspartnerschaften – Grundlagen, Strukturen, Begründungen." In *Erziehungs- und Bildungspartnerschaften. Grundlagen und Strukturen von Elternarbeit*, edited by W. Stange, R. Krüger, A. Henschel, and C. Schmitt, 12–39. Wiesbaden: Springer VS.

SVR (Sachverständigenrat) deutscher Stiftungen für Integration und Migration. 2013. Segregation an Grundschulen. Der Einfluss elterlicher Schulwahl. Accessed April 18, 2018. http://www.svr-migration.de/wp-content/uploads/2014/11/Segregation_an_Grundschulen_SVR-FB_WEB.pdf.

Tyrell, Hartmann. 1987. "Die 'Anpassung' der Familie an die Schule." In *Pädagogik, Erziehungswissenschaft und Systemtheorie*, edited by J. Oelkers and H. E. Tenorth, 102–124. Weinheim: Beltz.

Ulrich, H., and S. Strunck. 2012. *Private Schulen in Deutschland. Entwicklungen, Profile, Kontroversen*. Wiesbaden: Springer VS.

Waldow, F. 2014. "Von der Meretokratie zur Parentokratie?" *Zeitschrift für Erziehungswissenschaft (ZfE)* 17 (3): 43–58. Elite und Exzellenz im Bildungssystem: Nationale und internationale Perspektiven

Weiß, M. 2001. "Quasi-Märkte im Schulbereich. Eine ökonomische Analyse." In *Zukunftsfragen der Bildung*, edited by J. Oelkers, 69–85. Weinheim: Beltz.

Zymek, B., and J. Richter. 2007. "International-vergleichende Analyse regionaler Schulentwicklung: Yorkshire und Westfalen." *Zeitschrift für Pädagogik Jg* 35 (3): 326–350.

Practising autonomy in a local eduscape: schools, families and educational choice

Martin Forsey [ID]

ABSTRACT
Portraying a localised educational system as part of broader global flows of policy ideas and practices emanating from multiple sources – an eduscape– the paper focuses on family practices shaped by global policy flows and the return impact of families on the translation of these policies into local school formations. Under scrutiny are the decentralising or devolutionary directives, linked so often to choice and competition, which took hold in Western jurisdictions in the 1980s, the influences of which are still strongly felt. The conceptual links spread to a mobile 'second modernity', implicating many a family in movement associated with choices they are obliged to make, and which are often correlated to family achievement and success. The observations reported here are framed conceptually by an interest in the synthesis of Beck's individualisation thesis and Bourdieusean practice approaches in order to portray and comprehend social being and social change.

1. Once more into the eduscape

This paper centres attention on Western Australia (WA), the largest of the Australian states. More theoretical than empirical in its content, the ambition of this paper is to connect the inevitably complex systems built up around formal education, in WA in this case, to broader global flows of policy ideas and practices emanating from multiple sources. The great is often found in the small (Flyvbjerg 1998), so the paper proceeds with the assumption that amidst the peculiarities of WA, this case study resonates out into other places where similar reforms have taken place.

Consistent with the themes of this collection the focus here is on how family practices are shaped by global policy flows and in turn how families impact the translation of these policies into local educational practice, simultaneously reinforcing and reshaping the educational systems they are entwined within. The most notable policy formations under scrutiny are the decentralising, devolutionary directives, linked so often to choice and competition, which took hold in so-called Western jurisdictions in the 1980s (Whitty, Power, and Halpin 1998), and were instigated in the Western Australian government schools system in the late 1980s (See Forsey 2007).

The links between educational policy and family decision-making spread to a mobile modernity (Corbett 2009; Forsey 2017, 2015a), or more pertinently to a mobile 'second modernity' that implicates many a family, but most obviously the 'middling sorts', in movement associated with choices linked to family achievement and success (Ball and Nikita 2014: Corbett and Forsey 2017). The data highlighted in this paper are drawn from a variety of mainly interview-based studies among parents, students, teachers and administrators that concentrated on educational choices exercised by families and education professionals in a range of settings (see for example Forsey 2015b, 2017, 2008). Within this variety, the most pertinent contrast in the spectacularly metrocentric State of WA lies between families and schools located in rural and urban settings. However, when it comes to school choice research it is difficult to escape socio-economic differences and their effects on the sorts of choices families take, and are able to make (Ball, Bowe, and Gewirtz 1995; Breidenstein et al. 2018; Comber 2015; Corbett 2009; Corbett and Forsey 2017; Windle 2015). The intersecting impacts of place and social class on life chances and family decision-making form major focal points in this study of policy in practice (Levinson and Sutton 2001).

The research observations reported here are framed conceptually by an interest in the synthesis of Beck's individualisation thesis and Bourdeausean practice approaches to portraying and comprehending social being and change (Bourdieu 1977, 1998; Beck and Beck-Gernsheim 2002). Thinking of human action as a continual form of practice, where 'objective structure' impacts human agency in everyday decision-making and social action (Bourdieu 1978), poses some interesting challenges for the reporting of social research. It invites the researcher, and hopefully her/his readership, to co-construct understanding of the ways in which social systems and structures form, and are formed, by social actors (including the researcher) as they creatively use a world that is using them (Ortner 1989).

'Reflexive habitus' is a useful way of articulating understanding of combinations of practice and individualisation, offering a conceptual window on larger social processes of distinction and human formation as a practice of 'cultured structured agency' (Forsey 2015a), which are often disguised as matters of individual choice alone. According to Beck and his colleagues, as the apparent certainties of the post-war settlement centred around the welfare state in Western nations fade and reconfigure, new cultural imperatives arise requiring individuals to take responsibility for their own destiny in ways that have not been apparent before (Beck and Beck-Gernsheim 2002). The notion of reflexive habitus affords recognition of the habituation of this imperative (Sweetman 2003; see also Boström, Lidskog, and Uggla 2017; Rasborg 2017; Threadgold and Nilan 2009), and is articulated further in relation to devolutionary reform in WA discussed later in the paper.

The earlier reference to global flows signifies connections to Appadurai's (1996) influential ideas about the irregular effects of globalisation, recognising the ways in which 'Locality is itself a historical product and the histories through which localities emerge are eventually subject to the dynamics of the global' (18). The *flow* metaphor captures a dynamic movement that is continual rather than eventual. In motion are ideas, ideals, values and practices, capital, material goods, and people in all sorts of regular and irregular ways, impacting with varying force and speed into the interstices of locales and the existing formations they are part of. While the focus here is on structures of schooling, it is generally the case that the ideas and practices in motion lose at least some of their internal coherence when incorporated into local systems (Appadurai 1996, 36).

Embracing the dynamics of global flows expands upon the idea of an eduscape[1] articulated recently with colleagues in relation to international schools in Berlin (Breidenstein et al. 2018). By implication, and thence by definition, eduscapes are emplaced; they are 'local'. It is perhaps easiest to imagine an eduscape physically, as a complex or a system comprising a wide range of institutions, including schools, universities, bureaucratic offices, as well as ancillary organisations such as policy think-tanks, tutoring businesses, support organisations and so on. But it is not simply material and/or structural, the eduscape is embodied, occupied and activated by students, teachers, parents, bureaucrats, politicians, consultants, researchers, and opinion-makers. At the same time, these persons are activated around various educational apparatus such as curricula, examinations, sports carnivals, community events, and academic league tables, all of them energising and structurating components of the overall eduscape. Putting it more simply, the eduscape is a complex of structures, policies and practices, texts, curricula, and persons spread across a geographic space varying in scale from town or city to region, State or province, all the way up to a nation state.[2] A single school is too small, too singular, to isolate as 'a scape', and a national or regional system offers the widest range of useful focus; it seems to defeat the purpose of the conceptual tool to contemplate the intricacies of a global eduscape as some sort of world system; that was certainly not Appadurai's intention. As Felder (2002, 164) points out in conceptualising global phenomena from local perspectives Appadurai 'explores the impact of globalisation on everyday worlds ... on the question of how popular imagination is transformed with the context of globally embedded everyday life'. Depending upon the locus of concern, one may speak of the Berlin or Mumbai eduscape, Arizonian or Quebecan formations, and our attention can also be drawn towards the Vietnamese or Australian eduscapes; although, given the federal realities of Australian political life, it is likely more productive to focus on the various State-based systems of educational organisation than on the national scene.

The eduscape metaphor offers possibilities of appreciating education systems as enacted *practices* of administration, education and sociality, especially in considering the wide varieties of impacting forces and agents affecting the perceptions and the realities of these localised policy formations. For example, the economic upswings and downbeats, the shifting ideas and the imaginaries of curriculum and teaching practice that are inevitably local inflections of sets of ideas moving around the globe in and from a variety of directions. Most significantly, it allows appreciation of the shaping influences, however small, of the people who enact local educational structures as they occupy and vacate its buildings, shift their allegiances from one school to another, move into (or away from) the spaces surrounding the schools and universities, attend the meetings, participate in classes, disrupt the classrooms, care for the students, discipline them, withdraw them, advertise and lure them.

While drawing analogies between educational systems and landscapes can too readily naturalise the accompanying imagery, recognising both the socially constructed nature of the eduscape and the different ways it is apprehended by its 'audience', (a reality the originating metaphor of landscape should not escape either) helps mitigate the risk of misrecognition.

2. Into the Western Australian eduscape

2.1. A metrocentric state

The State of Western Australia occupies just over 2.5 million square kilometres in area; spatially it is close to a third of the Australian continent. The State's capital – Perth – is located in the south west, some 2,215 km from it farthest township of Wyndham in the north east. Climatically Perth is located in a narrow band stretching along the coast to the north and south of the city described as 'warm temperate'. The weather adds to the attractiveness of the capital city, particularly when compared with the very hot summers and warm winters characterising the north of the State, and the hot summers and cold winters occurring throughout much of the central east. These different geo-climatic conditions *help* explain a simple, stunning fact: at the time of the 2016 National Census, 79% of WA's 2.5 million residents lived in greater Perth. The starkness of these figures point to the imaginative organisational feat involved in designing, building and maintaining any social system aimed at addressing the needs of a place so large, so sparsely populated, and so strongly metrocentric.

Metrocentrism characterises much of the Australian nation; a phenomenon evident since European settlement in the late eighteenth century. While the extent of the spatial and climactic difficulties faced were arguably starker in WA than the other colonies (which became States of the Federation in 1901), the general metrocentric theme prevailed throughout the developing nation into the present. The similarity of the conditions, coupled with much policy borrowing across State boundaries, led to the formation of tightly-bound educational formations, described by Chapman and Dunstan (1990) as some of the most centralised education systems in the world. The central offices of the State-based educational systems held complete control over staffing allocation to individual schools; they also obliged students enrolling in government schools to attend the school allocated to them by the geographical boundaries, or 'catchment areas', drawn around individual schools.

2.2. Equity across distance

Reflecting global ideals about educational practice translated into local geo-political realities Australia's various education systems were partly designed to deal with equity over distance, or at least to ameliorate some of the inequities arising out of the uneven distribution of educational resources across a vast and unevenly populated jurisdiction. Teacher shortages in rural and regional areas of Australia is arguably the major resource concern faced by educational bureaucrats, posing a perennial problem for Australia's state-based education systems, across both government and non-government sectors (Boylan and McSwan 1998; Downes and Roberts 2017). A standard approach used to help State-run education departments meet obligations to the regions obliged teachers seeking permanent employment in government schools to complete extended periods of satisfactory service in a rural school (Hudson and Hudson 2008). The contracts are often short; even so, many freshly graduated teachers do not complete their term. Even among those who do complete their allotted time, more tend to move on than stay (Boylan and McSwan 1998; Cuervo and Acquaro 2018; Downes and Roberts 2017). As a result, many of the State's rural students are educated by young, early-career teachers, which of course has its advantages in terms of ongoing vitality and refreshment of up-to-date ideas and practices (Boylan and McSwan 1998). However, as Downes and Roberts (2017) review of school staffing issues in rural, remote and isolated schools indicates, many studies point to the problems triggered by having relatively high proportions of new teachers in difficult to staff schools, particularly given the teachers' lack of experience with their subject matter, coupled with tendencies to being obliged to teach outside their areas of expertise because of staff shortages the lack of suitably qualified teachers evident in schools at some distance from the metropolitan core.

The employment strategies just outlined have strong implications for rural parents, particularly when it comes to secondary schooling, a time when the vulnerabilities associated with the inverse correlation between distance from Perth and the probability of their child qualifying for university can be felt more strongly (Forsey 2015a). Rural families experience the possibilities of education failure for school-aged children more acutely than their metropolitan counterparts (Abbott-Chapman, Johnston, and Jetson 2017). Such concerns have had profound effects on the Western Australian eduscape. As is discussed later, all too often the net result is further concentration of the metropolitan focus and practices of its citizens.

2.3. Loosening control: education bureaucracies in second modernity

Chapman and Dunstan's (1990) description of the highly centralised systems undergirding the various Australian State-based systems created in the first half of the twentieth century captures local inflections of a more global phenomenon. Bureaucratic control is a defining feature of national governance created in response to the 'great transformations' triggered by the rise of industrial/market capitalism as the dominant mode of production. Identifying bureaucracy as one of modernity's quintessential creations, we can recognise the critique and rejection of the rigid, regimented centres of control occurring in the final quarter of the last century as post-modern – or at least as a movement beyond what *was*, which Beck, among others, was keen to conceptualise more as continuity than breach though the use of terms like second, late or reflexive modernity (Beck and Lau 2005; Giddens 1991). Articulating a portrait of a second or reflexive modernity is Beck and Lau's (2005) conceptual response to dissatisfaction with the rupturing metaphors of post-modernity. Interestingly, and usefully, Beck (2016:, 262) posited individualisation as 'the social structure of the second modernity', one that overtook a more collective social order once underpinned by the apparent certainties of strong public and communal institutions, clear career paths, a job for life, enduring marital partnerships and their accompanying sexual division of labour (Beck and Lau 2005, 526).

Clearly bureaucracies have not simply disappeared. It seems more useful, therefore, to think of the current period as an inflection of the period of post-WWII 'high modernity' rather than a radical breach. As with modernity, bureaucracy has become reflexive – 'directed at itself' as much as those it purports to serve (Beck, Bonns, and Lau 2003, 1). In neo-liberal inflections of second modernity education bureaucracies are instructed to diminish their power through legislation and empowerment of individual schools and families. Bureaucratic control of finance and governance of schools remains a defining feature of many an education system, with the global up-take of testing regimes providing a major locus of government control of schooling in decentralising times – all in the name of quality guarantees and parental satisfaction.

The individualising impetus identified by Beck and his various colleagues is strongly evident in educational policy reformations focused, often simultaneously, on devolution and parental choice. In both instances the aim, if not necessarily the result, is to shift decision-making responsibilities away from collective formations of education systems catering for a national or State citizenry to the practices of individual schools in relationship with family units. While these cultural and structural shifts in responsibility are often associated with neoliberalism, it is also useful to think of them in broader cultural and structural terms (Forsey 2007). Rose (1993, 298) offers some useful leads in describing the practices of advanced liberalism as freshened formations of relations between political subjects and policy managers through which 'the injunctions of the experts merge with our own projects for self-mastery and the enhancement of our lives.' Reflexive habitus is a useful way of describing this phenomenon – a *practice* of autonomy where practice is understood in conventional Bourdieusean terms as a dynamic synthesis between social structures, cultural perceptions and individual action (Bourdieu 1998). The logic of neoliberalism is underpinned by a belief in the ability of individuals utilising and applying market logics to ensure educational improvement (Bartlett et al. 2002; Harvey 2005), a logic internalised by many an individual and enacted often through the minutiae of everyday decision-making. Reflecting the cultural imperatives of the reflexive modernity in which they are formulated, policies enacting the devolution of school systems and promotion of parental choice help manufacture systems of individualisation.

The ongoing changes of the final quarter of the twentieth century into the first quarter of the 21st can be read as a movement away from various forms of solidarity produced through the class compromises forged in first modernity towards a riskier, more individualised present. This presents some useful ways of comprehending changes that have taken place in the delivery of education systems in various setting across this same period of time. In Western Australia the flow of ideas enmeshed in articulations of education policy focused on devolution was said to result in better schools for the State.

2.4. Second modernity and better schools in Western Australia

In 1987 the Minister of Education in the Western Australian Labor Government, approved the implementation of a report revealingly titled *Better Schools in Western Australia: A Programme for Improvement*. Produced as a glossy pamphlet, filled with colour photographs of students and their teachers, brief overviews and many dot-points, the marketable 'lightness' of *Better Schools* obscured a serious and far-reaching intent. 'Whereas once it was believed that a good system creates good schools' declared the Minister, 'it is now recognised that good schools make a good system' (Ministry of Education 1987, 5). The decentralising rhetoric of the document reflected trends apparent both nationally and internationally at that time (Caldwell 1990; Chapman and Boyd 1986; Chubb and Moe 1990; Whitty, Power, and Halpin 1998). Replicating the devolutionary ideals undergirding the document, *Better School's* advocated for school-based decision-making instead of centralised approaches. The authors offered two main reasons: firstly, autonomous decision-making encourages increased levels of teacher professionalism; secondly, it allows schools to better respond to community needs and the requirements of individual students (Ministry of Education 1987, 5).

A common-sense view about centralisation and bureaucratisation being 'substantially at odds with the effective organisation of schools and the successful provision of education' (Chubb and Moe 1990, 142) reflects broader patterns linked easily enough to neoliberalism (Forsey 2007). However, it is useful to recognise the broader patterns of social-cultural change linked to decentralising reforms particularly those associated with a growing reflexive individualisation in 'second modernity'. As the argument goes, disillusionment with the grand consensus associated with the welfare state built in the 1950s and 60s have triggered responses among those living in European societies and their offshoots, to actively chip away at the grand institutions of the nation-state and its associated welfare system – aspects of it at least (Beck, Bonns, and Lau 2003). Increased governmental commitment to education and the other institutions of social advancement and protection strengthened in most Western nations during the long boom of the post-war era produced 'a more predictable, institutionalised childhood, greater consistency in the period when children grow up and leave home, a narrowing of childbearing years and a clearer demarcation between when working life begins and when it ends' (Higgs and Gilleard 2006, 230). This institutionalisation of the life-course brought greater predictability to the lives of most citizens, especially those located in the broad and growing range of the middle classes. According to Higgs & Gilleard, increased emphasis on individualisation flowed readily enough from the conditions produced out of this predictability and stability, triggering a new political consensus centred around the production of more autonomous organisations and individuals. In turn, this increased the possibilities of, and desire for, the exercise of flexibility and choice. In other words, the class compromise that helped build the first modernity paved the way for the destruction of the consciousness that produced it. Or, as Beck and Lau (2005) put it, the welfare state created the conditions for its own demise; or at least parts of it.

Refocusing on the decentralising urge of the WA government in the late 1980s, it becomes apparent that the shifting of responsibility for the production of 'good schools' away from 'the system' onto the schools themselves, is attributable to late modern commitments to autonomous organisations and families, with both institutions operating with some degree of remove from the benevolence of state support when compared with the situation during the heights of post-WWII modernity (Forsey 2009; Walford 1996; Whitty, Power, and Halpin 1998). There is a double play operating in this reform as 'the system' also shifts the expectations of the families it serves to greater and lesser degrees. In ceding control to individual schools, allegedly in the service of efficiency and superior outcomes (Chubb and Moe 1990), the government applied this logic to families tasked with making very local decisions about their childrens' education. School choice became one of the key political slogans emerging from this newfound focus on parental 'rights', an alluring concept opening up to individual family units the promise of autonomy, liberty, immediacy, efficacy and control, moves made all the more attractive by allusions to the compulsory, regulated, rigid and distanced realities of bureaucratic control (Forsey 2009; Forsey, Davies, and Walford 2008). An embracing of competition and market forces is part of what happens in this sort of choice regime, captured neatly enough by Haley[3], interviewed as part of a school choice project in 2004/05:

> To me it's a bit like buying a car – you go and you shop around for the best deal or whatever. And it's the same like I've never felt that I would send all my children to the same school; just

> because one was there, the others had to go there, you know! I really think if somewhere offered a particular thing that was really good for one of your children be it State or be it Private then that's what I'd go and look at it. And it may be that the other ones might be better off somewhere else.
>
> That's how I think you should see it, they're offering you a service and you go and check them out. You line them up against everybody else.

On the surface, it is difficult to argue against the promise of choice as Hayley reports it, especially in an era valorising individualised responses to opportunities and challenges. There is a flip-side, however, as Brown (1994) pointed out:

> The deregulation and privatisation of schools shifts the responsibility for educational outcomes squarely on to students and parents ... If one's child does not perform and achieve to the expected level, then, as a parent one must look to oneself for the reason. Perhaps it is because insufficient attention was paid to the 'choice of school', or perhaps some spare cash was spent on a holiday rather than invested in education (63).

With the right to choose, comes the responsibilities for choices made; therein lie some possible routes to increased anxiety, as well as to intensification of social inequality, themes hovering around any contemporary discussion of educational choice.

2.5. The public/ 'Private' mix in the Western Australian eduscape

In addition to the network of government schools running through WA, there is an elaborate network of Catholic and Independent schools to consider. In many instances, these add significantly to the choices available to families. While a Catholic school system is fairly self-explanatory, the Independent label refers to a loose collective of mainly Protestant church schools, with some Indigenous community schools, Islamic schools, a Jewish school and a variety of community institutions such as Steiner and Montessori schools as part of the mix. Almost all schools in both sectors receive varying levels of funding from both Federal and State governments, so they are not private, even though this is the term most commonly used to describe Catholic and Independent schools in general conversation. The Independent Schools Council of Australia (ISCA) declare government funding to be a means of promoting pluralism in the nation, allowing families of different ethnic, religious and cultural identity to 'choose a school to best meet the needs of their child and their own values, within a frame of common social values'.[4]

This is not the place to go into the intricacies of Australia's funding policy regime and it peculiar history (see Campbell and Proctor 2014; Sherington and Hughes 2014); however, the Independent School's defence of pluralism should not be simply brushed aside. Government subsidy does allow some parents to more readily enrol children in schools compatible with deeply held beliefs and values that are educational in focus as much as religious. That said the statement from ISCA elides the fact that some of their most prominent schools already charge fees exceeding the funding made available for individual students enrolled in any government school. And, as Chesters (2019, 80) recently showed, '20% of those with university-educated parents attended independent schools compared to just 8% of those whose parents held no post-school qualifications'; while, 'almost one-third of those in the highest family wealth quintile attended an independent school compared to just 5% of those in the lowest wealth quintile'. There is a high level of social stratification in Australian schooling and elite independent schools are very much at the 'pointy end' of the educational hierarchy, allowing wealthy families to 'choose' the sorts of schools that help safeguard class privilege. Acknowledging previous research showing that attendance at private schools markedly increased one's chances of attending university (Dockery, Seymour, and Koshy 2016; Marks 2010), Chesters (2019, 83) concludes her analysis by observing that 'Australian education systems segregate students according to family wealth, with children from wealthy families being more likely to attend private schools and children from low wealth families being more likely to attend government schools'.

In recent decades Australia has the dubious distinction of producing larger concentrations of 'disadvantaged students in disadvantaged schools' than similar OECD countries (Nous Group 2011, 20). There is a general loss of confidence in such schools, diagnosed by various forms of race and class-based flight away from them (Windle 2015). The reduction of certain schools in particular places to the status of 'places of last resort', sometimes referred to as a process of residualization (Preston 1984) is invariably associated with government schools in the poorer parts of town. Drilling down into this disturbing reality Lamb et al. (2015) report that, of the three educational sectors, government schools increasingly enrol disproportionately high proportions of students with disabilities and schooling disadvantages (see also Forsey, Proctor, and Stacey 2017). This phenomonon has intensified in recent years, causing a number of scholars to link these residualising outcomes, that are both cause and effect, to neoliberal reforms in Australian schooling (Comber 2015; Windle 2015).

The social facts of residualization result in no small part from a reshaping of parental behaviour initially triggered in the 1970s by a guarantee of funding for all schools. This particular trigger almost certainly contributed to accelerating systems and practices of individualisation related to schooling at least in a reflexive second modernity. Suggestions of this phenomenon are evident in Figure 1 which captures the net flow of students away from the government sector towards the larger variety of non-government schools that opened up in the final quarter of the twentieth century. The vast majority of this movement towards the Independent school sector is clearly linked to the aspirations of many a middle class family in Australia (Beavis 2004; Forsey 2008; Windle 2015).

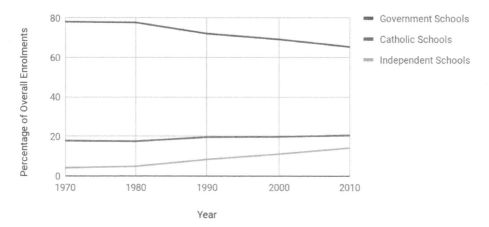

Figure 1. Proportion of Australian school students enrolled in schools according to sector 1970–2010.

It is a mistake to think of the flow of students in the last three decades or so as being simply from government to independent schools. The movement away from certain marginalised schools can also be to other government schools, an increasingly popular move made possible through 'The Better Schools' agenda. Moves towards autonomy and competition in government schooling triggered a relaxation of previously rigid school boundaries more or less determining the schools government school students would enrol in. The market logic accompanying these changes in policy and practice were quite clearly aimed at improving educational outcomes through competition (Forsey 2007). As the logic goes, 'market competition forces schools to continuously improve their standards in order to attract parent consumers of the educational "product" they are offering' (Angus 2015, 395). Consequently schools in socially marginal areas, characterised predominantly by high unemployment, lost students to more desirable schools. This, in turn, limited their ability to offer academic enrichment programmes, increasing their vulnerability to further middle-class flight and so the residualising spiral continues (Forsey 2006; Windle 2015, 114–116). The opposite applies in the more affluent suburbs and towns where government schools, often with strong academic reputations, attract interest well beyond their normal catchment. This enables such schools to limit enrolments to families located within the school catchment, although exceptions are evident through acceptance of students of exceptional academic talent, or other desirable skills depending upon any specialist curriculum programmes offered by the school. Parental demand has reshaped school practices in a variety of ways as they scramble to attract what one Principal described to a teacher I interviewed as part of a long term ethnographic study of devolution in practice at an inner city school as 'the right sort of student' (Forsey 2007). As far as the teacher was concerned, the principal was quite clearly referencing students from 'middle class' families as the 'right sort'.

2.6. Parents responding to the pull of the private

I return to Jim, an 'old friend' in my writing at least, interviewed as part of a project focused on students, parents and teachers who had chosen to change systems – from non-government to government or vice versa (Forsey 2008; 2014). His insight as a parent who had recently shifted his son out of low fee church-run school to the prestigious government school in which he worked as an Industrial Arts teacher helps highlight not only the implications of choices being made between government and non-government schools, but also between different government schools (see Forsey 2008; 2010). 'A generation ago we wouldn't have worried about where my son went to school', exclaimed Jim, 'most people would have been happy with the local government school'. Continuing this train of thought, and casting his eyes around his workplace where the interview took place, Jim suggested 'Schools like this probably reflect what people were getting 20, 30 years ago to a certain extent... What a lot of people are paying for now... is what they got for free 30 years ago'.

Aware of how the choices he was making for his children were influenced by forces sweeping Australian society, Jim spoke of his working class roots, his attendance at local Catholic schools until Year 10 and the apprenticeship following this. In the recent choices and decisions taken on behalf of his son, he was very conscious of the effects of a dominant ethos of competition and materialism, and the discomforts they created in him. However, alongside these critical edges, he was very conscious of his son's need to be competitive in a difficult employment marketplace.

Jim's ambivalence about the educational choices he had made is emblematic of many of the conversations captured in the changing school systems project (Forsey 2008). There was Jonelle with two children enrolled at a Catholic school on music scholarships, who expressed strong commitment to public education, not least through bumper stickers displayed prominently and proudly on the back of her car:

> Just because I don't want to send my kids [to government schools] to be the so called sacrificial lambs to fix the problems doesn't mean I don't care about the kids in there. It's still got to be fixed and I think a lot of us have still got to lobby to get them fixed particularly for the funding.

Hayley, whose thoughts likening the choosing of a school to choosing a car were shared earlier, expressed a strong, if vague commitment to governmental schooling, not least because she was a teacher in a government school. She spoke of feeling a little hypocritical – 'You know, you're in one system but you've got your kids going somewhere else. And I do sort of think a lot about why you make those decisions but it's always the same, there's never anything really conclusive'. Kelly, who was also teaching in a government school alongside her husband, reflected similarly on the hypocrisy of enrolling her child into a non-government school. Consistent with Jim's observations about the lack of thought or awareness of choice in times gone by, she suggested 'twenty years ago you just went to the local school, but now, we just expect more'. Expressing a belief about private schools having better resources and more competent teachers, especially when compared with the government schools in her area of residence – one of the more marginalised areas in the metropolitan area – she concluded 'if I want to give my daughter every opportunity I will be hypocritical'. We can hear in each of these reflections from the parents who volunteered to share their thoughts about choosing a school for their child, a sense of being part of a shifting sensibility – in the past we would have just gone to the local school but we now expect more and are prepared to 'shop around'.

But these are all city stories. When one shifts attention to the areas beyond the large metropolitan capitals of any of the six Australian States, where there are less shops and they are usually much smaller, different sorts of choices and shaping of family experience become very apparent due to the quite different spatio-structural realities faced in these rural and/or remote spaces.

2.7. In the rural edges

The majority of rural townships in Australia are focused on agricultural production. As is the case in many a nation-state, many of these towns are in decline as the compounding effects of prolonged droughts, mechanised farming, the massification of farms, the closure or rationalisation of major institutions such as banks, hospitals and schools, alongside youth out-migration, take hold (Cuervo and Wyn 2012, 68). These factors combine to render rural youth among the most vulnerable of their cohort to the 'shifting demographics and community restructurings of the Australian economy' (Alloway and Dalley-Trim 2009, 49). As their children transition into early adulthood, rural families tend to experience a range of educational disadvantages highlighted by a list of limitations, including access to schools, curriculum variability, quality teaching and resources, as well as the ready availability of tertiary education, further training and youth employment (Alloway and Dalley-Trim 2009).

In these circumstances of disadvantage families with a preference for rural spaces and lifestyles find themselves having to make significant decisions when it comes to where they are to live; education forms a major focal point for such decision making, rarely in positive ways (Forsey 2015a, 2017). That said, it is important to recognise the variability in rural and regional towns throughout Australia. There are significant fluctuations in economic opportunities between and within townships, with prospects often at a premium in mining areas that are often centred around townships in some of the more remote regions of the State.

The economic health of Western Australia is heavily reliant on resource extraction; in 2018–19 mining contributed 36% of the Gross State Product (GSP), compared with a 2% contribution from agriculture, forestry and fishing (Government of Western Australia 2020). Contrasting with the steady decline of Australia's agricultural township in recent times, mining towns tend to be more volatile in their population fluctuations. In 2010 I conducted a project in Karratha, a town/city some 1200 km north of Perth. The town was booming at the time: wages were among the highest in the nation, real estate was exorbitant, goods costly, unemployment just about nil. Forms of residence were mixed between semi-permanent home occupancy, or an arrangement often termed Fly-in-Fly-out (FiFo), involving a period of weeks working 12 h shifts in the company site while being accommodated in company camps, followed by elongated periods of leave. While the various companies were actively using FiFo to recruit and manage their workforce, the four gas extraction companies, merged into the North West Shelf Joint Venture (NWSJV), were very concerned to maintain a more permanent workforce. Unlike the iron-ore extraction companies of the region, the NWSJV required a staff well qualified to deal with the many technical issues associated with gas extraction, processing and delivery and were significantly more reliant upon university educated personnel to maintain their outputs. In a town of high resident 'churn' – the number of people staying in the town for less than five years was more pronounced than in many other parts of WA –in 2010 the NWSJV reported employee turnover to be costing $M15 annually. A survey of employees conducted by the NWSJV at that time pointed to high school transition for the children of these workers as a key turning point in family decision-making regarding residence in the town. The NWSJV worked keenly with schools in attempting to improve academic results and their overall image, donating significant amounts of money for supplementary programmes known as the Karratha School's Project (see Forsey 2015a, 2015b).

The majority of parents I spoke with outlined their distrust of the two local high schools, one a State school the other Catholic, especially when it came to getting their children into university. Remembering the difficulties associated with attracting teachers to rural towns and remote places identified earlier, I heard from one of the Deputy Principals at the government high school of how in a two-year period they turned over, '56 heads of department, 32 deputy principals and four principals'. The Catholic school was not immune from these difficulties either. The former principal of St Luke's (which had a full staff complement of 40), described employing close to 60 new teachers in his four years at the school: 'I had probably four or five stayers but there were only five I hadn't appointed by the time I left'. Quality of housing, the cost of living, distance from Perth and the difficult teaching environment were among the main reasons teachers offered for this spectacular teacher churn. Leadership issues were among the reasons offered by one senior teacher I spoke with. But whatever the reasons, since their inception maintaining quality staff has been a significant issue for Western Australian rural schools; Karratha in the first decade of this century captured this dilemma in a particularly emphatic way.

I conducted 20 interviews among 25 parents who were living in Karratha, and 6 with parents who had lived there recently but had moved to Perth. While schooling of their children was not the only concern of those who had moved, for each of them it was of at least some concern. Of the parents still living in Karratha in 2010, most were looking to stay there indefinitely, although close to half of the group signalled their intent to move as or before their eldest reached secondary school age. Staying did not mean the parents were comfortable with their decision in relation to their child's education. One woman I spoke with, Naomi I have called her, expressed clear commitment to her family staying together. They had lived the FiFo lifestyle in another job in another country, and it was not for them. The family could afford boarding schools, but the children were not interested in this option:

> And it's a hard thing because a lot of people think the schools in Perth are definitely better and therefore they're doing the right thing by sending their children away. [And we don't know, we're not from here], but I think a lot of education comes from home, and our children have said, 'there's no way they want to be away from us', so that isn't an option for them. And I'm quite happy to have them near me, but that means I've then got to take whatever education's offered, whether it's good or bad or indifferent. It is challenging.

Naomi's reflections stand as a reasonably representative articulation of the concerns and insecurities expressed by most I interviewed. Only four interviewees thought their children were receiving an educational standard equivalent, or in one case better, to what they would receive in Perth. For the majority, who worried about the effects choosing to stay had on their children the consequences were indeed perplexing, creating challenges accentuated by being in a small town so far removed from the State's capital (see Forsey 2015a, 2015b).

3. Shaping parents, shaping schools in second modernity

In closing, my thoughts return to Jim, the industrial arts teacher who had arranged for his son to join the prestigious government school in which he was teaching. His speculative reflections and generalisation about parents of the previous generation sensing no need to think about where to send their child to school, seems plausible. Catholic schools were in financial trouble, they were struggling to keep afloat and were still very parochial in nature. The schools in the Independent sector, such as it was, catered to elite families and were not known for the excellence of their product. In and around the long economic boom of the post war era, the government school system was the safer option for many families. During this period, the ideals and practices of the welfare-state held to a large extent. There was little choice available to families and they were not really looking for alternatives; they were not structurated to do so (Giddens 1991). Options have opened up through the funding guarantees for all schools, a subsequent expansion from the Independent sector into low and moderate fee schools, and government schools opening up to market models of organisation. There has been a concomitant shift in the expectations of parents and students towards choice, a phenomenon reflecting the conditions of second modernity, with the certainties and rigidities of the post-WWII era giving way to greater pluralism, deinstitutionalisation and deregulation, as well as increasing consumerism. This has brought a growing sense of uncertainty and risk, stemming in no small part from government withdrawal from the social body, 'governing at a distance' as Rose (1996) picturesquely describes current formations of governance. The old order, built around a strong centralised system, has been inverted; now the idealised model is one of strong individual schools connected to their local community helping build networks of excellence.

Bourdieu (1998, 26) reminds us that the structuring structures are structured structures; it is a mistake to think of individual families simply falling into line around the policy formations in the eduscape. The structures of governance are as much led by cultural change as they lead them. To greater and lesser degrees we are all neoliberal subjects (Larner 2005); the logic of choice is difficult to resist in any sort of complete way and all citizens are implicated to greater and lesser degrees in a system characterised by there being no choice but to choose (Forsey 2008; Giddens 1991). That said, it is important to recognise the metrocentrism of such thinking. For people living 'in the bush' the withdrawal of the state from the nation building projects of the first 70 years or so of the Twentieth Century – guaranteed milk prices for farmers for example, or state-run banks, schools and health care centres in as many towns as possible – further undermines their ability to choose like a city person. The opening up of markets and closing down of subsidies characterising this later rendering of modernity, further reduces local viability. For rural people, with few educational options to begin with, their choices are dwindling to the point where it often feels like there is no choice but to move if they want any kind of decent service. But of course not everyone wishes to make this 'choice'.

Following Beck and his various colleagues (Beck and Beck-Gernsheim 2002; Beck, Bonns, and Lau 2003; Beck and Lau 2005), referring to the final quarter of the twentieth century as the beginnings of *a mobile second modernity* is undesirable in its clumsiness. However, it is a useful term for linking the disembedding of individuals, often as part of a family unit, from particular locales as a consequence of culturally embedded desires and ambitions for social and economic advancement, or in other cases for simply making do and getting by. Writing about rural Canada Corbett (2009) exposes formal education as a key institution of 'disembedding' (see Giddens 1991). It 'loosen[s] ties to particular locales … promoting out-migration' (Corbett 2009, 1). Put another way, formal education helps frame a modernity in which individual progress and achievement are increasingly linked to the sheer physical act of movement (Forsey 2015a). The movement does not have to be as drastic as to the next town, or to the capital city 1500 km to the south, the shifts can be more subtle and slight, crossing from one school zone to another on a daily basis for instance, or moving across the city to attend the fee paying school of choice. These are all movements for which the middle classes are culturally primed, far more so than those of working class background (Abbott-Chapman, Johnston, and Jetson 2017; Ball, Bowe, and Gewirtz 1995). For the middle classes physical mobility is linked to social progress and mobility, with commitments to embodied motion reinforced and valorised through formal education (Forsey 2017; 2015a).

The allegedly decentralised eduscapes of second modernity influence the families within 'the scape' to take responsibility for the educational outcomes of their children. At the same time the same families help reshape the schools and the systems they are located around in order that they respond to their needs and desires. These structuring structured structures offer the promise of allowing specialised service for individualised children, a promise affecting the labour of educators in sometimes impossible ways. The force of ideas and practices, ideals and ambition swirling around the schools and universities and organisational spaces of these institutions, reshape, renovate and sometimes even wear away some parts of the educational assemblage – some schools disappear in the devolved rationalities of second modernity.

It is an obvious point, but useful to make – the system is never obliterated. All change is undergirded by continuity (Saussure 1959) in processes of ongoing re-production. Eduscapes across the globe are built around the need for safe and reliable child care, for basic literacy and numeracy for the majority of citizens, for instilling commitment to broader societal goals, and for the training and sorting of the talents of teenagers as they transition into adulthood. The conditions, around which these outcomes are more or less guaranteed shift with the social conventions and the political consensus driving them. In an individualising, mobile modernity, the relationship between schools and families becomes more personal and the mutual shaping of both key social institutions are more immediate and palpable than they once were as parents take increasing responsibility for the education outcomes of their children. The idea of the eduscape helps capture the dynamic and ever-developing connections between families and schools as part of a broader system of relationships and structures that affords some comprehension of the uneven shaping of local terrains caused by the impacts of ongoing and ever changing process of global modernisation in all of its imperfect glory (Breidenstein et al. 2018).

Notes

1. Appadurai used the *scape* suffix to capture the flow of people, materials/capital and ideas characterising globalisation, inserting the suffix into three terms: *ethnoscape*, *financescape*, and *mediascape*.
2. To avoid confusion between references to the nation state and the six States that make up the Australian federation, references to the state apparatus of the nation will be written in lower case. When State is capitalised it refers to one or all of the six States comprising the Australian Commonwealth.
3. The names of all interviewees cited in this paper are pseudonyms.
4. Go to http://isca.edu.au/about-independent-schools/parents-and-school-choice/.

Disclosure statement

No potential conflict of interest was reported by the author(s).

ORCID

Martin Forsey http://orcid.org/0000-0002-2532-2132

References

Abbott-Chapman, J., R. Johnston, and T. Jetson. 2017. "Rural Parents' School Choices: Affective, Instrumental and Structural Influences." *Australian and International Journal of Rural Education* 27 (3): 126–141.

Alloway, N., and L. Dalley-Trim. 2009. "'High and Dry' in Rural Australia: Obstacles to Student Aspirations and Expectations." *Rural Society* 19 (1): 49–59.

Angus, L. 2015. "School Choice: Neoliberal Education Policy and Imagined Futures." *British Journal of Sociology of Education* 36 (3): 395–413. doi:10.1080/01425692.2013.823835.

Appadurai, A. 1996. *Modernity at Large: Cultural Dimensions of Globalization*. Minneapolis: University of Minnesota Press.

Ball, S., R. Bowe, and S. Gewirtz. 1995. "Circuits of Schooling: A Sociological Exploration of Parental Choice of School in Social Class Contexts." *The Sociological Review* 43 (1): 52–78.

Ball, S., and D. Nikita. 2014. "The Global Middle Class and School Choice: A Cosmopolitan Sociology." *Zeitschrift für Erziehungswissenschaft* 17 (3): 81–93.

Bartlett, L., M. Frederick, T. Gulbrandsen, and E. Murillo. 2002. "The Marketization of Education: Public Schools for Private Ends." *Anthropology and Education Quarterly* 33 (1): 5–29.

Beavis, A. 2004. "Why Parents Choose Public or Private Schools." *Research Developments* 12: 1–4. ACER. https://research.acer.edu.au/cgi/viewcontent.cgi?article=1010&context=resdev.

Beck, U. 2016. "Varieties of Second Modernity and the Cosmopolitan Vision." *Theory, Culture & Society* 33 (7–8): 257–270.

Beck, U., and E. Beck-Gernsheim. 2002. *Individualization: Institutionalized Individualism and its Social and Political Consequences*. London: Sage.

Beck, U., W. Bonns, and C. Lau. 2003. "The Theory of Reflexive Modernization." *Theory, Culture & Society* 20 (2): 1–33.

Beck, U., and C. Lau. 2005. "Second Modernity as a Research Agenda: Theoretical and Empirical Explorations in the 'Meta-Change' of Modern Society." *The British Journal of Sociology* 56 (4): 525–557.

Boström, M., R. Lidskog, and Y. Uggla. 2017. "A Reflexive Look at Reflexivity in Environmental Sociology." *Environmental Sociology* 3 (1): 6–16.

Bourdieu, P. 1977. *Outline of a Theory of Practice*. Cambridge: Cambridge University Press.

Bourdieu, P. 1998. *Practical Reason: On the Theory of Action*. Cambridge: Polity Press.

Boylan, C., and D. McSwan. 1998. "Long-Staying Rural Teachers: Who are They?" *Australian Journal of Education* 42 (1): 49–65.

Breidenstein, G., M. Forsey, F. La Gro, O. Krüger, and A. Roch. 2018. "Choosing International: A Case Study of Globally Mobile Parents." In *Elite Education and Internationalisation - From the Early Years Into Higher Education*, edited by C. Maxwell, H.-H. Krüger, U. Deppe, and W. Helsper, 161–179. Palgrave Macmillan.

Brown, Philip. 1994. "Education and the Ideology of Parentocracy." In *Parental Choice and Education: Principles, Policy and Practice*, edited by J. Mark Halstead, 51–67. London: Kegan.

Caldwell, B. 1990. "School-Based Decision-Making and Management: International Developments." In *School-Based Decision-Making and Management*, edited by J. Chapman, 3–26. London: Falmer Press.

Campbell, C., and H. Proctor. 2014. *A History of Australian Schooling*. Sydney: Allen & Unwin.
Chapman, J., and W. L. Boyd. 1986. "Decentralization, Devolution, and the School Principal: Australian Lessons on Statewide Educational Reform." *Educational Administration Quarterly* 22 (4): 28–58.
Chapman, J., and J. Dunstan. 1990. "Introduction." In *Democracy and Bureaucracy: Tensions in Public Schooling*, edited by J. Chapman, and J. Dunstan, 1–7. London: Falmer Press.
Chesters, J. 2019. "Egalitarian Australia? Associations Between Family Wealth and Outcomes in Young Adulthood." *Journal of Sociology* 55 (1): 72–89.
Chubb, J., and T. Moe. 1990. *Politics, Markets and America's Schools*. Washington, DC: The Brookings Institution.
Comber, B. 2015. *Literacy, Place, and Pedagogies of Possibility*. New York: Routledge.
Corbett, M. 2009. "Rural Schooling in Mobile Modernity: Returning to the Places I've Been." *Journal of Research in Rural Education* 24 (7): 1–13.
Corbett, M., and M. Forsey. 2017. "Rural Youth Out-Migration and Education: Challenges to Aspirations Discourse in Mobile Modernity." *Discourse: Studies in the Cultural Politics of Education* 38 (3): 58–69.
Cuervo, H., and D. Acquaro. 2018. "Exploring Metropolitan University Pre-Service Teacher Motivations and Barriers to Teaching in Rural Schools." *Asia-Pacific Journal of Teacher Education* 46 (4): 384–398.
Cuervo, H., and J. Wyn. 2012. *Young People Making it Work: Continuity and Change in Rural Places*. Melbourne: Melbourne University Press.
Dockery, A. M., R. Seymour, and P. Koshy. 2016. "Promoting Low Socio-Economic Participation in Higher Education: A Comparison of Area-Based and Individual Measures." *Studies in Higher Education* 41 (9): 1692–1714.
Downes, N., and P. Roberts. 2017. "Revisiting the Schoolhouse: A Literature Review on Staffing Rural, Remote and Isolated Schools in Australia 2004–2016." *Australian and International Journal of Rural Education* 28 (1): 31–54.
Felder, S. 2002. "Review of Modernity at Large: Cultural Dimensions of Globalization." *Social Analysis: The International Journal of Anthropology* 46 (2): 164–166.
Flyvbjerg, Bent. 1998. *Rationality and Power: Democracy in Practice*. Chicago: University of Chicago Press.
Forsey, M. 2006. "Australian Public Schools and the Eloquent Fiction of the Free Market." In *Thinking Down Under: Australian Politics, Society and Culture in Transition,* , edited by G Willett, 59–73. Trier, Germany: Wissenschaftlicher Verlag.
Forsey, M. 2007. *Challenging the System? A Dramatic Tale of Neoliberal Reform in an Australian High School*. Charlotte, NC, USA: Information Age Publishing.
Forsey, M. 2008. "No Choice but to Choose: Selecting Schools in Western Australia." In *The Globalisation of School Choice?, Symposium Books*, edited by M Forsey, S Davies, and G Walford, 73–93. Oxford, UK: Symposium Books.
Forsey, M. 2009. "The Problem with Autonomy: An Ethnographic Study of Neoliberalism in Practice at an Australian High School." *Discourse: Studies in the Cultural Politics of Education* 30 (4): 457–469.
Forsey, M. 2010. "Publicly Minded, Privately Focused: Western Australian Teachers and School Choice." *Teaching and Teacher Education* 26 (1): 53–60.
Forsey, M. 2014. "The School in the State and the State in the School: The Social Re-Production of Education Systems in a Mobile Modernity." *Zeitschrift für Erziehungswissenschaft* 17 (Supplement 3): 95–112.
Forsey, M. 2015a. "Learning to Stay? Mobile Modernity and the Sociology of Choice." *Mobilities* 10 (5): 764–783.
Forsey, M. 2015b. "Blue-Collar Affluence in a Remote Mining Town: Challenging the Modernist Myth of Education'." *Ethnography and Education* 10 (3): 356–369.
Forsey, M. 2017. "Education in a Mobile Modernity." *Geographical Research* 55 (1): 58–69.
Forsey, M., S. Davies, and G. Walford. 2008. "The Globalisation of School Choice? An Introduction to Key Issues and Concerns." In *The Globalisation of School Choice?, Symposium Books*, edited by M. Forsey, S. Davies, and G. Walford, 9–25. UK.

Forsey, M., H. Proctor, and M. Stacey. 2017. "A Most Poisonous Debate: Legitimizing Support for Australian Private Schools." In *School Choice and Private Schools: International Perspectives*, edited by T. Koinzer, R. Nikolai, and F. Waldow, 49–66. Wiesbaden, Germany: Springer VS.

Giddens, A. 1991. *Modernity and Society: Self and Identity in the Late Modern Age*. Cambridge/Oxford: Polity Press.

Government of Western Australia. 2020. *Economy*. Perth: Department of Jobs, Tourism, Science and Innovation. May 2020. https://www.jtsi.wa.gov.au/about-the-state/quality-of-life/economy.

Harvey, D. 2005. *A Brief History of Neoliberalism*. Oxford: Oxford University Press.

Higgs, P., and C. Gilleard. 2006. "Departing the Margins: Social Class and Later Life in a Second Modernity." *Journal of Sociology* 42 (3): 219–241.

Hudson, P., and S. Hudson. 2008. "Changing Preservice Teachers' Attitudes for Teaching in Rural Schools." *Australian Journal of Teacher Education* 33 (4): 67–77.

Lamb, S., J. Jackson, A. Walstab, and S. Huo. 2015. *Educational Opportunity in Australia 2015: Who Succeeds and Who Misses Out*. Melbourne: Mitchell Institute.

Larner, W. 2005. "Neoliberalism in (Regional) Theory and Practice: The Stronger Communities Action Fund in New Zealand." *Geographical Research* 43 (1): 9–18.

Levinson, B., and M. Sutton. 2001. "Introduction: Policy as/in Practice – A Sociocultural Approach to the Study of Educational Policy." In *Policy as Practice: Towards a Comparative Sociocultural Analysis of Educational Policy*, edited by M. Sutton, and B. Levinson, 1–22. Westport: Ablex.

Marks, G. N. 2010. "School Sector and Socioeconomic Inequalities in University Entrance in Australia: The Role of the Stratified Curriculum." *Educational Research and Evaluation* 16 (1): 23–37.

Ministry of Education. 1987. *Better Schools in Western Australia: A Programme for Improvement*. Perth: Ministry of Education.

Nous Group. 2011. *Schooling Challenges and Opportunities: A Report for the Review of Funding for Schooling Panel*. Melbourne: Melbourne Graduate School of Education.

Ortner, Sherry B. 1989. *High Religion: A Cultural and Political History of Sherpa Budhism*. Princeton, NJ: Princeton University Press.

Preston, B. 1984. "Residualization: What's That?" *The Australian Teacher* 8: 5–6.

Rasborg, K. 2017. "From Class Society to the Individualized Society? A Critical Reassessment of Individualization and Class." *Irish Journal of Sociology* 25 (3): 229–249.

Rose, N. 1993. "Government, Authority and Expertise in Advanced Liberalism." *Economy and Society* 22 (3): 283–299.

Rose, Nikolas. 1996. "Governing "Advanced" Liberal Democracies." In *Foucault and Political Reason: Liberalism, Neo-Liberalism and Rationalities of Government*, edited by A. Barry, T. Osborne, and N. Rose, 37–64. London: UCL Press.

Saussure, F. 1959. *Course in General Linguistics*. New York: Philosophical Library.

Sherington, G., and P. Hughes. 2014. "'Money Made US': A Short History of Government Funds for Australian Schools." In *Educational Heresies: New and Enduring Controversies Over Practice and Policy*, edited by H. Proctor, P. Brownlee, and P. Freebody. New York: Springer Publishing.

Sweetman, Paul. 2003. "Twenty-First Century Dis-Ease? Habitual Reflexivity or the Reflexive Habitus." *The Sociological Review* 51 (4): 528–549.

Threadgold, S., and P. Nilan. 2009. "Reflexivity of Contemporary Youth, Risk and Cultural Capital." *Current Sociology* 57 (1): 47–68.

Walford, G. 1996. "School Choice and the Quasi-Market in England and Wales." *Oxford Studies in Comparative Education* 6 (1): 49–62.

Whitty, G., S. Power, and D. Halpin. 1998. *Devolution & Choice in Education: The School, the State and the Market*. Canberra: ACER Press.

Windle, J. 2015. *Making Sense of School Choice: Politics, Policies and Practice Under Conditions of Cultural Diversity*. New York: Palgrave MacMillan.

Index

Note: Figures are indicated by *italics*. Endnotes are indicated by the page number followed by 'n' and the endnote number e.g., 20n1 refers to endnote 1 on page 20.

Agency for School Development *(Myndighetenf örskolutveckling)* 73
AJ International School 20, *25*, 26–7, 29n17
amateurs 96–8
A Nation at Risk (ANAR) 49–51
anganwadi 15, 16, 19–24, *22*, 29n22
Anglosphere 9
Annual Status of Education Report (ASER) 28n2
Appadurai, A. 108
architecture of trust 7, 78, 79, 84, 88–9
aspiration 3, 16, 17, 19, 23, 27, 43
attitude 6, 16, 19, 27, 28n10, 34, 40, 64, 65, 74, 87, 97, 100, 101
Australia 2, 3, 7, 9, 10, 79, 102, 107, 109–19
A World Ready to Learn 18

Bæck, U. K. 35
Beck, U. 113, 120
Bendixsen, S. 5
Bergen: researching parents 36–7
Better Schools in Western Australia: A Programme for Improvement 112
Bhattacharjea, S. 28n9
Bihar 3, 5, 15, 19, 29n13
Bourdieu, P. 120
Bourdieusean 112
Breidenstein, G. 8, 10
Brown, P. 4, 114

capitalism 17, 111
caste-class distinctions 27
casteism 16–17, 20–1, 26, 27
Chapman, J. 110, 111
Chesters, J. 114, 115
Chicago 7, 49, 54
Chicago Public Schools (CPS) 52–3, 56, 59, 61
children's education 5, 24, 41–3, 45, 54, 70, 87, 96, 99
Children's Rights Convention 70, 71
Children's schooling 2, 4, 11, 33, 34, 37, 41, 45, 52, 57

children's *vs.* parents' rights 69–72
China 82
Chiong, Charleen 8
Christensen, Ditte Storck 6–8
class-caste distinction 23–4
Corbett, M. 120

Danielsen, H. 5
democracy 3, 6, 7, 59, 60–1, 63, 69, 70, 74, 82; Swedish concept of education 67–9; technocracy 60–1
Democracy Committee 68
democratic education 66, 67, 69
democratisation 33
devolution 7, 9, 79, 112, 116
Dimmock, Clive 8
discipline 16, 21, 24–7, 44, 59, 82, 109
Dodillet, Susanne 6–8
Dom community 19, 29n19
Dunstan, J. 110, 111

early childhood care and education (ECCE) 15–17, 20; in Gajwa 21–3; and school readiness 17–19
Early Childhood Education and School Readiness in India (Kaul and Bhattacharjea) 28n9
educational responsibility 102–3
educational systems 4, 5, 9, 35, 41, 45, 65, 66, 70–3, 94–6, 102, 107, 109, 110
education market 93, 103
education policy 1–2, 6, 49, 51, 53, 61, 64–8, 70–3, 79, 89, 95, 112
eduscape 9, 107, 109–21
egalitarian 34, 95
Elementary and Secondary Education Act (ESEA) 52
Ethiopia 34, 37, 41
ethnoscape 121n1

Felder, S. 109
Fernandes, Leela 16

financescape 121n1
Fly-in-Flyout (FiFo) 118, 119
Forsey, Martin 9

Gajwa 15–25
Germany 8–10, 94–6, 102
Global Education Reform Movement 3, 10
globalisation 9, 82, 108, 109
government schooling 16, 24, 83, 85, 107, 110, 114–17, 119–20
Gross State Product (GSP) 118
Guha, Ranajit 24
Gymnasium 95, 99

habitus 9–10, 37, 108
hegemonic aspirations 16, 19, 23, 27
Heller, Patrick 16
homework 37–8, 40
human migration 3
hybrid neoliberal-developmental city–state 7

immigrant parents 41, 44
inclusive education 46
Independent Schools Council of Australia (ISCA) 114
India 2, 5, 15, 16, 18–20, 24, 28n4, 28n11, 29n15
inequality 2–5, 7, 27, 34, 35, 40, 45, 59, 60, 79, 81, 83, 89, 93, 114
Integrated Child Development Scheme (ICDS) 15–16, 20, 22, 28n11
intensification 2, 33–4, 36, 87, 114
intensive parenting 5, 33, 44, 45; parent-school relationship 35–6
international development 15, 17, 18
interrogation of the normative developmentalism 27
Iraq 34, 37, 41

juridification 64, 65

Karratha School's Project 118
Kaul, V. 28n9
K-12 education 51
kiasuism 81
Knowledge School 33
Krüger, J. O. 8–10
Kumar, Krishna 24

Lareau, A. 83
Lareau, Annette 2
Lau, C. 113
learning discipline 24–7
'liberal welfare' states 3
LSC (Local School Council) 55, 56, 58
Luhmann, Niklas 7

marketisation 20, 27, 64–5, 93, 96, 102
mediascape 121n1

mercantile society 79
meritocracy 80, 81, 89, 99
meritocratic educational systems 4
migrant parents 5, 34, 37, 41, 44–5
Ministry of Education (MOE) 80
mobile technology 79
modernity 108, 110–13, 115, 119–21
Mukharji, Projit Bihari 29n21
Mushahar, Pasi, Turi and Dom communities 19
Muslim communities 19
MySchool 102

National Early Childhood Care and Education Curriculum Framework (NECCECF) 19, 28n3
National Rifle Association (NRA) 54
neoliberal education reform 3–7, 10, 53
neoliberalisation 33
neoliberalism 2, 4, 10–11, 54, 79, 81, 84, 88–9, 112, 113
neoliberal practices 89
New Republic 60
New Zealand 9, 10
No Child Left Behind Act (NCLB) 2, 7, 50–2, 61
non-Nordic migrant parents 5, 11
North West Shelf Joint Venture (NWSJV) 118
Norway 1–3, 33, 35–7, 40, 41, 43–5

OECD's Programme for Student Assessment (PISA) 3, 95
omnicompetent citizen 60
Ong, Aihwa 79
Other Backward Castes (OBC) 19, 22, 29n15

PAC (Parent Advisory Council) 58
parental involvement 8, 33–5, 52–4, 59, 61, 63–7, 70, 74, 94; margins of 66–7
Parenting Cultures and Risk Management in Plural Norway 36
parenting for schooling 3, 5, 10
parentocracy 4, 81, 89, 93
parents 46; amateurs 96–8; clients 98–100; customers 100–2
parent-school cooperation 34–7, 44–5, 103; and intensive parenting 35–6; Norwegian welfare state 34–5
Parents' Council Working Committees (PCWC) 39, 42
Penn, Helen 18
The Phantom Public 60
policyscape 49; Angela 57–60; parents' responses 53–5; Phuong 55–7; risk and responsibility 50–3
political economy 16, 27
political trust 8, 78–9, 81–4, 88, 89
pre-school classrooms, AJ International 26
primary education 94–6
private schools 20, 23–6, 28n11, 64, 70, 96, 100, 114–15, 117

private tutoring 16, 20, 21, 24
professionalisation 66
professionalism 51, 66, 73, 74, 97, 99, 103, 112
prosperity-loyalty 82, 89
Public Opinion (Dewey) 60

Ravitch, Diane 50
reflexive habitus 9–10, 108, 112
reflexive subjectivity 84
Regulations to the Education Act § 20-1 states 34–5, 46n1
responsibilisation 2, 3, 7–10, 36, 44–5, 64–5, 71, 72, 79, 81, 84–6, 88–9; architecture of trust 88–9; child 84–6; parents 86–8
Right to Education Act, 2009 28n11
Roch, A. 8–10
Rose, N. 112

Sahayikas 20
Scheduled Caste (SC) 19, 29n15
Scheduled Tribe (ST) 19, 20, 29n15
school autonomy 9, 95–6
school choice 9, 10, 57, 64, 79, 81, 93–6, 103, 108, 113
schooling systems 1–3
school leaders 8, 35, 39, 94, 96, 102
school market 95
school readiness: class-caste distinction 23–4; learning discipline 24–7
School Readiness and Transitions 18
school readiness discourse 6, 15–27
science-based professionals *vs.* laypeople 72–4
self-reinforcing 82
Shuffelton, Amy 6, 7

Singapore 2, 3, 7, 8, 11, 78–9, 83–90; neoliberal-developmental 80–1; political trust, state-citizen compact and neoliberal fractures 81–3
sitting tolerance 24, 30n25
social democratic states 3, 34, 66, 69, 80
soft authoritarianism 80
Somalia 34, 37, 41
Sriprakash, A. 5
Sweden 2–3, 6–7, 63–7, 69–74
Swedish Education Act 64, 71
Swedish Institute for Educational Research *(Skolforskningsinstitutet)* 73

Tan, Charlene 83
technocracy 60–1
Three Worlds of Welfare Capitalism (Esping-Andersen) 3
Torsten Husén's theory 72

UNICEF 17–19
United States 2, 5, 10, 49, 54
'uthana-baithanasikhtehain' 26

welfare state 34–5, 70–1, 108, 113
Western Africa 34, 41
Western Australia (WA) 107; education bureaucracies in second modernity 111–12; equity across distance 110–11; metrocentric state 110; public/private 114–16; rural/remote spaces 117–19; second modernity and better schools 112–14; shaping parents, shaping schools in second modernity 119–21
Western jurisdictions 107

For Product Safety Concerns and Information please contact our EU representative GPSR@taylorandfrancis.com Taylor & Francis Verlag GmbH, Kaufingerstraße 24, 80331 München, Germany

Printed and bound by CPI Group (UK) Ltd, Croydon, CR0 4YY
17/12/2024
01807709-0011